# THE
# FIRST-TIME
# SUPERVISOR'S
## *Survival Guide*

# THE
# FIRST-TIME
# SUPERVISOR'S

*Survival Guide*

## George Fuller

PRENTICE HALL

PRENTICE HALL
A member of Penguin Putnam Inc.
375 Hudson Street
New York, N.Y. 10014
www.penguinputnam.com

LIBRARY OF CONGRESS CATALOGING-IN-PUBLICATION DATA

Fuller, George.
The first-time supervisor's survival guide / by George Fuller.
p.   cm.
Includes index.
ISBN 0-13-044066-3 (cloth)—ISBN 0-13-311432-5 (pbk.)
1. Supervision of employees.   I. Title.
HF5549.12.F825   1994   94-21271
658.3'02—dc20   CIP

Printed in the United States of America

10  9  8  7  6  5          20                                        (pbk)

# Also by the Author

*Supervisor's Portable Answer Book,* 1990, Prentice Hall
*The Negotiator's Handbook,* 1991, Prentice Hall
*The Supervisor's Big Book of Lists,* 1994, Prentice Hall

# *Table of Contents*

*Chapter 4*  THE ABC'S OF SUPERVISING OTHERS—*87*

*Chapter 5*  DEALING WITH EMPLOYEE CONCERNS—*117*

## *Chapter 6*  MANAGING WORKER JOB PERFORMANCE ISSUES—*149*

*Chapter 9*    **FIFTEEN SUPERVISORY MISTAKES AND HOW TO AVOID THEM—*231***

# *Introduction*

It's a wonderful moment when you are told of your selection for a supervisory position. There's certainly cause for you to take pride in your achievement, since your appointment is not only a recognition of your past accomplishments, but also a vote of confidence in your ability to do the job. As you begin your duties as a new boss, however, you will quickly discover that it isn't easy to manage other people.

Your new subordinates will have differing personalities, goals, and abilities. Furthermore, many of them won't have your own desire to work hard day after day. Dealing with the many problems a new supervisor faces isn't easy, but it doesn't have to lead to discouragement.

On the other hand, you may find yourself becoming frustrated at having to learn the difficult task of supervising people on a trial-and-error basis. Seeking the advice of more experienced supervisors isn't a simple solution, either. They have their own responsibilities to worry about, and just may not have time to help you out. Some may view you as another competitor for limited resources and future promotions. Even on the rare occasion when you find veteran supervisors willing to assist you, they might not have the answers to some of your more difficult problems. Managing people often presents unique problems that someone else hasn't had to deal with.

The purpose of *The First-Time Supervisor's Survival Guide* is to help you quickly overcome the many supervisory problems you will encounter in your new role as a boss. It focuses on providing easy-to-use advice that will make your job as a boss a lot less difficult. Furthermore, it concentrates on the nitty-gritty details that you, as a new supervisor, have to contend with. You won't have to scratch your head trying to understand complex theory or search for answers in books not specifically geared to your basic needs.

This is a book you can refer to time and time again for assistance as you perform your supervisory duties. To further simplify its use as your workday companion, every topic is clearly identified in the table of contents. This will help you to find what you're looking for without searching through page after page to get the answer you seek. Perhaps most important of all, it is the first book on supervision that recognizes the pressing concerns a new supervisor faces **and** offers practical solutions for dealing with them.

Naturally, you may have come to your first supervisory position by a different route than someone else. Many first-time bosses are promoted after demonstrating their abilities in nonsupervisory positions, while others are recent college graduates just starting their careers. Both the avenues for getting to the first supervisory assignment and the backgrounds of new supervisors vary widely. Different also are the industries and companies that new supervisors work for. This book has taken these variables into account, so the information is designed to serve the needs of every new supervisor, irrespective of where you work and what you do.

Above all else, as you attack your new supervisory responsibilities with enthusiasm, retain your composure even when you would be justified in losing your cool. Every people-related problem a supervisor faces can be resolved if you approach it in a calm and reasoned manner. It is hoped that this book will help you in that regard.

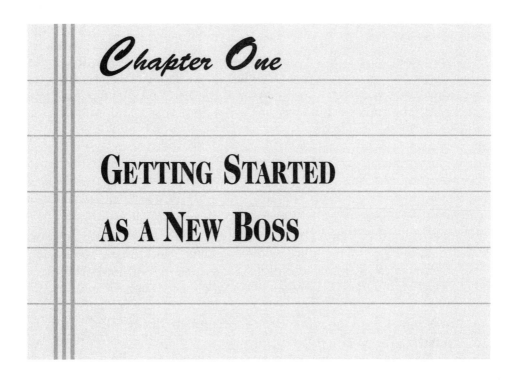

# Chapter One

# GETTING STARTED AS A NEW BOSS

*S*tarting a new job always brings a touch of excitement, a lot of anticipation, and perhaps even a bit of apprehension. These feelings are magnified when the new position is as a first-time supervisor. Once the initial reaction toward being a new boss wears off, however, reality sets in. You are now responsible for not only your own work, but also for the performance of the people you supervise. You may start to think about how people will react to you as a boss. Will they resent and resist your authority? If so, how can you deal with them successfully?

For better or for worse, the answers to your questions won't be long in coming. Those who desire to challenge your authority aren't going to wait around until you learn the ropes. Instead, they will likely seek to see what you're made of right at the start. For this reason alone, it's important to be prepared to establish yourself as the boss from the first day forward.

Even if you have the good fortune to avoid encounters with instigators and troublemakers at the outset, your initial days on the job will lay the foundation for future expectations—both for you and for those you supervise. Here, as everywhere else, first impressions count for a lot. It's imperative that you seize the initiative at the beginning and get off to a good start. The topics in this chapter focus on helping you to do that.

## OVERCOMING YOUR INITIAL ANXIETIES

The first hurdle you have to face as a first-time boss will come soon after you receive word of your selection for the job. Very likely, your thoughts will turn to the type of reception you will receive from the people you will be supervising. You might feel particularly uneasy and have visions of being totally ignored or, even worse, of a wholesale rebellion against your authority.

Although it's reasonable to be concerned about the initial response from people who will be working for you, your fears shouldn't be blown out of proportion. First, you're the boss who will control the work destiny of your newfound subordinates. Therefore, only the foolhardy among them will entertain any notions about giving you a hard time. Second, the people you supervise will most likely adopt a wait-and-see attitude about forming judgments until they get to know you. In fact, their worries will probably exceed yours—after all, you will be the one with the power and authority that goes along with a supervisory position.

Although becoming a new boss doesn't justify a lot of worry about your initial acceptance, it definitely requires some thought as to how you can get off to a solid start. Fortunately, there are some steps you can take that will help in this regard. The first is to learn what you can about the individuals in your new group before you even begin. Try to talk with the previous supervisor, since he or she best knows the details of the job and the capabilities of the people you will be supervising.

Of course, it may not always be possible to talk with your predecessor, either because the prior supervisor has left the company before you know you're getting the job, or because you're filling a newly created position. In circumstances such as these, the person who will be your own immediate boss may have enough working knowledge of the situation to bring you up to speed.

***Caution:*** Always weigh carefully what a former boss tells you about employees, since personal bias may outweigh objectivity. For example, there may have been personality clashes, or else a departing boss may decide to settle an old score by knocking someone when briefing you.

Another tool you can use is to review the recent performance evaluations and personnel files of the people you will be supervising. This type of information will at least give you enough knowledge about your subordinates to properly prepare yourself for your first days and weeks on the job.

Beyond learning as much as you can before you start your new position, one of the most important aspects of getting off on the right foot is your initial introduction to the group by your boss. In some cases, it may be nothing more than a simple announcement posted on a bulletin board. The preferred way, however, is for your boss to personally introduce you to the group.

A strong opening recommendation from your own boss sends a signal that you have the full support and cooperation of upper management. This is particularly significant if people in the group resent the fact that they were passed over for the job. They may be less inclined to be disruptive if they know you are held in high regard by higher levels of management. A show of support from your boss may also dissuade anyone who has plans to sidestep you and go directly to your boss for answers. Last, but not least, introductory praise from your boss to the group is an ego booster which can help you overcome your initial anxieties.

## SEVEN TIPS FOR GETTING OFF TO A GOOD START

How you start off as a new supervisor will to a large extent determine how difficult the adjustment to your new role will be—both for yourself and your subordinates. The following suggestions will help you to avoid some of the potholes that can trip up a new boss.

### 1. Be Yourself

You may find yourself to be the recipient of a good deal of unsolicited advice on how to handle your new responsibilities. Some of it may be useful, but much of it may represent someone else's notions of how a supervisor should act. The comments may include generalizations such as, "Show 'em who's boss right away," to specifics such as, "Watch out for Fred. He's a real back-stabber."

Ultimately, at least some of the specific advice you get may prove to be true, but it's crucial to start off with a clean slate and take nothing for granted. If someone is indeed a back-stabber you will find that out soon enough. On the other hand, an individual may be a back-stabbing victim of the person who gave you the advice. Therefore, although listening to what others have to say about your new position is useful, always assess the source of the information before you jump to conclusions.

Your subordinates will closely observe your reaction to them from day one, and one of the first impressions you want to create is that you're objective. As you get to know the job and those you supervise, any opinions you received about individuals will quickly be confirmed or refuted by their performance. In fact, workers who may not have gotten along with the previous supervisor might well decide to try harder to cooperate with a new boss. So, while some things you hear beforehand may ultimately prove to be true, other assertions won't pan out.

## 2. Start Slowly

You may have some good ideas about changes you want to make when you take over your new position. Tread carefully here, since change is difficult for most people to accept. This is especially true when someone new comes on board and immediately starts to make work reassignments and other changes that affect the way workers were doing things. At the least, you may be thought of as a "know-it-all" by subordinates. Even worse, you may make changes that don't work out which will peg you as incompetent.

Be yourself and don't fall victim to the notion you have to be a hard-charging leader from day one. You're much better off waiting to get a feel for your new job before implementing anything new. This will give you time to learn what will work and what won't. It also gives you breathing room to get to know your subordinates and solicit their ideas. Eventually you will have to make decisions that not everyone agrees with, but if your people have had a chance to be heard, future changes won't meet as much resistance.

## *3. Be Confident*

Although you essentially want to feel your way along in your new supervisory role, it's critical to show subordinates that you have confidence in your ability to do the job. For this reason, as problems are brought to you for resolution, don't appear indecisive. At the beginning, you may have to spend more time getting the facts before you act, and that is to be expected from someone in a new job. What you don't want to do is let decisions slide too long or to appear hesitant when you do act.

It's natural to worry about making mistakes when you're starting out—and you may make a few. Keep in mind that both your boss and subordinates know you're new on the job and are entitled to make an error or two while you're in the learning stages. The far greater danger is failing to act at all.

## *4. Be Visible*

Spend as much time as you can in the work area and as little as possible in your office. You may have an initial impulse to get control of your paperwork and the other desk-bound aspects of the job. There's also a certain comfort level for a new boss in sitting behind a desk and letting people and problems come to you. In fact, it's easy to hope that by staying out of sight, there's less likelihood of being asked questions for which you don't yet have the answers.

The advantages of making yourself seen are twofold. First, you get to know the people you supervise and their duties. Workers will be reluctant to enter the office of a new boss unless it's absolutely essential. Circulating throughout the work area will encourage exchanges of information as well as casual conversation. These, in turn, will increase your acceptance by employees.

Second, a visible supervisor encourages people to be more productive, since folks won't loiter at the water cooler too long if the boss is around. This helps to establish a pattern right from the beginning that should be maintained over the long term. Of course, when you become more involved with your routine, you might not be able to spend as much time out of your office. But even then, you should make it a regular practice to periodically walk around the work area.

## 5. Use Your Boss

Managers know that a new supervisor is entering uncharted waters. This is why your boss probably said something such as, "If you have any problems, let me know." Don't be reluctant to take your boss up on this offer, since the first few weeks are when he or she will be more receptive to your requests for guidance. The more experience you get, the less likely it is that a boss will take the time to offer assistance. After all, once you become a veteran supervisor you should be able to operate with a greater degree of independence.

The problem is that new supervisors don't always avail themselves of their boss's help. The natural feeling is that you don't want to appear not to know the answers—even when you don't. As a newly appointed supervisor, however, you're not expected to have all the answers. Therefore, seize the opportunity to obtain your boss's guidance whenever it's needed. Whatever your misgivings might be, the alternative of making unnecessary mistakes will be even worse. Furthermore, if you do make an error, you're liable to hear your boss say, "Why didn't you see me before you went ahead with that?"

Of course, your boss has other responsibilities, so the amont of assistance you can expect will be determined by that, as well as by the inclination of your boss to be helpful. You may find that you have a boss who preaches being available for guidance but who doesn't follow through in practice. In any event, you will quickly discover a boss's limitations, and if your boss seems irritated when you seek assistance, you'll know you have worn out your welcome.

## 6. Ask Questions

One of the keys to learning your new job is to ask lots of questions. For some people this comes naturally. Others are more timid about doing this for fear of showing how little they know about the operation they now supervise. If you are in this latter group, strive to overcome this tendency. First, it doesn't take workers long to figure out how much a boss does or does not know. Therefore, not asking questions won't hide a lack of knowledge for any length of time.

Second, what is often overlooked is that most workers want to demonstrate their knowledge to a new boss. As a result, a boss who is asking questions gives them an opportunity to display their skills. Beyond this, getting into the details of how your subordinates do their jobs will give you valuable insight for future use in deciding what needs changing and what doesn't. Finally, asking about operational details shows the kind of interest in what your people are doing that will encourage them to come to you when they have problems down the road.

The flip side of the coin is that if you're hesitant about asking questions, it may be assumed that you don't have any interest in knowing what your subordinates are doing. This can make them reluctant to come to you when problems pop up. And beyond anything else, the fewer questions you ask at the beginning, the longer it will take to feel comfortable about your job.

## 7. Be a Good Listener

Hand in hand with asking lots of questions is the need to be a good listener. This means you may have to spend more time than you would like listening to some of your subordinates ramble on. Later, as you get to know the individual traits of employees, you will find there are a few talkative individuals who sometimes have to be cut short.

With still others, you will probably feel like you're pulling teeth just to get them to say anything. In your first days and weeks, however, the best approach is to concentrate on hearing what people have to say. You might not be able to absorb everything that you're told right away, so don't be discouraged if you feel overwhelmed by what you're hearing. The pieces of the puzzle will fall together more quickly than you think.

Of course, being a good listener will bring complaints of one form or another right from the start. In fact, the workers who do the most talking to you in the beginning will likely be those people who are trying to convince you of the wisdom of their gripes. Naturally, unless there's an obvious need to deal with one or more of these complaints right away, you are better off waiting until you're more familiar with the situation before taking any action. Therefore, if you run into this sort of problem say something such as, "I want to talk more about this, so why don't you see me next week after I've had a chance to get settled in." This type of response will give you a little breathing room to check out the legitimacy of any complaint before you respond.

## DEALING WITH FRIENDS YOU NOW SUPERVISE

For many a new boss, their first supervisory position involves managing people they were working with before the promotion took place. This can lead to apprehension about how these people will react to having you as their superior. Usually it's needless worry, since both you and your former co-workers will quickly adjust to the change in your status. Nevertheless, there are a couple of potential pitfalls you have to learn to avoid.

The first is to not show signs of favoritism toward any friend whom you now supervise. The problem isn't so much that you would actually give special treatment to a friend, since the tendency is to be cautious about this when you assume a boss/subordinate relationship. The real dilemma is that other subordinates may think you're playing favorites simply because of your close association with someone who works for you.

In fact, someone you supervise may make a comment to you about favoritism. If so, it's likely to be done indirectly in a kidding manner—perhaps by smiling and saying, "Well, Todd, I guess your bowling buddy Brian will be getting the choice assignments." If this should happen, the worst thing you can do is to get mad. Instead, reply matter-of-factly by saying something like, "Ray, you know I'm not like that, so put your needle away."

Of course, the level of friendship influences the degree to which real or perceived problems of favoritism may arise. If it's nothing more than a workplace friendship based upon similar interests, such as rooting for the same sports teams or raising children in the same age range, the perception of favoritism may not arise. On the other hand, if it's a friendship that extends beyond working hours, there's a greater likelihood that some workers will suspect your friend is getting special treatment.

If you do have a friendship that extends beyond the workplace, you may want to be cautious about emphasizing that at work. Naturally, this means discussing the situation with your friend. Point out that you don't want your new position to harm your friendship, but that you don't want to go overboard in advertising the fact that you golf or play tennis together on weekends. In short, try to downplay your friendship at work, which shouldn't be that hard if you enlist your friend's cooperation.

On the other hand, don't go to artificial extremes to pretend the friendship doesn't exist, since no one will be fooled and it might even lead to heightened suspicions of favoritism. In essence, don't try to hide the friendship, but don't flaunt it in front of the other workers in your group either.

On rare occasions, you may notice that a friend you are now supervising is extremely uneasy about the new working relationship. Conversely, you may be the one who feels uncomfortable. Whichever it is, confront the issue by talking it out with your friend. If, however, over a period of time, the uneasiness continues, you may have to gradually phase out the friendship.

This sort of situation is most common when both you and your friend were in contention for the supervisory position for which you were selected. Despite the friendship, the other person may be resentful that you were the one who got the job. If this is the case, don't fret about it, since true friends would be happy for your success, after their initial disappointment at not getting the job wore off. So if you do face this dilemma, perhaps you will discover whether you have a true friend or just a casual acquaintance that can't survive the rough spots in a friendship.

No discussion of dealing with friends you supervise can ignore the aspect of romantic involvements at work. They are difficult enough to handle at work even when you aren't in a boss/employee relationship. But the problems are magnified when someone is dating an employee they supervise. Remember, these situations should be avoided if at all possible. Nevertheless, Cupid has a way of winning out over reason. It suffices to say that if you are romantically involved with someone you are now supervising, try to keep it as low key as possible.

## WHAT TO SAY IF YOU'RE NEEDLED ABOUT BEING A BOSS

It's to be expected that you will receive a little bit of good-natured ribbing about being a new boss. This is especially true if you're promoted to a position where you either supervise former co-workers or have otherwise worked with or known people you now supervise. This shouldn't be a major issue unless someone doesn't know when enough is enough.

For the most part, the best way to handle any ribbing you get is by accepting it with a smile. Keeping your composure is the surest way to put the teasing to rest. If you show the slightest sign of annoyance at being kidded, rest assured that a few people will see this as a signal to needle you even more. So although you may want to respond angrily, it's best to just bite your tongue and save yourself future aggravation.

Of course, there may be a few individuals who are jealous or otherwise unhappy about your selection and try to be vindictive under the guise of a little bit of friendly kidding. As a result, you may have to respond to let them know they've crossed over the line from good-natured teasing to maliciousness. If you handle this problem correctly, it will not only silence the agitators, but it will also end the needling from those who are just doing it in a good-natured way. Let's look at a few typical responses you can use to silence these mischief makers.

> *Remark:* "Things must be getting bad if they made you a boss."

> *Reply:* "I'll know they're getting worse, Joe, when I see you get promoted."

COMMENT: This is a quid-pro-quo response where you essentially imply that whatever negative applies to you also applies to the other person. This works well, since if you respond too sharply, the other person will likely say something such as, "Don't get uptight, I was only joking." But when you reply in kind, that's harder to do, since you can then say, "Who's getting uptight? I just did what you did." You can even carry it further by saying something similar to, "What's the matter? Don't you have a sense of humor?" Handling remarks in this manner in a joking way shows people that you can not only take a remark in good humor, but can also dish it out.

> *Remark:* "Don't take this personally, but I think Herb should have been promoted, since he has more seniority than you."

> *Reply:* "If I'd been working here as long as you have Al, I'd probably feel the same way."

COMMENT: People often think they can say anything by using a qualifier, such as "Don't take this personally." Actually, the use of the qualifier invites the result that it's pretending to discourage. It really only amounts to a verbal alibi for negative remarks.

Another tactic people use is to refer to someone else when they really are thinking of themselves. When Al talks about Herb's seniority, he ignores the fact that he is the senior employee. What he's really saying is that he should have been the one who was promoted to supervisor.

*Remark:* "I guess you have to know the right people to get promoted around here."

*Reply:* "I never thought about that. What do you mean?"

COMMENT: Replying in a noncommittal way with a question is a nice way to put the person on the spot. They are then forced to be more specific, which can make them look bad. As a result, they will generally just shrug or say something such as "Forget it, I was just kidding."

*Remark:* "I guess you have to be a good-looking woman to get promoted around here."

*Reply:* "Well Bill, that means you not only need a sex change, but a lot of plastic surgery as well.", *or*

*Reply:* (in a calm, but firm voice,) "Is that a sexist remark?"

COMMENT: Sexist remarks shouldn't be tolerated, but how you handle them is a matter of personal discretion. The first reply may be appropriate if you know the person is only joking—even if in poor taste— while the second response is aimed at putting the person on the spot. You may choose to discourage sexist behavior, while at the same time joke about the comment. If so, combining a comment on sexism with a jibe can work well. For example, say something, such as "If I didn't know you better, I'd think that was a sexist remark But I know you're not like that so you'd better get a sex change along with some plastic surgery."

*Remark:* (Said to someone else, but loud enough for you to hear.) "Just what we need around here—another greenhorn supervisor."

*Reply:*     "Hey, Smitty, I hear you talk a lot faster than you
            work. I'm sure planning to find out."

COMMENT: The fact that the person made the negative remark so you
would overhear it indicates you may have a behind-the-scenes troublemaker to deal with. You can call their bluff right away with a
response such as the one above. Alternatively, you might want to
ignore the initial remark but keep it in mind should the person try to
take advantage of your status as a new boss. If that happens, talk to
them privately and let them know you don't intend to tolerate their
nonsense.

All in all, any needling you get will cease rather quickly, so for the
most part it essentially involves taking a grin-and-bear-it approach.
People who persist or go beyond reasonable limits have to be dealt with.
But a smile or a quick retort will work well for most instances. If you do
have someone who is a particular pain-in-the-neck, rest assured that
other employees probably feel the same way you do. If you're forced to
take drastic action, you may receive more support than you might imagine from those you supervise.

## HOW TO HANDLE YOUR FIRST MEETING

As you start your new supervisory job, the moment when you have to call
your first supervisory meeting will fast descend upon you. You may dread
the approaching task, or at least view it with some degree of apprehension. This is especially true if you have never worked with any of the
employees you now supervise. On the other hand, if your new subordinates were former co-workers, you may envision some version of a
celebrity roast with you as the star attraction. In both instances, your
fears are out of proportion, even though you may not be sure of that until
after the meeting has taken place.

If you are nervous about your initial meeting, there are some measures you can take to make things easier on yourself. For starters, keep
your first meeting short. This is important for a couple of reasons. It not
only helps you to get it over with quickly, but it puts workers in a better
frame of mind when their new boss keeps meetings brief. Most people

either dislike meetings or accept them as a necessary evil. Lengthy meetings can create resentment, since workers often see them as absorbing time that could be better spent doing their jobs. So keeping the first get-together with your group short will make both you and your subordinates happy.

It's a good idea to look for something simple to be the topic of the first meeting. After all, who wants to announce layoffs at their first meeting as a new boss? Everyone blames the messenger when bad news is handed out, so control your destiny by picking an uncontroversial topic. One possibility is routine administrative information that has to be conveyed to all employees.

If you want to pick the topic, you can't postpone having a meeting indefinitely. Otherwise, you will find yourself forced to call a meeting to discuss a subject that isn't likely to please anyone. Even though you may be reluctant to chair your first official encounter with your group, put your qualms on the back burner and get it done on your own terms.

For the purposes of your first meeting, there are a couple of pointers to keep in mind. When you tell people there is going to be a meeting, let them know it will be brief. This isn't a big issue, but it puts people at ease when they know this. The time of the meeting will depend upon the specifics of your workplace, but it helps to schedule it about twenty or thirty minutes before the end of the workday. That way, you can hold a ten-minute meeting and then announce it's getting late and dismiss everyone. Say something similar to, "It's almost quitting time and some of you people have rides to catch, so let's wrap this up right now."

This has a couple of advantages. From your standpoint, people aren't going to prolong a meeting by asking lots of questions at the end of the day. Therefore, you're less likely to be asked questions about topics which you're not yet familiar with. Your newfound subordinates will also appreciate the fact that you aren't the type of boss who calls late afternoon meetings and doesn't worry about when they end.

Beyond this advice, both at your first meeting and subsequent ones, it's useful to do as much listening as you can until you get your feet on the ground. The only limit on this is to not let a meeting get out of control. It won't take too many meetings for you to overcome your initial jitters. In fact, just as you probably did before you were a boss, you will soon consider meetings to be just another boring necessity. The only difference is that when you're running them, you can limit the boredom by keeping them short and to the point.

## FIVE THINGS YOU SHOULD TELL SUBORDINATES RIGHT AWAY

Within the first week or two after assuming your new position, it's useful to hold a meeting with your group to essentially let them know what they can expect from you as their supervisor. But unless you feel comfortable doing so, don't make this the first get-together you hold as a new boss. As mentioned in the previous section, you're better off getting over the jitters by dealing with a simple administrative topic at your initial meeting. That way, you'll feel more comfortable when you hold this session to present a few general operating guidelines.

You essentially want to accomplish two things. First, you want to put the people you now supervise at ease in terms of knowing what to expect from you. Second, you want to establish your authority as the boss in a low-key way. You don't want to be too specific, since you don't really have a handle yet on the capabilities of individuals, or the overall efficiency of the unit. There are essentially five points you should cover:

- ✐ Reassure your new associates that everyone should continue doing their job as they have always done and that it's basically business as usual.

- ✐ Let them know that you have no preconceived notions about anything or anyone within the department.

- ✐ Emphasize that you believe in teamwork and cooperation in getting the job done.

- ✐ Point out that you will keep everyone informed as to anything you learn that will affect the group or any individual employee. Say that you expect them to be equally open about keeping you informed.

- ✐ Remind everyone that if they have any problems, they should be brought to your attention.

Let's go over the reasoning behind each of these points. Reassuring your subordinates will relieve some of the anxieties they have probably felt since you were appointed to the position. Just as you're anxious about getting off to a good start, the workers reporting to you have their own concerns. Foremost among these is apprehension about what sort of changes you may make in who does what in terms of both jobs and operating procedures. People are naturally resistant to change, so an initial reassurance that no immediate changes are going to be made will put these fears to rest.

Actually, from a practical standpoint, this early in the game you're not in a position to make any substantive changes anyway. However, on occasion a new boss will bring preconceived notions to a new job about what has to be done and immediately implement them. But even if you're familiar with the operation when you start, it's better to carefully assess the situation before you do anything. By moving slowly, you will be better able to enlist the support of your people when you do decide to revise operating procedures or juggle job assignments. In terms of implementing changes, the support of those affected is the most crucial element in achieving success.

The second point to be covered is to reassure people that you don't have any preconceived opinions about them. Doing this essentially gives anyone who had problems prior to your arrival a new lease on their work life. For any number of reasons, an employee may have had problems with the previous supervisor. In fact, you were probably briefed by the previous boss, your own supervisor, or even a friend, about one or more workers.

For the most part, these were probably accurate assessments. On the other hand, they could be exaggerations, or even flat-out wrong. Then again, they might just represent a personality conflict between two individuals. Even if the negative assessments were accurate, letting people know they're starting off from scratch gives anyone who needs it a new beginning. Therefore, a worker who may not have been hacking it previously, might decide to buckle down and do the job. If someone with bad reports doesn't turn the situation around under your supervision, you will at least be able to assess their performance for yourself and then act accordingly.

The third factor to discuss with your group is cooperation and teamwork. Doing this will send a signal that you expect people to work together and not at cross-purposes. Emphasizing this point now will make it easier later on to get people to cooperate with each other. Of more immediate value, it will discourage workers from coming to you with petty complaints about one another. And even if they do, you'll be able to reinforce the importance of working together as a team instead of engaging in petty politics.

The fourth point to make is letting employees know that you will be open about sharing any information that affects them, and that you also expect them to keep you fully informed about their problems and concerns. What you want to do here is set the tone for open lines of communication right from the start. Otherwise, workers may be reluctant to bring things to your attention, particularly if they don't know you. And when you get off to a start where workers hesitate to talk things over with you, it becomes much harder to get them to open up as time passes.

The last thing you should cover is that you want to hear about any job-related problems right away. Although this is essentially part of the process of open communication already discussed, it's worthwhile to emphasize this point. Workers are always reluctant to bring problems to the boss's attention for fear of being criticized for making careless mistakes or not doing their jobs correctly.

This sort of attitude can result in minor difficulties going unnoticed until they become major problems. Only then, when it's unavoidable, will you be advised—unless, of course, you have already uncovered the difficulty yourself. Be sure to point out that people have nothing to fear by bringing their dilemmas to your doorstep. Emphasize that you believe in working together to solve problems rather than looking to place the blame when things go wrong.

Letting workers know that open communication and bringing problems to your attention are important also has a more immediate benefit. It puts anyone who may be bypassing a new boss on notice that you expect to be kept informed. This makes it extremely difficult for a worker who is basically ignoring the fact that you're now the boss to later say, "I didn't know you wanted to know about that."

To recap, if you cover the five points discussed, you will succeed in letting your people know that they have a reasonable boss to deal with. In addition, you will have also established communication ground rules which, without saying so directly, establish your authority as the boss in an unthreatening way. There may be other matters that you want to point out at this meeting, but don't go overboard in either the number of things you cover, or the duration of the meeting. Keeping it short and sweet will avoid diluting the impact of the purpose of the meeting. Furthermore, until you have been on the job for a while, you don't want to say anything you have to backtrack on later when you discover that something wasn't the way you initially presented it. After all, there will be plenty of future meetings in which you can raise other issues. At this point, you're better off just laying the groundwork by setting forth your basic expectations.

## FIELDING QUESTIONS WHEN YOU DON'T HAVE THE ANSWER

One of the trickier aspects of being a new boss is trying to answer questions when you haven't been around long enough to know the answers. You shouldn't worry about this since anyone with an ounce of common sense doesn't expect you to have the same command of the job as a veteran supervisor. Then again, you probably have an employee who either doesn't realize this or who is merely baiting you. Whatever the case, avoid the pitfall of trying to immediately answer every question that comes your way.

There's a natural tendency for people to try to give an immediate reply to every question they get. It's assumed that whoever is asking the question will think you don't know what you're doing if you don't have an immediate answer. People sometimes fail to realize that giving the wrong answer is far more damaging in the long run. Actually, it displays a lot more self-confidence when you admit to not knowing something, as opposed to winging it and ultimately looking like a fool.

In any event, always keep in mind that, as a new supervisor, you're not expected to have the answers to every question at your fingertips. When you're not comfortable with giving an immediate reply, just say so. Then promise that you'll find out the answer and get back to the person. Since you're still feeling your way along, unless there's a specific reason for doing so, it's probably better not to give a specific time or date when you will respond. Simply say something like "Let me look into that for you."

***Important Point:*** When you promise to provide an answer at a later date, always follow up. Employees will quickly lose confidence in you if you don't get back to them. If something is taking longer than expected to resolve, let the employee know that you're still working on the problem. This is so basic, but it is worth repeating.

The nature of some questions is such that it's assumed a response may not be needed. One example would be an employee asking, "Will you let me know when the new forms come in, so I can pick them up in receiving?" As it turns out, you subsequently discover that the new forms weren't ordered, because a decision was made not to use them. In a literal sense, there's no need to respond to the worker, since there won't be any forms to be picked up in receiving. Nonetheless, the worker doesn't know that unless you tell him, and in the meantime he may think you just didn't bother to find out the answer.

There are all types of questions where it can be assumed a reply is needed only under certain conditions. And, there are actually many situations where an answer isn't expected. But, as a general rule, always let workers know the outcome of any questions they ask. That way, they won't misinterpret not getting a reply as a failure by you to keep them informed.

There are a number of other aspects of fielding questions in the early days of your new job. One thing to be particularly careful about is to always be sure you understand the question being posed. If there's any doubt in your mind, either ask that the question be repeated or paraphrase it yourself by saying, "As I understand it, Joanne, you want to know if you can carry over vacation time to the next fiscal year. Is that correct?"

Sometimes when you're asked a question in a group meeting, one of your subordinates will give the answer. When this happens, it's a good idea to ask the person who raised the question if they have the answer they need. Otherwise, you may assume the question was answered, while the employee may go away waiting for you to get back with a reply.

You may be unlucky enough to have someone working for you who asks questions only in an attempt to make you look bad. If you sense this happening, a good way to deal with it is to tell the employee to see you later. The best method for doing this is by using time for an excuse. Say "Bryan, it will take some time to deal with that, and I want to keep this meeting brief. See me later and we'll go over your questions all at once." The beauty of this is that the wise guy won't even come looking for you later, since he probably suspects you're on to his game. Even if he does, he's lost what he wanted—an opportunity to embarrass you in front of the group.

Incidentally, this is an equally good method for handling any situation where open discussion will lead to embarrassment or anger. Always keep in mind that privacy is the proper context for dealing with controversy. Employees will usually tend to argue longer and louder if they have an audience.

## TIPS FOR LEARNING THE ROPES QUICKLY

One immediate concern as you begin your new supervisory assignment is learning the details of the job as quickly as possible. But, don't become frustrated if everything doesn't come together as fast as you would like. There's a natural inclination in any new position to think "It's going to take forever to learn this job." These fears, however, are overblown, since even routine matters that are unfamiliar can appear to be more difficult than they actually are. As time passes, you will master the job to the point that what now seems difficult becomes routine. Nonetheless, there are a number of measures you can take to help you get off to a fast start. These include:

### 1. Identify the Priorities of Your Job

Concentrate on learning how to handle these tasks. You obviously can't learn everything at once, so it's important to focus your energies on what matters most. This won't be as hard as it seems, since anything of significance will generally be brought to your attention by your boss, subordinates, or other departments. All you have to watch for is to make sure your attention isn't diverted from these topics by the daily routine. So even though you may want to give every subordinate your undivided attention in the early stages of your new job, don't hesitate to tell people you're busy, and will get back to them as soon as possible.

### 2. Find Yourself a Seasoned Mentor

A veteran supervisor whose skills you admire is the best bet. Of course, there's the question of whether the person has the time or inclination to help you out. You can discover this easily enough by a little trial and error in approaching a couple of logical choices when you need a question answered.

If someone is helpful and extends an offer of future assistance by saying something such as, "Anytime you have a question, give me a holler," then don't be bashful. Of course, you don't want to abuse this generosity, so don't overdo it and be sure to express your gratitude. One good way to show your appreciation is to tell your boss how helpful so and so has been. This compliment will likely be mentioned to your mentor, which will help maintain a willingness to assist you.

   Assuming you're not able to connect with another supervisor, your boss is the next logical choice. However, the problem here is that it's hard to be as open with your boss, since there's a hesitancy about demonstrating how little you know. Furthermore, your boss may feel compelled to assist you even when he or she lacks the time to do so. This could cause resentment which carries over to the future if you have a boss who isn't very understanding. Therefore, play it by ear in terms of using your boss as a coach. If you sense any degree of impatience, limit yourself to approaching your boss with questions only when imperative.

   A third possibility for receiving guidance comes from the people you supervise. Although they can't help in terms of supervisory duties, they are the natural experts to consult in terms of how operations are conducted. After all, who knows a job any better than the person doing it? Here though, you have to be selective, since some workers don't always know their jobs as well as they think. It shouldn't take you very long, however,  to sort out who knows what, and you can go from there in choosing who to solicit advice from.

### 3. Listen

   Basically, the more you listen, the more you'll learn. At the beginning, you won't be able to absorb everything right away, because everything will essentially be new. Don't worry about this—it's to be expected. You can, however, hasten the learning process by being a patient listener along with combining listening with another effective learning tool which is discussed next.

### 4. Learn to Ask Questions

   Everyone loves to demonstrate their knowledge, so give the people who work for you that opportunity by asking two basic types of questions. The first are those that seek clarification of what someone is telling you. If you don't understand, ask specific questions that will require the speaker to give you more detailed information. For example:

   *Worker:*    "It takes too long to get information from shipping."

   *Boss:*    "Why do you say that, Peggy?"

   *Worker:*    "Because at least twice a week when I'm checking to see if an order has been shipped, I can't get a straight answer."

*Boss:* "What seems to be the specific problem?"

*Worker:* "Frankly, it's Joe. He always complains he has more important work to do than answer my questions."

*Boss:* "Do you have this problem with anyone else in shipping?"

*Worker:* "No, everyone else is pretty good about it."

COMMENT: By asking follow-up questions, the supervisor was able to establish that it was one person and not the entire shipping department that was at fault. Of course, the boss here has to do some more research before talking to the shipping department supervisor, but the point is to ask as many questions as are necessary to gain an understanding of what someone is telling you.

The second type of question are those you initiate yourself to learn more about the specifics of your new job. Basically, if you're curious about something, ask about it, and continue to ask questions until you have a satisfactory understanding of the subject. The biggest hurdle you face here may be your own reluctance to ask questions. But, unless you do, it will take you much longer to absorb the intricacies of your new position.

## 5. Review Written Materials

Mastering your job is aided by scanning procedures, regulations, reports, and other documents that will help you do your job more effectively. Don't immerse yourself, however, in reading lengthy material unless you're convinced it's really relevant, since you don't want to waste time on information that's of little importance. If there's a significant amount of material you feel compelled to read, then you may want to take some of it home with you. That's not a happy thought, but early on in your new job, you won't have much time to do any reading at work.

## 6. Observe the Workplace

Probably the best way to acquaint yourself with the people who work for you, as well as the operating practices of the department, is to get out into the working area and observe as much as you can. In addition to the practical knowledge you will gain, it also demonstrates an interest in your workers and their jobs. They will know you're not just going to be a figurehead boss who sits in an office waiting for problems to come through the door. This is important, since your subordinates aren't going to respect a boss who shows no apparent interest in what they are doing or how they do it.

## EASING OUT AN ACTING SUPERVISOR

As you start your new job one of the first items you may have to deal with is handling the transition from someone who has been acting as supervisor until your selection for the job. Of course, this isn't always a problem, since you may be appointed before the previous boss leaves the job. In other situations, you may be selected to temporarily fill the role until your promotion becomes effective.

Nevertheless, if someone else was filling in on an interim basis, the first thing you want to do is establish an orderly transition of responsibilities. This shouldn't be particularly difficult if the acting supervisor was someone who had no interest in being permanently selected for the position.

If an acting supervisor is friendly and cooperative from the start, then you may be able to benefit from his knowledge of the situation. Take advantage of the opportunity to learn everything you can from this person, and don't neglect to express your appreciation for any assistance you get. The only problem you will likely encounter in this area is that workers may continue to treat the other person as the boss.

Don't make a big issue of this initially, but instead, gradually wean workers away from going to the other person for supervisory matters that should be brought to your attention. When the individual you are replacing is cooperative, this shouldn't be difficult. In fact, frequently an acting boss has been saddled with supervisory responsibilities on top of a normal workload and is anxious to unload these burdens.

Snags can occur sometimes when someone has been serving in an acting supervisory capacity for a job which they wanted but you got. Some people will accept the fact they were an unsuccessful candidate and cooperate fully. Others will reap their revenge by giving you only minimal recognition as the new boss and refuse to volunteer any information that might help you in performing your duties. Sometimes this resentment will fade with time, while in other instances the person will eventually transfer out of your group, or seek employment somewhere else.

If you face this sort of difficulty in your new position, you are likely to find that workers may continue to treat the acting boss as their supervisor by going to him or her for guidance. Of course, some of this will occur naturally in your first days on the job, since people tend to adapt slowly to any kind of change—including having a new boss. In fact, frequently this happens not so much as a deliberate attempt to ignore a new boss, but rather because it's easier to deal with someone you already know.

For this reason, don't overreact initially if workers appear to bypass you and seek answers from the person who was acting supervisor. If you make it a major issue by publicly proclaiming that you want everything to go through you, it can come across as insecurity on your part. Instead, try to ease yourself into the picture by asking lots of questions. In particular, let the former acting supervisor know that you want to be kept informed on matters large and small. Do this in a nonchalant way by saying something such as, "Linda, please keep me posted if someone runs something by you instead of coming to me. I have confidence in your decisions, but when people upstairs (higher-level managers) ask me questions, I don't want to be caught short." Most of the time this approach will result in a fairly smooth transition of power.

If, unfortunately, diplomatic attempts to gain control are met with subtle resistance, then you may have to confront the person directly. Call them into your office if you can talk privately there and state your position clearly. Try to do so without being accusatory, since the person will only deny that he or she was trying to undermine your authority. Say something such as, "Linda, I know you have a lot of experience and for that reason people are inclined to go to you for answers. But my job is to supervise this group, and I can't do that when I don't know what's going on. Therefore, in the future when someone comes to you with questions or problems that need solving, please have them see me. I may then consult you on how to handle certain situations, but the important thing is that I'm in the loop. I know with your experience that you understand the problem. Can I look forward to your cooperation?"

Obviously, the person will respond affirmatively, since even if they have no intention of cooperating, they aren't about to openly challenge your authority. But let's suppose that after this meeting you still find people going around you. Then, take the matter directly to the person involved. For instance, if you find a decision has been made on something you should have been consulted on, talk to the employee involved and insist that they get future directions from you. Word will quickly get around after this happens once or twice, and workers will then start to see you, not the pretender to the job.

Alternatively, you can hold a meeting in which you let everyone know that you expect things to go through you and not someone else. If you use this approach, do it in a nonchalant way without actually implying that someone is trying to subvert your authority. Just say something such as, "I've had a couple of situations where I've been caught short, since something was done without my knowledge. Use your judgment, but if you feel you need to clear something first, make sure it's run by me before you go ahead."

As for the resistant individual who continues to challenge your authority after you put them on notice, if they're still working for you when performance review time rolls around, they certainly won't deserve a high rating for cooperation. Of course, if they don't fall into line in the meantime, talk to your boss about the situation and see about getting them transferred. If that's impractical, make their life miserable by giving them every dirty job you can dredge up. Always keep in mind that it's a lot easier to win any contest of wills when you're the boss. Most people realize that, so the likelihood of any prolonged resistance to your authority will be minimal.

## THE BEST WAY TO ESTABLISH YOUR AUTHORITY

Before you actually take over your new position, you will probably receive some well-meaning advice on how to be a boss. Most of it, naturally, will be from the perspective of the person who is giving you counsel. That can pose a problem, since relating to other people is based as much on the personality of the individual as anything else. Some people can readily assert authority, even though they're mild-mannered, while others can bellow and bluster and still be ignored. So acting like a drill sergeant isn't the answer.

On the other hand, if you don't show that you're in charge, your job will be much more difficult—if not impossible—to do. Doing this successfully won't be accomplished by any one action on your part. Instead, it will result from how you handle supervisory situations the first few weeks on the job. During this time, the people who work for you will be watching how you deal with them personally, as well as how you react in business matters involving those outside of your immediate unit.

Although any one action won't clearly establish your authority, there are certain things you can do to demonstrate that you're in command of the situation.

## 1. Be Evenhanded in Dealing with Everyone

Don't lose control of your emotions, since this can be interpreted by others as a sign you can't handle the job. So even when anger might be justified, bite your tongue and keep your cool.

## 2. Make Your Own Decisions

Don't automatically defer to someone else when you're not sure what action should be taken in a given situation. Instead, listen to what the person recommends, ask any questions necessary to clarify matters, and then make the decision yourself. Give credit to the person whose advice you've solicited, but make sure you're the decision maker. You might say something like, "That sounds good to me, Scott. Let's go with it."

What you want to avoid is giving people the impression you don't know what to do—even when you don't. You may need to ask a lot of questions before making decisions as you're learning the ins and outs of the job. Choosing the easy course by letting employees make decisions for you, however, can be habit forming and can make it hard for you to exercise any authority later on. This can happen if you continually say, "You know better than I do, Peter. Do what you think is best," or "Anything you want to do is alright with me, Linda."

The problem with doing this is twofold. First, it encourages those who work for you to take actions without consulting you. Second, by not raising questions so you understand what is going on, you prolong the period of time it will take to fully understand the job.

***Note:*** It's proper to let employees handle as much responsibility as they can, including making routine, and perhaps not-so-routine, decisions without consulting you. This is, of course, the right way to manage once you become familiar with the position. You can't establish the limits of what workers may do on their own, however, until you have mastered the operating fundamentals, as well as the capabilities of each worker. At the outset you have to be more of a hands-on manager until you're in a position to freely delegate responsibility with confidence in the outcome.

## 3. Learn the Facts

Don't let yourself be bullied by the managers of other departments who may try to take advantage of your status as a new supervisor for their own purposes. For example, another supervisor may push to get work done on a priority basis by telling you that's the way it's supposed to be done, even though you know otherwise. Alternatively, it may be asserted that the previous boss did such and such, which may not be true. If you're sure of your facts, stand your ground. Otherwise, you will face recurring problems with these individuals.

If you're not certain of the facts, tell the person you'll check it out. Say, "I'll have to look into that, Gino. If that's how it's done, then that's what we'll do." A pushy person might try to stampede you into immediately agreeing, but don't give in. Even if it turns out they were correct, they certainly aren't handling the matter reasonably. One way or another, you must let them know you're somebody who cannot be intimidated. This type of person probably won't give you too many headaches once you stand your ground. That's because they're probably smart enough to know that antagonizing you further will only make it harder to secure your future cooperation.

## 4. Demonstrate a "Can-Do" Approach

Show confidence in your ability to tackle difficulties. This works particularly well with problems involving personnel matters that affect those you supervise. If you show that you're able to quickly get answers from staff members on matters of employee concern, you will gain a good deal of respect from those you supervise.

Conversely, if you drag your feet on resolving personnel issues, the first impression gained by subordinates is of a boss who doesn't care or who doesn't have clout. This isn't fair, since you're so busy trying to learn everything about your new job. But people are seldom fair when it comes to matters that are of personal concern. Therefore, make an extra effort to promptly resolve employee problems of a personal nature; it demonstrates that you're a boss who cares about her people. It also marks you as the person to go to when something needs to be done. Beyond anything else, it's a sure-fire way to get subordinates to respect you. And once that happens, you will have soundly established your authority as a supervisor.

## What to Do if Your Authority Is Questioned

One of the hardest problems you may have to deal with in your new position is having someone challenge the very fact that you are the boss. Of course, this may not happen at all, so it isn't something you should lose any sleep over. Most people are willing to give a new boss every opportunity to succeed. At worst, employees will be hesitant about coming to you with problems and adopt a wait-and-see attitude before they commit to giving you their full-fledged support.

This is to be expected, since it's natural for people to be reluctant about running the slightest risk of getting on the wrong side of a new boss. After all, you're now in a position of power where you have control to a large degree over the work destiny of the people you supervise. You probably haven't thought of it that way, as you rightly concern yourself with how to get off to a good start. But the fact is, you're the one who assigns work, recommends people for promotion, processes pay raises, and, if necessary, takes disciplinary action. From the point of view of those who now work for you, those are very real reasons to exercise caution in dealing with you until they get to know you better.

This hesitancy on the part of workers can sometimes be construed as a challenge to the authority of a new boss, especially when they seek the advice of your own boss or take action without consulting you. Don't be too sensitive to minor transgressions of this nature—they may well stem from a reluctance to bring you problems rather than a deliberate attempt to subvert your authority. Once employees see that you're fairly reasonable and won't criticize them for bringing problems to your attention, this sort of difficulty will fade away.

Then again, if you're unlucky, you may find yourself having to handle a situation where someone just plain doesn't want to accept the fact that you're now their boss. This should be obvious, since the person will go over your head on even the simplest matters. When this happens, two separate actions are required to get things back in focus. First off, talk to your boss and explain that you can't supervise the unit if your people go over your head for answers. In fact, this step won't even be necessary if your boss is savvy, since an upper-level manager will quickly direct an employee back to the immediate supervisor when these end-runs are attempted.

Once you have your boss on board, it's time for a heart-to-heart chat with the culprit. Explain to the employee that you're the supervisor responsible for what happens in the unit. Emphasize that there's nothing that can be accomplished by going to anyone else, since the employee will be told to see you. If you've been told that the employee said something unfavorable about you—that you won't make a decision, or you never tell anyone what to do, or you don't listen, etc.—bring this up.

Don't be hostile, but state that you want to know why the employee feels this way. Do your best to get the employee to open up and lay the cards on the table. Above all, don't get defensive if the worker does start to say something that you don't particularly want to hear. Think about whether there is any basis for the gripe. It could simply be the result of poor communication resulting in a misunderstanding. Perhaps what you hear might lead you to change the way you deal with either the group as a whole or this person individually. Whatever the result, by directly confronting these situations you will soon be able to bring any offender into line.

Unfortunately, your own workers aren't the only ones you may find challenging your authority. There may be another supervisor who decides for one reason or another to make you look bad. This will generally take one of two forms. Either this person will try to put you down in a face-to-face confrontation, or he will ignore you and go directly to your subordinates. In either case, you have to let him know you won't tolerate such actions. Serious morale problems within your group result when employees feel they're being bossed around by another supervisor.

If the offending supervisor launches a verbal attack upon you, respond firmly by saying that you won't listen to anyone who refuses to discuss something in a calm and reasoned manner. If necessary, ask him to leave the work area. Once you prove you can't be pushed around, this classic example of bullying will cease.

The best way to deal with the problem of another supervisor going directly to workers is to tell him politely that you want him to come through you. At the same time, let your people know that they're not to accept work directions from another supervisor unless you have told them to do so. Tell them to refer the person to you if they are approached with a request to do work which you haven't authorized. Once in a while, you may find someone who accuses you of being overly sensitive or who asserts that the previous boss allowed them to go directly to your employees with work requests. Politely, but firmly, point out that whether you're sensitive or not, or whether a prior boss operated differently, this is how you want it done. Once you put people who try this on notice, you aren't likely to have further problems in this area.

## SOME BASIC STEPS THAT WILL EARN YOU IMMEDIATE RESPECT

If your employees don't respect you, you will never be able to gain their confidence and trust. If that happens, workers won't be willing to confide in you or to put forth any extra effort in doing their jobs. Although earning the respect and trust of your employees is a gradual process based upon your performance over time, the clock starts running from your first day on the job. Fortunately, there are basic values you can practice from day one that will quickly earn the respect of those who work for you. These include:

**1.** Deal honestly with your workers. Don't hedge on telling them something just because it may not be well received. There's a natural tendency to procrastinate about giving out bad news, but hesitating doesn't solve anything—sometimes it can make matters worse. This is especially true if the bad news leaks out and rumors start to spread. For example, if everyone will have to work on an upcoming holiday, grit your teeth and tell it like it is. Sure, there may be grumbling, but it will be even worse if people aren't told until the last minute.

**2.** Show workers you have confidence in their abilities by soliciting their advice. You may not always choose to follow employee recommendations, but the fact that you're willing to listen to suggestions will be respected by those who work for you.

**3.** Always be conscious of the need to express appreciation for the efforts of your workers. This is especially true for any assistance you receive in learning about the operations of the department. Employees will be far more willing to help you learn the details of your job if you express your gratitude for any assistance they give.

**4.** Listen carefully to employee concerns. Since you're new, you may well hear more complaints than you would like. In addition, you won't be familiar enough with what's going on to easily separate fact from fiction. Nevertheless, be patient with people, since it will take a while to know which complaints are valid. Of course, to the extent possible, try to quickly resolve any difficulties brought to your attention.

**5.** Don't let your department get shortchanged just because you're the new kid on the block. Other department heads may look upon your novice status as an opportunity to dump undesirable assignments on your group. If you let this happen, employees will decide that you're not able to protect their interests. It may seem difficult to oppose more experienced bosses in this area. Those who are trying these tricks, however, will respect you for it. If push comes to shove and a decision has to be made by your boss, the odds are you will win, since the boss won't want to overburden someone new to the job.

**6.** Even though you might not think so, you can earn the respect of your workers by putting your foot down with someone who is goofing off. You may well find that an employee or two will decide to slack off in doing their work, assuming you won't notice since you're too busy settling into your job. Let anyone you see goofing off know about it right away. You probably won't have to say anything much more than, "Al, is there a problem I can help you with?" for the worker to get the message. Other workers will respect you for not tolerating a goof-off. After all, they are the ones who have to pick up the pace because someone isn't carrying their fair share of the load.

## How to Initially Work with Other Supervisors

The quickest and safest approach to learning how to function as a supervisor is to essentially play "follow-the-leader" and take your cues from more experienced supervisors where you work. In doing this, it's wise to try and sort out those bosses who are conscientious from others who may be more or less going through the motions. Pay particular attention to whom your boss seems to respect. This will become evident in several ways: take note of whose counsel the boss seeks and who never gets closely questioned or criticized in supervisory meetings.

Cooperate as much as possible with other supervisors whose departments work with your group regularly. Whenever practical, go out of your way to be helpful if another boss faces a deadline which is dependent on work to be performed by your group. Being supportive in this manner will position you as someone who is easy to work with. This can pay dividends if you find yourself needing a favor in return at some future date. It will also hasten your acceptance as a supervisor by your peers.

Incidentally, it's useful to have lunch with other supervisors, especially if they tend to eat in a group. This will give you the opportunity to learn the latest scuttlebutt that's circulating through the supervisory ranks. It also gives you a chance to meet other supervisors whom you may not yet have been introduced to.

Although you may prefer to eat alone or use the time to catch up on work, joining other supervisors for lunch will keep you abreast of what's going on in the management ranks and give you information that you won't be able to learn in any other fashion. It also serves another purpose: to prevent you from being pegged as a loner. Even when it isn't true, it's a label that's hard to overcome. Besides that, the sooner you get to know other bosses, the easier it will be when you have to work with them.

If you are new to the company as well as to your supervisory role, do things the way they are done in this organization, even though that differs from the way they were done with your former employer. Above all, never offer a suggestion on how to do something better by saying, "This is the way we used to do it at Trendsetter, Inc." Your idea may be superior, but it poses a couple of problems. Along with implying that your peers don't know what they're doing, it also paints you as a "know-it-all."—and that's the worst impression you want to create when you're trying to learn a new job. Save your good ideas for down the road, after you have established yourself. By then, you will have gained the necessary credibility to get your ideas accepted.

*Caution:* Although you want to be cooperative in helping other supervisors, don't place unreasonable demands on your workers just to score points with another boss. Be practical in what you offer to do to help out, and keep your eyes open for the one or two people who may try to take unfair advantage of your willingness to be a team player.

## LEARNING TO DEAL WITH YOUR OWN BOSS

The person with the greatest control over your future as a supervisor is your own boss. How you manage this relationship will to a large degree influence your ability to master your job. The natural inclination of some-one new is to try to impress the boss. This is often interpreted to mean making suggestions and the like which will show the boss how smart you are. Surprisingly, this isn't the best or the brightest way to win the admiration of a boss. Why not?

In the first place, as mentioned in the previous section, since you're new to the operation you don't have the credibility that experience brings when you make suggestions. Second, and even more critical, is the fact that you haven't been around long enough to learn the ins and outs of why things are done the way they are.

For instance, you might have a sensible, well-developed idea for changing a procedure. However, unknown to you, the procedure you want to replace was developed by your boss. If, not knowing that, you recommend it be changed, not only will your suggestion be rejected, but you'll also irritate your boss. This is just one more reason why it's wise to keep suggestions on hold until you gain both experience and acceptance in your new role. Of course, if your ideas are solicited by the boss, that's a different story. But even here, make sure to throw your ideas out as pos-sibilities, without being critical of the way things have been done in the past.

If your boss isn't looking for your great ideas, then just what is expected of you? What every boss looks for is a smooth and efficient operation that gets the job done with a minimum of problems—in short, as few headaches as possible. This is essentially your target for satisfying your boss's desires. But to do this successfully, you need to know a num-ber of details. Otherwise you're just stuck with a general idea of how to please your boss, without the foggiest notion of how to accomplish such an ellusive goal.

Learning the specifics for pleasing your boss essentially involves using your own powers of observation and listening carefully to what other supervisors have to say. The first imperative is to get a quick fix on your boss's likes and dislikes on a wide-ranging number of details. For example, one boss may loath being besieged by paperwork, while another may want virtually everything to be put in writing. This is just one of the minor preferences of your boss you have to master. This may seem like small potatoes, but little things can make a big difference in terms of how your boss rates your performance.

There are any number of other factors that can make or break a good working relationship with your immediate superior. If you're not careful to learn these pet peeves, it can cause you problems. For instance, you may notice that your boss is always busy except early in the morning. Without thinking, it's easy to assume that this is the best time to get to see him or her. Unfortunately, if you jump the gun, you may discover the boss's office is empty for an hour after starting time for a very good reason, which is that this particular boss is a grouch before 10:00 A.M. It suffices to say that learning these aspects of a boss's preferences is an essential starting point in keeping your boss happy.

Overall, the best method for working effectively with your boss is to take your cues from what he or she says and does. It's also handy to watch how the most successful supervisors relate to your boss. Of course, since you're new, the boss will probably cut you a little more slack than a seasoned pro might get. In feeling your way along, you will doubtless make some errors in judgment. That's to be expected, but the essential point is not to repeat your mistakes.

As time passes, you will learn many of the nuances that affect how you deal with your boss. Until the moment arrives when you are secure in your knowledge of the boss's quirks and of the internal politics of the company, it's best to be known to your boss as a hard worker who doesn't rock the boat. That alone is a hard enough task to tackle.

# Chapter Two

# PRACTICAL TIPS ON HANDLING YOUR NEW RESPONSIBILITIES

There are many things you will have to learn to deal with in your new position. To do this successfully, you must first establish yourself with your subordinates and others. This means learning to sort out who knows what in terms of the differing abilities of your people, how best to gain their cooperation and the cooperation of other departments, and getting a quick fix on what's important and what isn't.

Beyond that, you need to get a handle on your paperwork so it doesn't bury you before you even begin. There may also be other problems you have to quickly resolve, such as clamping down on any worker who for one reason or another decides to make your life miserable right from the start. These tasks aren't easy to accomplish, but they can be done with relative ease if you approach them properly. This chapter covers how to do that without placing too much stress on yourself or those you deal with on a daily basis.

## WHY IT'S BEST TO MOVE SLOWLY AT FIRST

As a new supervisor it's natural to want to create a good first impression with everyone from your boss to your subordinates. This isn't easy—what makes you look good in the eyes of your boss may not always sit well with those you supervise. And, if you try too hard to please those who work for you, the end result may be satisfied subordinates but an unhappy boss.

This is just one example of some of the juggling acts you will face in doing your job. As you gain experience as a supervisor, you will often find yourself trying to balance the competing interests of various people. It could be two employees who both want the same vacation time, or perhaps two department heads, each of whom wants their work to receive top priority. Learning how to do this successfully requires having command of sufficient facts to make the right decision. Beyond that, you may also have to convince those who weren't happy with your decision that it was nonetheless the right one.

Once you learn the ropes of your new position, making these kinds of decisions will become second nature. Until then, however, you will have to feel your way along. This is only one of the reasons why you want to proceed cautiously in your first few weeks on the job.

For example, things aren't always what they appear to be. Making hasty decisions and judgments without knowing the details and other nuances of a situation can lead to mistakes. Unless you take the time to learn everything you can about both the operation and the people that you supervise, you may be pegged as someone who shoots from the hip without getting the facts first.

Another reason for moving slowly in taking any significant action is that your employees will react to you based upon their initial perceptions. What you do and how you do it during the first days and weeks at your job will go a long way toward creating how you are viewed as a boss. Furthermore, if you move ahead quickly before you have command of the facts, workers may decide they would be better off not letting you know when something is being done wrong. Alternatively, they may decide that exercising care in what they do isn't that important, since their boss tends to play things by ear. Furthermore, it is much more difficult to emphasize the need for quality work unless a boss demonstrates those characteristics by his or her actions.

For these reasons, even though you're anxious to quickly demonstrate your skills as a supervisor, don't do so at the expense of not learning what you need to know before you act. It's impossible to grasp all of the details of your new job at once. If you start slowly, you will be able to learn things gradually. This is preferable to plunging ahead and ending up winging it on everything. This requires some patience on your part, but don't forget that since you're new it's expected that you will take a while to get up to speed. Once you gain experience, you won't be given the luxury of analyzing things at any length, so you might as well take advantage of it while you can.

*Caution:* Taking as much time as necessary to learn your job applies to run-of-the-mill operating practices, personnel matters, and the daily routine in general. Naturally, any actions that have to be taken immediately should be handled promptly. If you're unsure of how to handle any such matter, consult your boss or an experienced supervisor for advice on how to avoid doing the wrong thing by virtue of your inexperience.

## HOW TO LOOK GOOD WHEN A WORKER TRIES TO MAKE YOU LOOK BAD

One unpleasant task you may have the misfortune to perform is dealing with a worker who is deliberately trying to make you look bad in front of other people. This can happen when someone feels she—not you—should be the boss. Amazingly, this isn't always someone who was in contention for the job. In fact, it may even be a dud who isn't performing up to par in her current position. Then again, it may be someone who had no interest in the job but is simply a troublemaker trying to undermine your authority. Whatever the case, it's necessary for you to set such people straight sooner rather than later, since the longer they are allowed to go unchallenged, the harder it becomes to rein them in. What do these jokers do that requires you to set them straight? Let's look at a few common tactics they tend to use:

- always correct what you're saying in front of the group
- constantly complain to anyone who will listen that you don't know what you're doing

✏ may deliberately ask you questions for which they already know the answer, and then answer it themselves if you give an incorrect response

✏ will ask hardball questions you're not likely to know the answer to, and then make a sarcastic remark about your lack of knowledge

✏ can continually badger you to accomplish difficult administrative actions such as getting more help

✏ might make subtle—or not so subtle—comparisons with the prior supervisor

✏ will challenge your authority at any opportunity

✏ may complain they're not being treated fairly, with remarks about too much work, getting the dirtiest jobs, and so forth.

The list of possibilities could go on and on, since this type of person can be guilty of a lot of mischief, including the ability to devise clever ways to get under your skin. This type of behavior is unpleasant to deal with, but it can't just be ignored, since if it goes unchecked it can create further problems for you. For one thing, other workers will watch closely to see how you deal with this harassment. If you don't silence the troublemaker right away, then your remaining workers may start to dismiss your ability to manage the group. Even worse, more cautious troublemakers will see this as a sign that you can be taken advantage of. Should that happen, it will become extremely difficult to regain supervisory authority.

Fortunately, there's a silver lining beneath the hassle that this sort of behavior creates for you. It gives you a golden opportunity right at the start to show that you're the one in charge and that you won't tolerate any nonsense. In terms of specifics, you don't want to jump all over the culprit the first time a negative remark is made. If you do, then you will receive a response such as, "I didn't mean anything by that," or "I was only kidding." If you lash out in response, then you may appear to be overly sensitive in the eyes of onlookers. This plays right into the hands of the troublemaker.

Yet don't let an initial remark go unchallenged if it was direct enough not to be misconstrued as anything other than a deliberate attempt to discredit you. Just casually ask the person to repeat what she said, as if you didn't really hear her. Likely, she will just mumble that it wasn't important. Of course, it takes a little longer to catch up with a troublemaker who doesn't make snide remarks in your presence but rather criticizes you behind your back. Whatever the person's mode of operation, once you recognize a definite pattern, it's time to call a halt to it. Tell the culprit you want to see her privately, and directly state that you're not going to tolerate her nonsense.

Let's look at how such a confrontation might be handled.

*You:*     "Tonie, on several occasions you have made remarks which I don't appreciate, and I want this behavior to end here and now."

*Tonie:*     "You're kidding me? I haven't said anything wrong."

**Note:** Jot down notes of these actions as they take place, because you will need them when the employee typically denies doing anything wrong and later on if events ultimately culminate in disciplinary action.

*You:*     "I don't intend to point out every time you tried to be a wise guy, and there's no point in you trying to be cute about it. I'm telling you for the first and last time that I won't tolerate your behavior. I'm perfectly willing to forget about what's happened up until now and get off to a fresh start in our working relationship. But as you know, insubordination is grounds for dismissal, and if you keep it up, it's only fair to tell you that may be the end result, since you appear to be heading in that direction. Do I make myself perfectly clear?"

**Note:** There are a couple of points to keep in mind when you lay down the law. The first is that your tone of voice should be firm, but avoid the appearance of anger, since this may provoke an angry response. The last thing you need is to lose your cool and get drawn into a shouting match. It will prevent you from thinking clearly, and it sends a message that the culprit was successful in getting under your skin.

Second, as far as mentioning the possibility of dismissal for insubordination, the purpose of doing this is to emphasize how seriously you take the matter. This may shock the subordinate to her senses, since she might not have expected such a drastic action would even be considered. However, be sure you couch it as a possibility, since (1) actual insubordination may not have taken place yet and, (2) there will be several steps in the formal disciplinary procedure that have to be taken before that occurs. Nevertheless, by merely mentioning what might ultimately happen, the subordinate will likely recognize that she's dealing with someone who isn't going to tolerate her nonsense.

In your mind, you may have thought about the possibility of asking the person if she wanted to be transferred out of the unit. Eventually, this might be a viable option depending on what happens in the future. But at this point, you shouldn't give the worker this option. In the first place, it might be just what the individual was angling for, and you don't want to reward bad behavior. Second, whether or not the person wants a transfer, it sends a message that you are taking the easy way out rather than dealing with the issue. Since you're new on the job, a transfer might be interpreted by the other workers in your group as a sign they have a weak supervisor. A transfer is a better option for experienced bosses, since they have already established their authority as a boss. Even then though, the only times transfers should be considered are situations such as personality conflicts, assuming the individual is otherwise a good worker. Otherwise, a problem employee is just being sent off to someone else who will have to deal with the same problems.

Once these troublemakers are confronted, they will either grudgingly fall into line, or at least go underground in their attempts to sabotage you. If they follow the latter course of action, then lower the boom by giving them the dirtiest jobs you can find and formally discipline them the first time they give you an opportunity to do so.

One item that can't be overlooked is if, or when, you should get your boss involved when you're dealing with a troublemaker. When you become more experienced, even if you do notify your boss, you will likely be told to do what you think is best. At this stage of the game, however, it's wise to alert your boss as to what you intend to do.

On the other hand, you don't want to give the impression that you can't handle the situation yourself. For this reason, the best time is probably after you have had your initial session with the culprit. Brief your boss on what has been happening and let him know that you held a meeting with the troublemaker to straighten out the problem.

Since you haven't yet taken any formal disciplinary action, there's no sense in seeing your boss first. If you did, the boss would probably tell you to do what you already did on your own initiative. By briefing the boss afterwards, you demonstrate your ability to exercise your supervisory authority. Your boss is likely to be impressed by your willingness to act without having your hand held. Of course, at what point you tell your boss about the problem will be determined by how often you meet to discuss matters.

If the practice is to go over virtually everything that happens on a daily basis, then you should mention the troublemaker giving you a hard time once you're certain this is what is taking place. But if you meet more sporadically with your boss, and the meetings are primarily concerned with operations rather than your supervisory duties, wait until you have had your meeting with the problem employee. In any event, be sure you brief the boss before attempting any formal disciplinary action, since procedures must be carefully followed for both legal and administrative reasons.

## How to Deal with Other Assorted Pests

Whereas the previous section dealt with a serious troublemaker who was deliberately trying to give you a hard time, there are all sorts of lesser fools you may have to deal with. They may not pose any major problems but instead waste their time—and yours—with a lot of silliness in one form or another. Their actions may not be deliberate, but rather reflect poor work habits or a difficult personality. These include pests who always bother you, as well as shirkers who always look for a way to avoid doing any work. Depending upon the nature of the behavior there are basically three things you can do:

✐ Tell them what they're doing that irks you.

✐ Put them in place with a little bit of sage advice or sarcasm as the situation demands.

✏ Put them to work so they can't practice their ploys.

Let's look at a few of the more common pests you may have to deal with. You may discover to your misfortune that you have a worker who continually annoys you as well as others. The person may be a good worker, but consistently interrupts people—including you—when you're busy. Just sitting down with someone like this and pointing out what they're doing wrong will often solve this problem.

Sometimes people don't recognize they are bothering others. Part of the reason is that there's a natural reluctance to tell someone they are pestering you, which is especially true if the individual is a likeable sort. This takes on an added dimension in the workplace, since it's generally a lot more pleasant to engage in small talk than to work. So when the office chatterbox interrupts people, they are often more than willing to kill a little time discussing the subject of the day. Naturally, a little bit of this is harmless and should be ignored. But when someone does this habitually and day after day bounces from one person to the next, a lot of productive time is being wasted. Furthermore, these interruptions can distract people from the work at hand so they lose their concentration on the task they were performing.

If you have someone who does this regularly, sit them down and tell them what they are doing wrong and that it is keeping people from doing their work. Usually, this is sufficient to cure the problem. If it isn't, give these individuals additional duties to keep them busy. If that's not practical, then perhaps you can move their work location, so they have less access to people they can bother. Another option is to relocate them closer to your office so you can keep a watchful eye on them.

You may find you have to repetitively remind someone such as this of their behavior, since it may well be a personality trait. This is especially true if the person is a good worker who just likes to socialize, rather than someone who is looking for an excuse to goof off.

A second type you may have to deal with is a worker whose sole goal in life seems to be giving you unsolicited advice on how to handle every aspect of your job. This may result from either the person having illusions about their knowledge of the operation, or merely result from an attempt to place themselves in good standing with their new boss. Although you should welcome all the help you can get in learning your new job, you don't have time to waste on an advice-giver who probably knows little or nothing about anything, including how to do his or her own job. Politely tell this sort of busybody that you appreciate their assistance, but you're too busy to talk with them. If this doesn't work, give them little chores to do whenever they bother you. At least this way, you will be getting some benefit out of them.

On a more unpleasant level, you may have a worker or two who is foulmouthed or otherwise demonstrates obnoxious behavior. Here, you shouldn't have any hesitancy or remorse about quickly putting them in place. Tell them their behavior is uncalled for and that you won't tolerate it. You may not even have to go this far, since a well-placed comment on your part may embarrass the worker into ending the distasteful conduct. For example, if you overhear someone using profanity, say something like, "Clean up your vocabulary, Jim," or "I'd appreciate it if you would refrain from using profanity at work."

These are just a few examples of the types of troublesome behavior you may find yourself forced to deal with. After all, many different kinds of personalities are thrust together in the workplace, so anything that happens shouldn't surprise you. Whatever it might be, the basic point is to keep these people busy and prevent them from bothering others. As a new supervisor there are two considerations to keep in mind when dealing with these problems. One is that you should be reasonable about what is acceptable and what isn't. All you need to do here is use a little common sense. In addition, the prior supervisor may have been lax in this area, so changing ingrained habits may take time. Consequently, don't waste a lot of time dealing with these people at the expense of high priority tasks.

Nevertheless, let those who work for you know right away about any practices you find to be unacceptable. This is one place where being new to the job is an advantage, since workers will be more likely to pay attention rather than start off on the bad side of a new boss.

## WHY IT'S IMPORTANT TO HAVE A SENSE OF HUMOR

The last two sections may have given you an inkling as to why a sense of humor is a valuable asset in your position. Make no bones about it, supervising people is a tough job. You have all kinds of people working together who aren't necessarily socially compatible. That alone can make it difficult to keep people working together as a team. But there are other aspects of the job that can try your nerves. For one thing, sooner or later you will have to make tough decisions that have a great impact upon your employees. Pay raises, promotions, job assignments, disciplinary actions, and perhaps even layoffs or firings all fall into this category.

From the standpoint of doing your job, you may from time to time be faced with unreasonable demands from upper management, coupled with a lack of resources to adequately do the job. But even beyond these trying situations, people naturally respond better to someone who can see the lighter side of life. So even on a daily basis, a little bit of levity can go a long way in boosting everyone's morale.

This isn't to imply that you should take a crash course in comic relief, since even if you're not good at humor, it's just as effective if you're able to recognize and respond to someone else's. If you're not funny, don't try to be. However, always try to be pleasant, even under difficult circumstances. Workers will react much more readily to a boss who is polite and pleasant in dealing with them.

Although encouraging a friendly atmosphere within your group is a good idea, there are a couple of precautions to take. First and foremost, any kidding that does take place shouldn't have any sexist, racial or ethnic overtones. Be perfectly clear at the start that this won't be tolerated. In addition, don't let things get out of hand to the point where some practical joker starts to get on people's nerves. After all, it's a workplace, not a funhouse.

From a personal standpoint, you will be much more effective in doing your job if you don't let the hassles and headaches of supervision get to you. Try to see the lighter side of things, and if you have to let off steam, do it away from work whenever possible. No matter how impossible a task may seem, take comfort in knowing you're not alone in feeling that way. Every supervisor faces seemingly insurmountable problems on occasion. So just do your best in dealing with each problem, and then forget about it. Many of the tasks that appear to be impossible to master in your first days and weeks on the job will become routine to the point of boredom after a while.

## GETTING OFF ON THE RIGHT FOOT WITH OTHER DEPARTMENTS

Beyond your boss and subordinates, the people within the company that you deal with most frequently will generally be those in departments that work closely with the group you supervise. Good relations with these people can make your job a lot easier. This isn't always easy to achieve, especially if you deal regularly with several departments that rely on work being done by your group. You will also have to learn how to get departments that provide support to your group to meet your needs in a timely manner. These working relationships can become filled with tension during times of peak workload, so your ability to exercise tact and diplomacy will be put to the test. Let's look at some measures you can use to establish and maintain good working relations with both other department heads as well as the key people who work for them.

First of all, go out of your way to get to know other supervisors you will work with on a regular basis. Ask them what concerns they might have or what previous problems they have had in dealing with your group. Solicit their advice as to what you can do to better serve their needs. Expressing a desire to be helpful will earn their respect. In fact, if they experienced difficulty in working with your predecessor, they may treat you as a long-lost friend. In any case, making it known that you are cooperative will serve you well.

For one thing, if other department heads have had trouble in the past working with the group you now supervise, they won't be inclined to be helpful. This could make for a rocky road in your dealings with them. So letting them know you believe in cooperation rather than conflict can deflect potential problems before they arise.

Furthermore, there will be times in the future when for one reason or another, such as a backlog of work or other priorities, your group won't be able to complete everyone's work as fast as they would like. This could cause all kinds of hassles and conflicts with other department heads. If they know you to be cooperative, however, there will be a greater willingness to listen to and understand your problems. There's no magic in this at all. The simple truth is that people are more willing to be tolerant of those who have previously demonstrated a willingness to be cooperative. So in any of your dealings at work, doing your best to be helpful will pay dividends when you need them most.

The longer you're at your job, the easier it will be to see that the people you deal with all have different methods of getting their work done. Some of the other groups you work with will have bosses who want everything done right away, while others just patiently wait their turn. However, you can't simply cater to the demanding ones, since the less demanding people may have higher priority requirements.

Until you get a handle on which jobs are more important than others, you're better off essentially doing the work on a first-in, first-out basis. If someone wants priority treatment, and it will mean slippage in doing someone else's work, get your boss involved if you aren't sure of the urgency expressed by the person claiming an immediate need. Otherwise, you may become the victim of someone just taking advantage of the fact that you're new. This will needlessly result in making those whose work gets shunted aside less than happy with you. Although you want to be obliging, don't be taken advantage of by someone who is using your inexperience as a means of getting preferential treatment they don't deserve.

Let's look at how you can handle such a situation.

## Background

Joe D., the supervisor of another unit comes to you with an urgent work request. In order for you to complete the work when Joe says it is needed, you will have to miss the due dates on work in progress for two other departments. Since you're not yet familiar enough with the work requirements, you can't be sure if Joe's job should take priority. You do know from the grapevine that Joe tends to be pushy in dealing with others.

## The Encounter

| | |
|---|---|
| *Joe D.:* | "I need 120 type 30AZ gizmos from you by Friday to meet a rush order." |
| *You:* | "Sit down and let me check my schedule, Joe." (You reach for your work schedule.) "We're pretty well booked for the week, Joe. The earliest we could finish them is next Wednesday. Can you live with that?" |
| *Joe D.:* | "Hey, this is urgent. Just put something else on the back burner." |
| *You:* | "I can't just arbitrarily slip a due date for someone else, Joe, even though I want to help you out." |
| *Joe D.:* | "Look, you're new here, so you don't know how we operate. Whenever something's priority, everything else gets put aside." |

*You:*  "That sounds sensible, but what tells me one job should take priority over another?"

*Joe D.:*  "I'm telling you. Who would know better than me?"

*You:*  "No one, I guess, Joe, but since I'm new around here I better check it out with Jack Burns. (the boss) If he gives the OK, I'll have my people drop everything and get right on your order."

*Joe D.:*  (Looking frustrated, starts walking away and says) "I don't know why you have to see Burns. After all, you're the supervisor."

(After Joe D. leaves, you head up the hall to see Jack Burns, your immediate boss.)

*You:*  "Sorry to bother you, Jack, but Joe D. was just in my office looking for 120 type 30AZ gizmos by Friday. I told him they couldn't be done before next Wednesday, since we're booked for this week. He claims it's a priority order, and I should slip my other delivery dates to meet his. I don't know the procedure for priorities, so I thought I'd better touch base with you."

*Burns:*  "I'm glad you did. Let me call his boss and see what the story is." (He talks on the phone a few minutes, hangs up and continues.) "Just what I thought. That order has about as much priority as day-old bread. Joe D. thinks everything he has to do is a priority. Furthermore, he knows the priority procedure requires his boss to sign off on a request and then it has to be approved by me. I'm glad you checked with me. I should have told you what the procedure was, but I didn't think anyone would try an end-run like that. In the future, nothing's priority unless I've signed off on it. If any other clown tries that, send him directly to me."

As the example demonstrates, there may be a few people who try to take advantage of your inexperience as a supervisor. For the most part, being cooperative with others will prove to be beneficial. Nevertheless, don't let anyone push you around, since it's equally as important to earn the respect of the people you deal with. Incidentally, although we have talked about this using other departments as an example, the people you deal with will vary with the specifics of your job. In your particular position, most of your contact might be with staff people or customers. Still, the principles of cooperation are the same.

## A GREAT WAY TO GAIN WORKER COOPERATION

Though you might not believe it, there is a sure way to gain the cooperation of those who work for you in getting the job done. It involves nothing more than earning the respect of your employees. You can do this from the start by following a few fundamentals. These are:

1. Always be fair in your treatment of those who work for you.

2. Stand up for your people when it's called for. Don't use them as an excuse for missed deadlines or low productivity.

3. Be as flexible as you can in meeting the needs of employees who experience problems. If someone needs time off to cope with a personal emergency, bend the rules a little if you have to. If you go out of your way for them, they will do the same for you when the workload gets heavy and you need that extra effort from everyone.

4. Be nice to people. You don't have to be everyone's friend, and in fact you're better off if you don't socialize with those who work for you. But you can and should show an interest in them, even if it's nothing more than a friendly greeting in the morning.

5. Try to make your people active participants in deciding how the work is done. The people doing the work know far more than many managers give them credit for. If they see you are willing to listen to their suggestions, it's likely you will discover many little ways to make the work done by your group easier and more efficient.

It's important to try and follow these principles from the start, since the initial impressions you create will be lasting ones. Admittedly, there may be one or two people who will try to take advantage of your enlightened style of management. With these people you should be firm but fair in insisting they follow the rules and do their jobs to the best of their ability. Even if you have to use disciplinary measures with someone, you will receive the support of those who are doing their jobs, since everyone knows a good boss when they see one. When your employees view you positively, they won't be very tolerant of a co-worker who is giving you a difficult time.

As a new supervisor, it's important to avoid using fear as a managerial weapon. In the past, all too many managers operated much like military drill instructors by issuing orders and expecting them to be carried out, with any failure resulting in a loudmouthed reprimand. Disciplinary measures and on-the-spot firings were used as substitutions for effective leadership. Although these tactics are becoming relics of the past, there are still bosses who believe in the stick rather than the carrot. People don't respond favorably to this sort of treatment, and any manager who still uses these methods will inevitably find that out. Even if you have an old-fashioned boss or two where you work, avoid mimicking their example. Always keep in mind that the reputation you earn as a rookie boss will be tough to shake even after you become a veteran supervisor.

## SORTING OUT YOUR SUBORDINATES' ABILITIES

It will take a few weeks at least, but one of the first items on your agenda should be to learn the relative strengths and weaknesses of those who work for you. Knowing who is good at what will help immeasurably in getting maximum productivity from your group. Basically, you will get to know the relative talents of the individuals who work for you by observation. You will also get some feedback from workers as to the jobs they like and dislike.

After a short while you will know which people are good at detail work and which aren't. There will be people who can pump out work in quantity, while others may be slower but do better quality work. Being able to identify these traits lets you assign work that best suits the talents of individual workers. For example, if you get a rush job, you don't want to give it to a perfectionist who is slow but sure. Alternatively, if the priority is quality, you will know who to go to.

Knowing these individual characteristics will be a big help in scheduling the unit's workload. This information is valuable in other ways too. For instance, it will give you some clues as to training needs and input into the potential of people for reassignment to other positions.

It's not always recognized, but one of the key ingredients to productivity is the ability to allocate work so you get maximum benefits from the talents of each individual. Some supervisors set the same expectations for every worker without even thinking about differences in ability. It's automatically assumed that workers who don't meet the pre-set standard aren't performing up to par. But a boss who recognizes these differences in performance levels can assign work accordingly. The end result will be greater output for the group as a whole. Knowing who does what best can make your job a lot easier to do.

This is true even if every worker performs the same tasks. As a minimum, there will be quality and quantity variables. Therefore, if you supervise an operation where all your employees have identical duties, you can still benefit from knowing which workers are superior from a quality standpoint, and which ones excel at meeting quantitative goals.

Of course, there are other influences that affect employee performance. The work ethic varies from person to person, so individual effort is a factor. And, naturally, experience and level of training also have to be considered. Before you even begin to think about these aspects of performance, however, you first should get a feel for the basic existing abilities of the individuals working for you.

***Pointer:*** Before you are on the job very long, you will soon notice that one or two or your workers tend to outperform the others. It's natural that as you go along, whenever you need a job done quickly, you will tend to assign it to these people. That makes sense from the standpoint of meeting deadlines and completion dates. However, always be sensitive to the fact that you don't want to overburden these individuals with work. In effect, that would be punishing them for being hard workers. Unless something is of the utmost urgency, try to assign some of the rush jobs to workers who may be a little slower, rather than constantly placing pressure on one or two people.

## How to Get a Handle on What's Important and What Isn't

Since everything is new to you when you begin your duties, one of the first things to think about is how to sort out what you have to do right away and what can wait until later. Some of these decisions will be made for you, such as your boss telling you he needs such-and-such a report by tomorrow morning. But for the most part, you will have a lot of work to tackle, with no immediate inkling of any specific priority. The main danger here is that deadlines loom ahead that you're not even aware of—at least until someone charges into your office looking for something that was due yesterday.

Naturally, there will be existing work schedules and the like which essentially resolve any questions on what's due when. On other occasions, people will tell you when they have something which has a degree of urgency attached to it. For anything you have a question on as to its priority, seek out the answer from someone knowledgeable on the matter. This will help to keep you from operating in the dark.

In more general terms, for those items that don't have a specific completion date assigned, you can mentally group most of them into the following categories:

- ✏ problems that have a potential impact on getting your unit's work accomplished (example: equipment breakdowns)

- ✏ general work flow actions (example: giving out work assignments)

- ✏ personnel matters (example: preparing timesheets)

- ✏ routine paperwork (example: reading new procedures)

For the most part, the above categories generally represent the order of importance that you should place on anything you have to do. Obviously, this is only a rough guide for you to use in deciding what to work on first. There could be any number of situations where what is routine one minute becomes priority-plus the next. However, barring exceptions, always place the most importance on getting the job done. On the other end of the scale are all kinds of routine paperwork that detours onto your desk—instead of heading directly to a recycling plant where it belongs.

The problem of assigning priorities to your workload will fade into the past as you learn the details of your job. However, there is one issue in this area that even veteran supervisors sometimes overlook. This is the importance that your subordinates place on matters affecting them. These can range all the way from working conditions to someone having a mistake in their paycheck.

Don't blithely brush off workers when they come to you with problems, even if they seem relatively insignificant. What's essentially meaningless to you may have great importance attached to it by someone else. A good way to look at these problems is to try to put yourself in the shoes of the other person. Obviously, you will have people come to you with petty complaints. But even here, unless the individual is a chronic complainer, at least listen sympathetically, although there is essentially nothing that can be done to satisfy the employee. Your willingness to listen will encourage workers to come to you with problems. Some may be valid, others less so, but by openly communicating with your subordinates, you avoid the danger of being unaware of something that is of consequence. By doing this, there's far less chance of looking foolish in front of your boss because you didn't know what was going on in your own department.

## THE GOLDEN RULE ON WHAT TO DO FIRST

No matter how good you become at being able to determine what should be done next in terms of your workload, there is an overriding consideration that can't be ignored. This is when someone in a position of power wants something done, which except for the person's status in the company would be considered routine. Sometimes these requests are obvious, such as when your boss says, "Drop everything right away and work on this."

Naturally, what the boss wants, the boss gets. But even here, you have to be careful, since your boss like everyone else can be forgetful. If you're already working on something significant when you receive such an edict, make the boss aware of this if the new assignment means the initial project won't be completed when promised. Say something such as, "Do you want me to drop work on...(whatever the project is) and do this first?" All you're doing here is giving yourself a little insurance in case one of the two priority projects aren't finished on time. This forces a choice as to which job comes first, since your boss (1) may have forgotten about the first assignment, (2) might be assuming both will be completed on time, or (3) may not even know about the other priority item.

There are other occasions when you will have to consider juggling normal priorities because of demands from someone in a position of power within the company. Outside of your boss, these requests will usually originate with higher-level managers. Practical politics and diplomacy come into play when you're placed in this situation. For instance, if a high-level manager asks for something to be accomplished right away, don't directly raise the issue of conflicting priorities. In the first place, the manager might not even care about what else you're doing. Besides that, since you're new on the job, any attempt to convince a senior manager that you have more important work to do won't be warmly received. Instead, after the person leaves, bring the problem to your boss's attention. Since position and power generally rule in determining what gets done first, chances are your boss will tell you to give the senior manager's work higher priority.

These situations can get tricky when you're relatively new and aren't aware of the power structure within a company. For this reason, any time you are unsure about whether to give work a higher priority because of the status of the individual making the request, don't argue the issue, but immediately consult your boss when the person leaves. The *general rule* of what to do first is determined by which is the most important priority in terms of meeting sales goals, production quotas, or whatever the standard is which applies to the duties of your particular job. But the *golden rule* which keeps you out of trouble is to give top priority to requests made by higher-level managers, no matter how trivial the assignment is in comparison to your other work.

***Caution:*** When it comes to power within an organization, there are people who wield considerable influence apart from their formal position in the company. These folks can cause you headaches if you're not aware of their power. They ask you to do something in a hurry and you rightly refuse because it doesn't deserve to be done ahead of other projects. The next thing you know, your boss is at your shoulder telling you to do such-and-such for so-and-so. What's the deal? It's that these people have connections, either through friendships or by working for someone influential within the company. Once you learn who these individuals are, treat them with respect, since they often have the ability to make your life difficult if you give them a hard time.

## A Few Basic Tricks for Controlling Your Paperwork

If you happen to be sitting at a desk overflowing with paperwork as you're reading this, you probably hope the first recommendation is to throw everything in the barrel. It's not, but it's almost as good. Frankly, in your first days and weeks on the job, you should ignore most of your paperwork. Your first priority as a new supervisor is to focus on learning the operational aspects of your job and getting to know those who work for you, as well as others you will be doing business with on a regular basis. Only deal with paperwork that is essential to keeping things running smoothly. Most of this will be obvious, such as work orders, timesheets, and memos from your boss. Just quickly scan everything that comes your way, and set aside anything that doesn't have an immediate necessity attached to it. Let this paperwork sit until you have satisfied yourself that everything is sufficiently under control so you can spend some time going through it.

An abundance of paperwork can be conquered if you tackle it with a plan in mind. Even experienced supervisors have trouble keeping up with their paperwork, and this problem is compounded when you're new to the job. Much of what comes across your desk is unfamiliar, so your first problem is just figuring out what to do with it. A veteran boss can be a big help to you in this regard, but you can't be asking them questions twelve times a day. However, this problem is already solved, since you can sort through what you have accumulated and group it by category. This way, one question will essentially get you the answer you need on how to handle an entire category.

One fear everyone has about letting paperwork sit around is that something important will be overlooked. This is unlikely, since your initial scanning will pretty much be able to identify anything that's obviously important. But if by chance, a document that requires immediate action does get inadvertently overlooked, there are safeguards. First, someone will either call or come looking for your reply. You can then say something such as, "Let me look through this paperwork and get back to you." Then, dig it out of the pile and answer it. If that isn't feasible just say, "I thought I'd answered everything that had a due date on it. I apologize if I goofed, but being new, I'm still trying to get caught up." Although someone may be unhappy, this is a reasonable response and it should get you off the hook.

The irony of worrying about paperwork burdens is that a lot of the paper that comes your way is of little or no value to you. Some people have a lazy habit of sending information out without making any effort to determine who needs it. So a lot of what you will receive doesn't even have to be read. Other material, such as procedural updates, just need to be filed away for future reference. Once you are able to discern which is which in terms of useful and useless material, you will soon tame the paperwork monster.

## WHY IT'S SMART TO BE AVAILABLE AND VISIBLE

Keeping a diverse group of people working together as a cohesive unit isn't easy, and with many supervisory duties to perform you don't have a lot of time to spare. But right from the first day on the job, it's important for employees to know you're available whenever they want to see you. Some managers attempt to meet this need by establishing an "open-door" policy and encouraging workers to see them in their office. This in itself isn't enough, since there's a natural reluctance to entering a boss's office. A worker's thinking might go like this:

- The boss may want to be left alone.

- Someone else is always in the office.

- I better stay away, since I'm likely to get more work handed to me.

- What if I'm asked about something I don't have the answer for?

- Seeing the boss means I might get asked to work overtime.

Of course, there are all sorts of reasons such as these that have a common theme which is, "If you leave a boss alone, the boss will leave you alone." This tends to diminish the value of an open-door policy to some extent. As a result of this hesitancy, workers will avoid taking the initiative to go to the boss's office unless it's absolutely essential to do so. This is even more likely when workers are dealing with a new boss. It's essentially the same as walking up to a stranger and striking up a conversation. This isn't easy to do for most people. And a boss is even more difficult to approach—unlike a stranger, a boss has the power to make a worker's life miserable.

Therefore, although having an open-door policy is fine as far as it goes, it's far better to combine this with the habit of circulating throughout the work area as much as possible. Adding visibility to availability has many advantages for a new boss. Walking around and talking with workers gives both you and them the opportunity to develop a familiarity with each other. It will definitely hasten the process of learning about both the people you supervise and the working procedures they follow.

There are also other benefits to be derived from making yourself visible in the work area. For one thing, it discourages workers from goofing off. In addition, it can give you a jump in spotting and solving small problems before they become big ones. Naturally, you have other duties which won't always give you the luxury of circulating in the work area as much as you might like. But in the initial stages of your job, abandon your office as much as possible and get out on the floor. If you do this, you'll learn the fundamentals of your new job a lot more quickly.

# Chapter Three

# Basic Tactics for Mastering Supervisory Skills

*L*earning how to save time and effort in performing routine duties will make your job a lot easier to do. For example, meetings can drag on forever and accomplish little if they're not properly controlled. Other chores, such as briefing your boss, can be painless or painful, depending upon your level of preparation. In fact, there's a whole laundry list of items which individually aren't of great consequence, but taken together they can eat up a big chunk of your time.

Given the amount of effort required to master your new role as a supervisor, it's useful to know the shortcuts for handling these matters. That way, you won't be spinning your wheels on minor details, all the while wondering if things will ever fall into place. The following sections contain many pointers that will help you get started in the right direction.

## Basic Steps for Holding a Meeting

Most of the meetings you're responsible for scheduling will be with the group you supervise. These will be pretty informal and should cause no particular difficulty as long as you're able to avoid the pitfalls that can make any meeting a waste of time. The potential hazards are easy enough to deal with, but frequently get overlooked. If you get in the habit of using a few simple techniques during your initial meetings, however, they will set the tone for future get-togethers with your workers.

The most basic consideration involving any meeting is whether it should be held at all. This particular point is of more significance for people who from time to time conduct larger, more formal meetings involving participants from different groups within the company. This shouldn't be a task you ordinarily have to do, but if the nature of your position requires this sort of meeting, be sure to explore alternatives before scheduling these gatherings. Otherwise, you'll be committing the time and energy of people to a meeting that may not be necessary in the first place.

Although it's a good general rule to keep meetings to a minimum, as a new supervisor a regular meeting with your own group can help immensely in several ways. First, it can serve as an ice-breaker forum where both you and your employees get to know each other. It will allow you to express your ideas and expectations, as well as provide an opportunity for workers to give you feedback.

Second, holding a regular meeting will give you an opportunity to more rapidly familiarize yourself with both subordinates and operating practices. These get-togethers also encourage the open and ongoing lines of communication which will help in effectively managing the operations you supervise. When practical, it's worthwhile to schedule these group meetings once or twice a week for your first couple of months on the job. Later, as both you and your employees settle into a routine, you may find they can be scheduled less frequently, or perhaps only sporadically when specific topics have to be discussed.

In planning these unit meetings, don't overlook the following factors:

1. Schedule the meetings for a time when they will cause the least disruption of everyone's work. At the start or end of the day is generally best.

2. If you have specific items you want to cover, jot them down so they won't be overlooked when the meeting gets under way.

3. Make the meetings brief. Ten or fifteen minutes should be sufficient, although at the beginning you may want to let them run longer, since the familiarization process will involve longer discussions. Once you start to notice a drop-off in the topics you or your subordinates want to talk about, however, establish a set length of time for each meeting and stick to it.

4. Keep the meetings focused and avoid drifting into casual conversation.

Since you will be the one responsible for chairing these meetings, the responsibility for keeping them under control will be yours. After your employees get to know you, the only repeating problem you'll have is to keep the meetings focused. In any meeting, there's always the possibility of the conversation drifting off the subject entirely. When this happens, you will have to be alert to interrupt and get it back on track. Simply say, "Let's get back to (whatever the topic is) or we'll be here all day."

There are additional difficulties that you may have to deal with in your first few meetings, until workers see how you react to these situations. These include:

- someone giving you a hard time;

- a worker monopolizing the conversation; and

- disagreements about a subject becoming overheated.

Here's how to handle each of these situations:

### Someone Baiting You

> *Paul:* "How come no one in our group ever gets any awards?"
>
> *You:* "What do you mean, Paul?"
>
> *Paul:* "Smitty's group always has one or two people who get cash awards for outstanding performance every year. We never get any."

*You:* "Being new, I don't know the answer to that. However, if over time any of you qualify for any awards, I'll certainly put you in for them."

*Paul:* "What do you mean over time. How long do we have to wait?"

*You:* "I certainly can't recommend someone for an outstanding performance award until I've been here long enough to know they deserve it."

*Paul:* "I've been here five years and never gotten anything. Why should I bust my butt for nothing?"

*You:* "Paul, I can't speak for what's happened in the past, but I do know that anyone working for me who deserves recognition will get it."

*Paul:* "I've heard that before. Just how long do I have to prove myself?"

*You:* "Paul, you seem particularly upset about this. Does anyone else feel this way? (No one else responds) Well Paul, rather than spend any more time discussing this issue now, if you have anything further to add, see me later. In the meantime, let me quickly cover a couple of other things, so we can get back to work.

COMMENT: There are any number of personal gripes that someone may choose to air at a general meeting. Whatever the topic may be, it should be resolved privately. Therefore, if you have to handle such a problem, avoid getting drawn into a long discussion at a group meeting. Simply tell the employee to see you later. There are a couple of reasons for doing this. First, since it's an individual gripe, it's unproductive for the group to be wasting time while it's discussed. Second, these personal issues often require things to be said that are best done in private, such as the employee doesn't have a beef because his or her performance is subpar. You don't want to embarrass an employee by airing these facts in public—even though the worker chooses to raise the issue before the group. Finally, you won't always have the facts you need to respond on the spot, since you may have been unaware of the matter until it was raised in the meeting.

On occasion, you might not be sure whether it's a personal or general gripe the individual is raising. That's why, in the previous example the supervisor asked if anyone else felt the same way. When no one responded, it was reasonable to assume it was an individual complaint. Of course, if others had chimed in with similar complaints, it would become an issue you would have to deal with on a group basis. But even then, after everyone has been heard, you would essentially tell them that you would look into the matter. Don't let workers trap you into making commitments before you have had a chance to get the facts you need to make a decision. Once in a while, one or more workers may try to take advantage of the fact that a supervisor is new and try to pull a fast one. If this happens to you, once it's recognized that you're not going to bite at the bait, this nonsense will cease.

## Someone Monopolizing a Meeting

Another common difficulty that often occurs at meetings is when one or two talkative individuals monopolize the conversation so no one else can get a word in edgewise. When this happens, you have to tactfully quiet them down. Here's one way of doing it.

**The Scenario:** Imagine you're having a group meeting to discuss the need to rearrange the layout of the working area, which will affect everyone. As the discussion evolves two employees (Ned and Valerie) get involved in a long two-way discussion of the subject and interrupt whenever anyone else starts to express their thoughts. You want everyone's opinion of all of the pros and cons, so you have to diplomatically quiet these two people down without discouraging them from raising valid issues.

*Valerie:* "You're better off by having your desk near the copier, Ned, since you use it more than anyone else."

*Ned:* "No way, I don't want to be interrupted every two minutes by someone using the copier."

*Alice:* "I think we ..."

*Valerie:* "Well, neither do I, Ned, and since you use it more than anyone else, it only makes sense for you to be near it."

*Frank:*     "Can I say something here?"

*Ned:*       "Wait until we finish this, Frank. Who says I use it more than you, Valerie?"

*You:*       "Look Ned and Valerie. No decision has been made on anything yet. The purpose of this meeting is to get everyone's thoughts about the new layout. You two have made your feelings clear about the copier. Let's hear what Alice and Frank have to say. For now, let's put where the copier goes on the back burner. Alice, what was it you started to say?"

COMMENT: Anytime someone tries to monopolize a meeting, use your authority to quiet them down and allow others to participate. You may also want to encourage people to contribute by asking for their opinion. By doing this, you can get less talkative people involved in the discussion. Some people are essentially shy and won't say anything unless they are encouraged to do so. Don't overdo it, but try to get them to participate—they may have valuable contributions to make.

## Stopping Heated Disagreements

There may be times at meetings where two employees start to get involved in a heated disagreement over a subject. Once you notice they're becoming emotional, interrupt and calm things down. There are a couple of good ways to do this. If it's practical, try to restate their positions in such a way that they both can agree. Say something such as, "You both have good points. Why don't we use both of your suggestions by doing this..."

Of course, that's not always a feasible approach, and another tactic is to suggest they both meet with you privately after the meeting. An offshoot of this is to have them both submit their ideas to you in writing. This is especially effective if you don't fully understand what they are talking about, or if what one or both want to do doesn't make sense. Having them commit their thoughts to writing will force them to think through what they're saying. Incidentally, this tactic has the added benefit of discouraging people who like to disagree for the sake of disagreement. If they find themselves having to justify their ramblings in writing, they may well choose to control their argumentative nature at work.

Beyond meeting with your own group, you will likely have to attend staff meetings conducted by your boss with the supervisors who report to him. Since you're new to the job, you won't be expected to make major contributions to the discussions. Nevertheless, when such a meeting is to be held, you want to be prepared for any eventuality. All you have to do is think about:

1. What questions are you likely to be asked about your group's work?

2. What, if any, information should you bring with you? For example, if the meeting is about production goals, or some other measure of performance, you might want to have the figures with you.

3. Who will be there? Knowing this can clue you in as to possible questions coming your way from someone other than your boss. For instance, supervisors of other departments may ask about work your group is doing for them.

*Caution:* Be careful here, since someone may try to put you on the spot, especially if they have already expressed their displeasure to you about some aspect of the work being done for them. Typical examples would be completion dates and the quality of work produced by your group. If this happens, calmly state your position. Incidentally, if you have already talked about this topic with the other supervisor, let this be known in your reply. Say something such as, "As we've already discussed, Susan,..." Doing this lets your boss know this isn't a new issue, but rather an attempt to embarrass you in front of the boss.

*Note:* You may have to deal with a supervisor or staff person who tries to be cute in their dealings with you. Typical behavior of this nature includes attempts to make you look bad in front of others, as was just discussed. For this reason, it's wise in your private meetings with your boss to mention when someone appears to be unhappy about work you are doing for them. Then, when they try their tactics, what they're doing will be obvious to the boss.

## SIMPLE WAYS TO WRITE SHORT MEMOS

You can read book after book on business writing, but the essence of a good memo boils down to a few basics:

- Be brief.

- Get to the point.

- Use easy-to-understand language.

- If you're asking for someone to take action, tell them what it is you want them to do.

- If you're taking action on someone else's request, tell them what you're going to do.

If you master these techniques, you'll never run into problems writing memos. Let's look at each of these elements.

**1.** You want to be brief for a couple of reasons. First, the longer a memo is the greater the chance it will be confusing. Second, people get impatient if they don't understand something right away. This means your memo may be put aside to be read later if it's lengthy. Being new on the job, you have to resist the temptation to show people how much you know when you respond to them in writing.

**2.** Long or short, a memo is useless if the reader can't easily understand what is being said. Tell them what you have done, or want them to do, right away. Then, if necessary, fill in the background. For example, "Jim, the Acme gizmos you asked about will be delivered on February 2. I'll call you when they come in." If it's relevant you can then continue with additional details, which in this example might include why February 2 was the earliest delivery date you could get. The important point is to give people what they want to know right up front. Imagine that this was a longer memo which had to contain a lot of detailed information, and the delivery date was put at the end. The reader would then have to go through the whole memo to find out what they wanted to know.

**3.** Use easy-to-understand language, or you risk confusing people, along with irritating them. This means short words, sentences, and paragraphs. Remember, you're furnishing information to people who are probably buried in paperwork.

**4.** Be clear about what you want the recipients to do if you're asking them to take action. Otherwise, they will decide for themselves, or even worse, do nothing.

**5.** In the same vein, if you are the action taker, be specific about what you will do. Otherwise, you're going to get a phone call or a written reply asking for clarification. Not only does this involve more work for you and the other party, but it also leaves the other person unhappy over having to follow up.

Another confusing issue with memos is who, if anyone, should receive copies. The general rules such as copying anyone directly involved in or working on the subject of the memo are good general guidelines, but they don't always apply. For one thing, it's not always easy to identify these individuals. As a result, some people go to the extreme and send copies to everyone who has even a remote possibility of needing the information. This causes problems, since people (1) don't want to waste time figuring out why they received a memo they shouldn't have gotten, and (2) it will waste your time fielding questions from people who are confused about a memo they received.

The practical approach until you're on the job long enough to be able to distinguish who should and shouldn't be on a distribution list for routine memos is to follow the practice of your predecessor. The correspondence files should serve to fill you in as to who gets a copy and who doesn't.

If you have a nonroutine memo and can't figure out who should be copied, check with your boss or someone else who would be knowledgeable on the matter. Another approach when you're not certain whether to send a copy of a memo to someone is to ask them directly if they want one. But always avoid doing this with senior managers, since they may not know anything about the subject matter of the memo. They may also wonder why you can't make a decision without contacting them. Last but not least, senior managers may say yes, and subsequently get involved in a project they weren't aware of, including asking lots of questions to the extent that your own boss is unhappy about their oversight. In other words, you don't want to get someone involved unless they should be—it can cause a lot of unnecessary complications.

## TACTICS FOR BRIEFING YOUR BOSS

One of the tasks you will want to master is being able to satisfactorily brief your boss when called upon to do so. These briefings may be periodic reviews of your group's output or a presentation on a specific topic. They may be conducted with you alone, or as part of a broader briefing by others who also report to your boss. Being successful at this isn't difficult once you learn how your boss tends to operate. While some bosses want lengthy, detailed explanations, others want to know little more than the minimum necessary to do their job.

The best way to learn your boss's preference is to observe his or her reactions in the first briefing or two you attend where more experienced supervisors are also participating. Watch for whether more information is requested, or whether impatience is displayed if someone gives a lengthy presentation. Also notice the types of questions that are asked to see if you can detect any obvious patterns. It also helps to pick the brains of a helpful supervisor as to the best approach.

Beyond individual preferences, there are a few basic rules to follow. The most important is not to avoid giving the boss bad news. No boss likes surprises that arise because they weren't informed by those reporting to them. Just as you feel this way, so does your own boss. Always be forthright about any existing problems. It's far better for your boss to hear about potential trouble from you than from someone else at a later date.

Always try to anticipate any questions that will come up at a briefing. It may mean being ready to answer questions that don't come up, but this is preferable to being caught unprepared. Since you're new, you will probably be unsure of yourself at the beginning. But if you don't know the answer to a question just say, "I'll look into that and get back to you." This is far better than stumbling around trying to fake an answer. The boss will easily see through you, and it certainly won't help you build any credibility. Remember, since you are new on the job, you're not expected to have all the answers.

One last thing to be careful about when preparing for briefings is to be sure your workers are giving you the right information. After you get to know your people, it will be easy to recognize who levels with you and who tends to be evasive. Until then, always try to double check information given to you by a subordinate if you feel it may not be correct. Otherwise, you may find yourself being embarrassed when something you say at a meeting is challenged as inaccurate. Don't forget, it's your reputation that's on the line, so don't stake it on what a subordinate tells you unless you're comfortable about it being correct.

## How to Communicate Effectively with Your Subordinates

How easy or difficult your new supervisory position turns out to be will to a large extent depend upon your ability to establish open and honest two-way communication with your subordinates. Many veteran bosses wonder why they can't get workers to perform up to their limits. Sometimes this failure is attributed to factors beyond the supervisor's control, such as low pay, poor working conditions, and a dozen other reasons.

Of course, these factors do come into play. But many times, employees don't give their utmost to the job simply because they don't have any respect for their boss. This is sometimes overlooked because it's not always apparent. After all, workers who value their jobs aren't going to risk offending their immediate supervisor, with the exception of a few problem employees who either don't know any better or don't care whether they lose their job. For the most part workers will plod along doing the minimum necessary to keep the boss happy.

This lack of trust and respect for a boss largely results from a failure to communicate effectively with workers. It's admittedly not an easy thing to do, since a supervisor has to walk a fine line between what employees want and the best interests of the company. On the other hand, a boss who takes the time to explain why something can't be done may not persuade workers of the merits of the decision but will nevertheless earn their respect by leveling about the reasons why a request must be denied.

As a new supervisor, you have a big advantage going for you in establishing good back-and-forth communication with your group. Being new, you have an opportunity from the start to prove your credibility as someone who will be open and honest with them. Let's look at some approaches you can take to do this successfully.

First of all, avoid being vague when you tell workers what you expect from them. You may find your message doesn't always get through the first time. If this happens, exercise patience, since some workers have to be told something more than once before it finally sinks in. This is especially true when people are asked to do something differently than what they have become accustomed to.

It's also wise to avoid letting things slide when work is being done incorrectly in the hope that it won't be repeated. If employees are making mistakes and you ignore them, it's assumed you approve of what is being done. Then, when you do decide to take action, they are bewildered as to why you're suddenly making a fuss about something. Don't wait when you see anything being done wrong. Instead, tell the worker right away and explain why it should be done the way you want.

When you talk to subordinates about their work, don't arbitrarily insist the work be performed in such-and-such a way. Solicit suggestions from workers, and even if you disagree with their recommendations, always show respect for their opinions. Then, explain why you want it handled differently without belittling the worker's idea. For example, say, "That's not a bad way to do it, Linda, but the quality standards require that it be done differently. I know it's hard to change your routine, but you'll get the hang of it after a day or two."

Incidentally, there will be times when workers have a better idea as to how something should be done. When this happens, be ready to accept their suggestions rather than fall back on the old "this is the way it has always been done" argument. And don't forget to be appreciative of employee efforts to improve how the job is performed. When workers see you're not being arbitrary about how things are done, they will object less to your requests for them to do something differently than what they are accustomed to.

If your employees see you constantly striving to create open lines of communication, they will soon learn to confide in you. To do this effectively on a daily basis, frequently engage in one-on-one conversations and small group discussions, rather than limiting yourself to formal meetings. This daily interchange of ideas will then become second nature. Even when there isn't anything work-related to discuss, engage in small talk. People relate better to people who are friendly, and when a new boss projects this attitude, workers feel more confident about their supervisor.

## How to Be Fair when Making Work Assignments

When you're assigning work to subordinates, a primary goal is an equitable distribution of the workload. This isn't difficult to do if everyone performs the same tasks on a routine basis and there's little or no variance in the difficulty of the work. But even if you're supervising this type of operation, there are occasions when nonroutine work has to be assigned to someone. If you're supervising a unit where there are a wide variety of tasks of varying complexity, it becomes more of a chore to achieve an even distribution of the workload. Whatever your particular circumstances, you always have to be fair in parceling out the work. Otherwise, workers will openly grumble or silently assume you play favorites.

The problem is that when you're starting off, it's not always easy to know whether you're distributing the work so some workers are overburdened, while others aren't as busy. Of course, when this is obvious you can make adjustments. But frequently it isn't easy to tell when you're new on the job. This problem is compounded by the reactions you get from workers. A few workers will readily accept any assignment, while at the other end of the spectrum are those who will habitually complain. Furthermore, when you're starting out in a new supervisory role, it's sometimes difficult to separate fact from fiction in terms of the comments workers will make. A few typical reactions when you make work assignments may sound something like this:

- "Jennifer usually does that job."
- "I wasn't trained to operate that machine."
- "I'm overloaded with work. Can you get someone else to do it?"
- "If I do that, I won't be able to finish my other work on time."

The types of excuses workers will give can be endless. Naturally, you can pretty much tell them to just do the job anyway. However, that doesn't solve anything, since some of the reasons you're hearing will be valid. Unfortunately, you can't always spend the time and effort to determine which excuses are valid and which are not. As a result, you may take the practical approach when you get objections and assign the work to the few people who never give you an argument.

This will get the job done, but it can have far-reaching consequences over a period of time. For one thing, once the good workers see they are bearing the brunt of the burden, resentment will set in. Since they are competent and willing workers, their talents are in demand. Therefore, they may eventually seek work elsewhere within the company, or with another employer. Over time, this leaves you with nothing but duds.

Of course, that's an extreme example which will only happen if you continually accept every excuse as valid. Naturally, once you're on the job a while, you will be able to sort out the difference between the valid reasons and the phony excuses. And although you can't get a handle on the trickier alibis you hear in your first weeks on the job, there are some steps you can take to limit this practice to only the cleverest malingerers. And those few will have their day of reckoning once you are settled into a routine.

What can you do right from the start? First of all, don't let worker protests go unchallenged. Although you don't want to accuse them of lying, you do want to know whether they're passing the buck or leveling with you. When an employee makes a fuss about an assignment, carry the discussion further, rather than accepting the worker's claim as a fact.

For example, when someone tells you another worker always does the particular job you're giving to him, say, "Sorry, Fred, I didn't know that. Let me check with Cathy." Assuming you hear a different story from Cathy, which can be verified with others, go back to Fred and say, "Fred, I talked with Cathy and she's working on a priority job right now, so she can't handle this. I want you to do it. If you need any assistance, ask Cathy what to do. Incidentally, I'm glad you told me she was the only one who ever did this job. I don't like to have just one person knowledgeable about anything, so with you learning how to do it, there will be two of you who can handle it."

Even though Fred probably knew how to do the job, there was no need to confront him on that, since it would only be pitting one worker against another. Incidentally, this example points out another problem which you can deal with at a later date. Although it wasn't true here, there are times when a worker will validly claim he or she wasn't trained to do a certain type of job. If you hear this excuse frequently, make a note of it, since you may want to cross-train people to do other jobs, rather than rely on one person having the knowledge. By doing this, you won't be caught shorthanded when people are sick or on vacation. Ideally, all of your workers should know how to do each others' jobs. In some instances, this may not be practical, but to the extent it is, cross-train them so they have multiple skills.

As time passes, you will be able to figure out who is being uncooperative when they're asked to do something, as opposed to those with legitimate complaints. But initially, you don't want to crack down on the excuse-makers, since the risk of being wrong is higher until you master the working routine and the work ethic of individual workers. If you wrongly challenge someone in the beginning, a good worker who is leveling with you won't respect your judgment. So take your time in dealing with excuses. After all, those who are making them will continue to do so, thereby digging a deeper hole for themselves. And when the time comes, you may derive a little pleasure from gaining a bit of retribution.

One other point on being fair with assignments is not to take undue advantage of an extremely competent and cooperative worker. When unusual or difficult tasks come up, you may find yourself asking the same person to handle them time after time. If you see this happening, but find it to be temporarily unavoidable, let the person know you're aware of this. Say something such as, "Jean, I know I keep asking you to do the tough jobs, and I don't want to overburden you. I wouldn't do this, except I'm so confident in your abilities. If I'm working you too hard, be sure to let me know. I'm really appreciative of the way you pitch in to get the job done." This gives hard workers a chance to beg off if they are being overloaded, and it also shows that you appreciate their efforts. Of course, once you learn the ropes, make a more equitable distribution of the workload rather than relying time and again on one or two top performers.

## WAYS TO USE YOUR TIME EFFECTIVELY

Since the newness of everything during your first weeks on the job won't leave you time to do much serious thinking, it isn't practical to do any detailed planning on how to manage your time effectively. Furthermore, until you learn all the ins and outs of your duties, it's impossible to know where you can take some short cuts. Therefore, any serious time-management planning can be left until you become more familiar with your job.

Right from the start there are a couple of steps you can take to give youself some flexibility to work on the priorities of your new job. First, enlist the help of everyone you can, so you're not spending extra time trying to figure something out that could be explained to you by someone with knowledge of the subject matter. If it's a supervisory duty you're struggling with, ask a willing and knowledgeable peer to explain what you should do. Most people like to show off their knowledge, so you won't be rebuffed too often. However, unless you are able to enlist a willing and able supervisor to act as a mentor, don't keep going to the same person too often. After all, you don't want to wear your welcome out.

The biggest hurdle you will face in this area may be your own reluctance to seek assistance. Don't hesitate because you think people will feel you're lacking the skills or ability to do the job. Every supervisor starts off somewhere, and no one expects you to be an expert. In fact, the greater danger lies in not seeking help, since every other boss knows you are new, and not asking questions may lead them to believe you think you know everything about the job. So rather than you needlessly feeling foolish about asking questions, it's more likely you will be pegged as a know-it-all if you don't.

Second, you can help conquer your time constraints early on by delegating tasks to subordinates. Don't do this arbitrarily though, since there's little to be gained by giving a task to someone who is ill-prepared to handle it. When this happens, the end result is likely to be spending more time explaining how to do something than would be spent if you did it yourself. Therefore, once you get a handle on who your more competent workers are, delegate some of your more routine work to them.

Another tactic you can use right from the start is to group similar chores together and do them all at once. This is time-effective, since you avoid the process of gearing up to think about a particular task every time you handle it. Simply put, every time you do something, you consciously or subconsciously have to think about what you're going to do. When you do like items together, you only go through this process once.

One good example of this is when you have to write a memo. It probably takes a few minutes to assemble your thoughts before you even get started. But if you work on two or three similar memos, one after the other, the later ones come more easily. On the other hand, if you did one in the morning and another one later in the day, the second memo would require you to think through the process again from the start.

Another simple tactic is to keep one or two minor chores handy on your desk that you can do during downtime periods such as waiting for meetings to begin. For example, making out overtime schedules or filling out timesheets are the types of minor items you can do while you're waiting for a meeting to start. It might even be something as simple as preparing a "things-to-do" list in a notebook you carry with you. The point is to utilize every bit of available time to the maximum. A few minutes here and there may not seem like much, but it adds up quickly over an extended period.

Beyond these tactics, there isn't a lot you can do to use your time more effectively until you master your job enough so you can look for tasks that can be combined or eliminated. Nevertheless, don't get frustrated if you feel the time demands of the job are overwhelming. This is natural with any new position, and as time passes many of the duties that seem to take forever will become simpler and shorter when viewed from the perspective of experience.

## HOW TO HANDLE RUSH JOBS

One of the headaches of being a new supervisor is that everybody seems to want everything in a hurry. Different aspects of determining what jobs should be done first were discussed in Chapter 2. Here, the focus is on the mechanics of handling a rush job so it's completed on time. The first step starts with being sure you promise a completion date that can be met. When someone comes to you with a request for work to be done in a shorter time than is normally required, don't make careless commitments to meet the required date. Also be wary of individuals who will tell you that the requested time frame has been met in the past. People on the hook to complete a project may be perfectly willing to let you be the sacrificial lamb when a deadline can't be met. Therefore, if they can persuade you to accept an unrealistic completion date, you will be the one blamed when the job isn't finished on time.

To prevent being unfairly blamed, when a job with a deadline is presented to you, get the facts before you make a commitment. Since you're new, it's likely you won't have a good feel for the time required to do various projects. Consult with subordinates to get their input, and if there is still doubt remaining in your mind, bring the matter to your boss for resolution. If the work will depend upon the assistance of people outside of your department, you will also have to confer with them to be certain you will have all of the necessary support and resources to do the work. Then, and only then, should you agree on dates for completion of rush projects until you gain enough experience to know for yourself.

Once you do agree to complete a rush job by a certain date, you will have to do the following:

1. Make assignments to the workers who will be working on the project. If the project will be lengthy, you may want to hold periodic meetings with those involved to monitor the progress of the work.

2. Coordinate with anyone outside of your group who will be furnishing parts, materials, or any form of support services. Make certain they understand both what you need and when you need it.

3. Follow up closely on a daily basis to be certain there are no slippages in the schedule. This is important, since if someone starts to fall behind there may be a reluctance to let you know about it.

4. If any hitches develop which threaten to derail the project, get everyone involved together right away and brainstorm for options to deal with the difficulty.

5. From start to finish, try to remain calm and display an air of confidence even if prospects aren't looking good. Not only does this allow you to think clearly, but your composure will carry over to the people working on the task.

6. Keep your boss briefed as the work progresses, since it won't be pleasant if he or she is suddenly surprised with an announcement that the date won't be met. For this reason, avoid simply saying "Looking good," or "It's right on schedule," when there are potential problems looming ahead. Sure, you may be confident they can be resolved, and those working on the job may have given you every assurance this is so. Nevertheless, keep the boss posted on all possibilities, and you won't have to listen to, "Why didn't you tell me that before? I could have..." What follows may then be a Monday morning quarterback assessment of how the boss could have solved everything if he or she had known what was happening.

7. When a rush job is completed, go out of your way to thank everyone involved for their efforts. This includes outsiders as well as your own workers. Let your boss know the names of those who did a good job, since workers love to hear that their supervisor has been praising them to others.

## WHY IT'S BEST NOT TO SOCIALIZE WITH SUBORDINATES

One of the tricky aspects of being a first-time boss is figuring out how to handle relationships at work. You may recall the discussion in Chapter 1 on supervising friends. This may not even be a problem for you if the new job involves supervising people you didn't know before. However, with every passing day on the job you will get more and more familiar with the people you now supervise. Unfortunately, this familiarity can lead to problems if it's not handled properly.

This is a particular challenge when you first arrive on the scene. You don't want to appear to be antisocial or unfriendly. Nevertheless, you don't want to become too close to your subordinates. After all, there will come a time when you have to make hard-nosed decisions on discipline and other distasteful topics. These are hard enough to do without the added influence of emotional involvement.

The major dilemma you face is wanting to be a friendly boss who communicates openly with people. On the other hand, this can lead to invitations to socialize after work, as well as a failure to recognize you as the boss when it's time to do so. Of course, the alternative of being stand-offish and aloof may gain you respect on the surface, but the underlying feelings of workers will be of a new boss who thinks he or she is a hot-shot. This won't lead to the kind of teamwork and "can do" spirit you want to elicit from your group.

So far, this seems like a no-win proposition. It isn't, but in terms of relationships with those who work for you, there's a fine line you have to learn to walk. What you have to do is be friendly while you avoid crossing that narrow line which transforms you into being a friend. The key to success is consistency in your actions. Learn to routinely turn down requests to socialize with people who work for you. Do this politely and consistently and people will soon realize you have other interests to pursue.

Of course, you can and should attend company sponsored social events, such as holiday season parties, summer outings, and so forth. The biggest problem you will face in these situations are coping with people who have consumed one too many alcoholic beverages. This can always lead to problems, so when you see this happening, avoid the individuals involved. In fact, you may want to make it a practice to bow out early if things appear to be getting out of hand.

If you're new to the company as well as your job, however, make an effort to attend company events. It will give you an opportunity to meet people from throughout the company you might not otherwise know. These contacts can come in handy at a later date. If you don't go to company functions, you may be pegged as antisocial, which is a label that's

hard to shake when you're new on the job. Even if you're not the party-
ing type, push yourself to go through the motions.

## OVERCOMING THE PROBLEMS OF
## SCHEDULING OVERTIME

If you're supervising a group where overtime work occurs on a fairly regular basis, there are a couple of potential pitfalls to avoid. First of all, in
terms of being receptive to working overtime, your subordinates will have
differing viewpoints. At one end of the spectrum will be those who want
all of the overtime they can get for financial reasons. On the other end of
the scale will be those who want nothing to do with working beyond their
regularly scheduled hours.

Of course, it's ideal if you have enough people who want to work, so
you don't have the hassles of scheduling people who don't want to be
there. However, this sort of luck is usually more a dream than a reality. In
fact, even those workers who jump at the opportunity to work overtime
will become less willing after a prolonged period of overtime work. So,
the first problem you face with overtime will likely be scheduling. With
any luck at all, there may be a scheduling practice in place when you
come on board. If there is, at least initially, just go along with it as long
as no problems are apparent.

If, however, there was no set arrangement, you will be forced to set
up an overtime schedule. You want to be fair to everyone, so the best bet
is to schedule everyone in rotating order. Keep a provision that workers
can fill in for each other as long as you are kept informed. This will allow
people who want to work to substitute for those who don't.

Incidentally, keep an eye out for workers who try to build up overtime pay at the expense of doing their work during regular hours. A few
workers may try to take advantage of the fact they have a new supervisor. If you see this happening, you should let people know that overtime
won't be worked to compensate for anyone taking it easy during the day.
If you tell a worker who is an overtime hog that you're concerned about
this, you shouldn't have any further difficulty. After all, the culprits won't
want to be prohibited from working any overtime. As a result, they will
probably pick up the pace during regular working hours. All you have to

do is monitor the situation closely to keep them honest. Let's look at how you might let it be known that you're concerned about people loafing during the day so they can work overtime.

| | |
|---|---|
| *You:* | "Fred, I don't want to point fingers at anyone in particular, but a couple of people seem to take it slow during the day, and then ask to work overtime to get caught up. I'm thinking about talking to Jim Erickson (your boss) about eliminating overtime." |
| *Fred:* | "Well I know I'm going full speed during the day, boss, and I'm pretty sure everyone else is as far as I can see." |
| *You:* | "Maybe so, Fred. Being new, I guess I'll just have to watch things a little more closely." |

It's virtually guaranteed that Fred will spread the word about the conversation, and any worker who was slacking off will be more careful in the future. By doing it this way, you're sending a message without making any direct accusations.

There are a couple of other aspects of overtime work you may have to deal with. The first is to be sure to let workers know as far ahead as possible when overtime will be scheduled. The other problem is you may have one or more workers who face real problems with their personal lives if they have to work extended hours. This is pretty common with working parents, especially if they have to pick their kids up from school or daycare. Whenever possible, try to accommodate the needs of employees in this area. If overtime is a normal requirement of the job, be sure any job applicants you interview are aware of this.

## HOW TO DECIDE ON USING THE PHONE OR MEETING FACE-TO-FACE

It may not seem particularly important whether you telephone someone within the company or meet face-to-face to discuss a particular topic. In most circumstances it isn't and it simply boils down to using the most expedient means of communication. Ordinarily this would be the telephone or its voice mail and computer message counterparts. However, there are a number of circumstances where it's to your distinct advantage to meet face-to-face with someone. This is especially true where you're new to the job and an unknown quantity to those you are dealing with. Here are a few situations where a personal meeting is preferable.

1.  Probably the most crucial time when it's better to meet directly with someone is if you're explaining away a mistake. It's much easier to be persuasive in person than by phone or e-mail.

2.  Always handle disciplinary measures in person—and in private.

3.  Whenever you want to add emphasis to something you're saying, your presence will enhance the chance of getting the point across.

4.  As a new supervisor, whenever it's practical try to make your initial contact with anyone you will be working with on a regular basis a personal visit.

5.  When someone tries to pull a fast one on you by leaving a message in the hope you won't respond, visit them instead of picking up the phone. One example of this kind of situation would be another supervisor leaving a note asking you to complete a job earlier than is feasible. Sometimes actions of this nature will be harmless, but on other occasions people will try to sneak things by and hope you won't notice.

6.  When an inquiry is made for which the explanation is better handled in person. For example, you may have paperwork supporting your response, or perhaps you want another person to participate in answering the question.

There are, of course, other instances where a personal meeting is preferable to a telephone call. This will depend on the specifics of what you're dealing with. The important point is not to use the telephone or e-mail if personal contact will be more effective. Naturally, the flip side of the coin is not to waste time meeting with people if other means are more expedient. If you have difficulty deciding which way to go, take a moment and ask yourself what is gained or lost by using the phone instead of a face-to-face meeting.

## FIFTEEN BASIC PRACTICES THAT WILL MAKE YOU A BETTER BOSS

Mastering a list of techniques in and of itself won't guarantee your success as a supervisor. However, if you make an effort to practice the following fundamentals, they will help you to become a better boss a lot sooner than might otherwise be the case. You should also keep in mind that the following practices are geared toward getting you off to a good start as a new boss. Therefore, they are essentially building blocks that will lay the foundation for your future performance. There's nothing complex about them, but as a whole they are valuable components in making the transition from a novice boss to an experienced supervisor.

### 1. Handle Employee Complaints Promptly

If you don't, workers will think you're only interested in getting the job done, and have no regard for their concerns. This is always an important factor in keeping morale high, but it's especially true when you're a new boss. In fact, one or more workers may put you to the test right away to see if you're willing to go to bat for them. In addition, someone who hasn't gotten satisfactory results from the prior supervisor will be quick to seize the opportunity when you come on board. Therefore, go the extra mile to resolve any employee complaints you get when you first arrive on the job.

### 2. Be Informed

Keep up-to-date on rumors and office gossip, as well as present and forthcoming actions that may affect your group. By doing this, you will be viewed as a reliable source of information by your subordinates. This will make it easier to combat rumors and will lessen the amount of time workers engage in scuttlebutt. What you want to establish in the minds of your subordinates is that you are the one reliable source of information they can count on. Of course, you won't always have the answers at your fingertips, but when you don't, display a willingness to track the necessary information down. By establishing this practice in your first few weeks on the job, you will convey the impression of a boss who intends to be on top of every situation.

### 3. Don't Let Minor Irritants Distract You

Early on in your tenure, you may find yourself getting aggravated over the habitual actions of one of your subordinates. It won't be anything of a serious nature, but rather one of those nagging little habits that can drive you up the wall. For example, perhaps you have noticed a worker who seems to spend a lot of time chatting with other employees. You don't know for sure, and you are too busy learning the job to carefully monitor the situation. Should you focus in on this and put a stop to it? Eventually you should, but as long as everyone is doing their work, this isn't the type of problem you can afford to waste your time on in the early stages of learning your job.

As the days blend into weeks in your new position, there will be a variety of minor problems you start to notice which will require action on your part. But at the beginning, it's crucial to concentrate on getting the work out and learning the most significant duties of your job. This won't give you time to do other matters which are secondary in importance. If you get trapped into spending time on monitoring who loiters at the water cooler, it will divert you from tackling the essentials. For this reason, be on guard against letting relatively petty matters keep you from your main mission. As you gain experience you will eventually find the time to handle some of the issues you initially put on the back burner.

### 4. Don't Dodge Unpleasant Duties

Although you don't want to get bogged down with minor irritants, major matters requiring supervisory action can't be ignored simply because they're unpleasant and you feel insecure about dealing with them. For example, you can't let events requiring potential disciplinary action go unchallenged. Such matters as fighting, insubordination, and the like must be dealt with promptly. However, being new, you can't be expected to tackle the problem without assistance.

Therefore, if something significant requiring immediate action comes up, consult your boss as to the proper action to take. Don't feel as if you're not doing your job, since even when you become a veteran boss, serious disciplinary matters require consultation with both your boss and the personnel department. Often there are legal and union ramifications involved, so it's not the type of issue where you have the sole responsibility for dealing with the problem.

The greater danger lies in letting these actions slide, since those involved may be encouraged to continue their irresponsible actions by your failure to deal with them. This will make it even more difficult if action needs to be taken at a later date. So get all of the help you need, but don't let this sort of problem slide simply because it's easier to ignore than to confront the perpetrators.

## 5. Prevent Little Problems from Becoming Major Issues

You may run into minor work-related difficulties that have the potential for becoming more serious if they're not dealt with right away. The problem here is that it's not always easy to recognize the potential consequences, especially since you haven't been around long enough to distinguish the difference between the relative importance of every aspect of the operation you supervise. In this regard, it's vital to heed any warnings you get from subordinates.

For example, if a worker tells you a machine is on the verge of breaking down at any time, don't wait for it to happen before taking action. This seems like simple common sense, but when you have a zillion things to do, it's easy to ignore subtle warning signs. After all, if the machine's still running, there's no immediate problem. If it breaks down suddenly and causes production delays or some other major headache, your boss and others will want to know what happened. You don't want to be in the position of having a subordinate say, "I told the boss about this machine three weeks ago."

To avoid these hazards, when a problem with some aspect of work is brought to your attention, look into it at least to the extent of determining whether it has the potential for causing serious problems. If so, bring the matter to the attention of your boss. He or she may well say, "Don't worry about it." Whether they do or don't doesn't matter, since you have alerted them to the problem, and it's no longer a potential disaster in the making for which you have to shoulder the blame.

## 6. Have Confidence in Your Subordinates

It will take a while to learn the relative strengths and weaknesses of those who work for you. For this reason, it's easy to be hesitant about accepting some of the initial advice you get from subordinates. At the same time, whether you want to or not, your inexperience forces you to place a great deal of reliance on the capabilities of employees. This can have positive results which extend beyond your first weeks and months on the job. When workers see you're willing to accept their advice, they are far more likely to have a positive outlook toward both you and their own jobs. So even though you may be nervous about not having as much control as you would like over the situation, there are benefits to be gained.

The flip side of the coin is that you don't want to make any major decisions unless you have confidence in the source of the information. However, it's relatively easy to double-check something a worker says with other employees to see if you get the same response. In any event, it won't take very long for you to figure out who pretty much knows what they're talking about and who tends to be less reliable.

## 7. Don't Worry About Looking Foolish

It's easy for anyone's ego to get in the way when they start a new job. It pretty much boils down to not wanting to look stupid. As a result, there's a tendency to avoid asking lots of questions for which answers are needed. It's hard to accept the fact that everyone knows you're new on the job and aren't expected to know everything. Try your hardest to overcome any fear of asking about anything you want to know. Otherwise, it will take much longer to learn the details of your job.

## 8. Don't Dwell on Any Mistakes You Make

Everyone makes mistakes, but you would never know it by the way some people are bothered by making an error. The ironic thing is that people with a lot of experience and training behind them are more likely to take a mistake in stride than those who are in the learning stages. Yet everyone expects the beginner to make errors as part of the learning process, while experienced hands aren't supposed to make mistakes—at least not very often.

You will have your share of mistakes while learning the job, but that's to be expected. They generally won't be of any great significance, and are usually correctable without a lot of difficulty. Take them in stride as part of the learning process, since the far greater danger is to be hesitant for fear of making an error.

## 9. Listen Carefully to Everything and Everyone

The next chapter will deal with how to listen, as well as the importance of listening carefully to what your subordinates have to say. It suffices to say here that in the learning stages, it's vital to pay particular attention to what you're being told. It's equally useful to pick up valuable tidbits of information by listening to conversations your peers and others have about work. The more you listen, the more information you will be able to gather about all facets of the company in general and your job in particular.

## 10. Show Your Gratitude for Assistance

You may at times start to think you're being a pest by continually asking various people about some aspect of your job. Don't let this bother you. Most folks love to demonstrate how much they know, and by asking questions, you're giving them an opportunity to show off. Of course, people may not view it quite that way and would prefer to think they are doing you a favor. So let them have it both ways by being sure to express your thanks when anyone gives you assistance. You will be surprised by how often you hear some variation of, "No problem. Anytime I can help, let me know." Whenever you get a response that appears to be genuine, take advantage of it, but make sure you let such people know you appreciate their efforts.

## 11. Maintain Your Confidence

As you go about trying to absorb as much knowledge of your job as possible, you may find yourself getting discouraged. Do your best to keep your confidence up, since it can have an impact on those around you. Workers tend to take their cues from the boss, so if you don't appear to be confident when handed tough assignments, they can't be expected to believe the challenge to get the job done will be met. This isn't easy to do when you're relatively new and don't have the experience of overcoming the necessary hurdles to get the work out. But always grit your teeth and project a "can do" attitude—it will add the encouragement workers need to succeed.

## 12. Try to Avoid Mood Swings

Everyone has their good days and bad days, but unfortunately workers remember when a supervisor snarls at them once, while forgetting a month's worth of being greeted by a cheerful boss. With the pressures of learning a new job, it's harder to keep your emotions on an even keel at all times. Do your best to maintain your composure, however, since it just brings added pressure when you explode in anger at a worker. Incidentally, if you do slip up and are rude or abrupt with someone, go out of your way to apologize at the first opportunity. No one likes to be yelled at, but everyone appreciates anyone who makes an effort to make amends.

## 13. Don't Try to Do Everything at Once

Your desire to succeed may lead you to attempt to do more than is practical in a short period of time. Resist this temptation, since as the learning process proceeds everything will fall into place and your workload will whittle its own way down to a manageable level. If you overextend yourself, it will only lead to making more errors than are necessary, which in turn will result in an even higher level of frustration. Concern yourself with mastering the priorities of your job first. Only then should you work toward getting a handle on lesser chores which have been accumulating.

## 14. Don't Volunteer for Anything

There's a lot to be said about the advantages of volunteering for projects and chores in terms of giving your career a boost. Save that for later. Right now, you're interested in learning your job, not advancing to the next level. It may seem unlikely that you would be asked to volunteer for anything until you get your feet on the ground. Generally, this will be true. However, there may be an occasion when another supervisor tries to get you to assume duties beyond those you already have.

It may be unintentional, or perhaps some wiseacre sees a chance to dump something on a greenhorn. Whatever the situation, don't voluntarily assume any more responsibilities than you already have. And don't be fooled by statements such as, "There's nothing to it. It won't take any time at all." If that's the case, then let the person making the statement do it. If you get an argument, suggest the matter be discussed with your boss. Someone who is trying to be cute about unloading a can of worms will back off rather than go to the boss and have their scheme revealed.

## 15. Don't Make Your Life Miserable Over the Job

Above all else, don't let worrying about learning your job become all-consuming. Leave it at work, and pick it up again the next day, rather than having it constantly on your mind. Since you are busy, it's more important than ever that you don't become fatigued by working long hours in trying to learn everything at once. When the workday ends, relax and enjoy yourself. Above all, don't let the pressures get to you to the extent that your discouragement carries over to your family and friends. Experienced managers know when to let the job go, so this is one more technique you can learn right from the start.

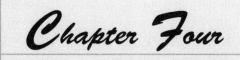

# Chapter Four

# THE ABC'S OF SUPERVISING OTHERS

*S*upervising people in the performance of their duties is a lot easier if you master a few fundamental tools for one-on-one communication. You will develop these by trial and error over a period of time, but knowing the basics right from the start will speed the process immeasurably. One of the keys to success is developing an ability to listen to what your subordinates are saying. This may seem simple, but most people aren't particularly adept at listening to others. The prime reason for this is because it seems so easy to do that it's taken for granted.

There are several other aspects of communicating with your subordinates that can contribute to your initial success as a supervisor. These include techniques for handling employee questions, the proper way to praise people, and how to respond when a worker disagrees with you. Beyond this, you should know how to effectively delegate work, conduct follow-up, and consistently build a level of trust with your group. All of these techniques are covered in the pages that follow.

## WHY IT'S IMPORTANT TO LISTEN
## TO SUBORDINATES

Throughout your career as a supervisor, it's imperative to establish effective two-way communication with the people who report to you. Otherwise, the level of cooperation and teamwork necessary to achieve high levels of productivity will never be reached. Establishing open channels of communication with workers means you have to keep employees fully informed on any and all issues affecting them. Equally crucial is the need for you to listen carefully to what workers have to say. This latter requirement takes on even greater significance for the new supervisor.

If a new boss isn't willing to listen to workers from the very beginning, it's extremely difficult to turn this situation around later on. Once workers sense a boss has no interest in what they have to say, it's assumed the supervisor thinks they have nothing worthwhile to contribute. This can have a number of unpleasant ramifications.

For starters, employees aren't likely to volunteer any advice if they see the boss is going about something the wrong way. This can lead to a series of otherwise avoidable blunders when you're just starting off in a new position. Furthermore, workers aren't likely to keep you informed of potential problems until they become a full-blown crisis. Beyond that, when workers think a boss doesn't want to hear what they have to say, even their response to direct questions will be as brief as possible. This means that if you're not asking the right questions, the answers you get won't be expanded to tell you what you want to know.

Therefore, to generate the type of feedback you need to operate effectively, you have to learn to listen to what your workers have to say. Otherwise, you'll be flying solo without a parachute in trying to figure out what's going on in the group you supervise.

## A FEW SIMPLE TIPS FOR BECOMING
## A GOOD LISTENER

Although listening to what people have to tell you will speed the process of learning your job, it can't be done halfheartedly. Otherwise, you won't assimilate the information you need to know. Therefore, it pays to practice a few basic listening skills, so you become an accomplished listener rather than just going through the motions. There's nothing particularly complicated about being a good listener, but it does require more than just sitting down and saying, "Go ahead, I'm listening."

The first step in being an effective listener is to have an open mind about what you're hearing. If someone isn't really listening, but is just going through the motions as a formality, then everyone's time is being wasted. If you think about it, this happens continually in all facets of life. People have a habit of shutting down their thought processes when someone tries to tell them something they don't want to hear. This may be because they disagree with what the speaker is saying, or perhaps they have already made a decision and aren't about to change their mind.

Therefore, always be attentive when you're listening to someone. This is particularly true when a subordinate is making a suggestion on some aspect of work. Even though you know it's impractical, hear the employee out. Then, and only then, explain why the idea can't be used. Otherwise, if an employee realizes you aren't really paying attention, other ideas which have real merit aren't likely to be suggested in the future.

Along the same line, don't ignore what someone is saying simply because it doesn't seem to be of any importance. This can happen when workers come to you with minor gripes, especially if you have heard the complaint before. Hear them out, since the gripe may have real merit in the eyes of the worker. You may not agree with them, but the fact you're willing to listen may be enough to pacify the worker. After you have heard the employee out, carefully explain why the gripe can't be resolved to his or her satisfaction.

By this point you may be wondering if you have to spend all of your time listening to every petty complaint imaginable. That of course isn't necessary, and as you get a better feel for the personalities of the people working for you, it will be easy enough to figure out who the chronic complainers are. Once you have this figured out, just listen long enough to be polite, and then calmly bring the discussion to a close. Let's look at how this can be done:

## Background

Almost from your first day on the job, a worker named Sarah has been complaining about the air conditioning. From her viewpoint, it's been too hot or too cold continually even though the temperature is automatically controlled and everyone else is comfortable.

> **Sarah:** "It's freezing again in here. Can't you do anything about it?"
>
> **You:** "Sarah, we've talked about this before, and I even had Fred from the maintenance department check the thermostat to see if it was working properly. It was then and it is now. I'd suggest you bring a sweater or jacket to work for when you feel it's too cold. I really want to help, but in this situation there's nothing I can do."
>
> **Sarah:** (Refusing to drop the issue) "One day it's hot and the next it's too cold. That doesn't make sense."
>
> **You:** "Look Sarah, no one else has this problem except you, and I can't spend any more time discussing it. Try wearing a sweater when it gets too cold for you. Other than that there's nothing further I can say to help."

You are sure to face various gripes of a similar nature as time passes. Once you have covered the subject thoroughly, you have to abruptly call a halt if a worker continues to make an issue of the matter. The constant complaining will generally be confined to one or two workers. Needless to say, when you're dealing with this sort of problem, the best thing that can happen is to arrive at work one morning and find the person in your office requesting a transfer. If that happens, don't even wait to take your coat off before signing it.

One of the main requirements for being an attentive listener is the ability to exercise patience. Some people take a while to get their point across. This is particularly true when the topic is something the speaker is hesitant to bring up. For example, some employees might find it difficult to ask for a raise or inquire about a promotion. Other people just naturally take a while to get to the point.

Although you don't want to interrupt people when they're trying to say something, if it becomes obvious someone is having trouble ask a question or two to help them along. This has to be done carefully, since interrupting at the wrong time may be seen as an attempt to silence the speaker. Let's look at an example of how you can gingerly nudge the speaker along.

## The Situation

Andrea, a long-time employee has asked to see you and has been talking for five minutes about her personal financial situation, how hard she works, and how difficult it is to get by on her salary. By now, you sense she may be looking for either a pay raise, a promotion, or perhaps is explaining why she is taking a better paying job somewhere else. You decide to ask a question or two to get her to say what she wants.

*You:* "From what you're telling me, Andrea, you seem to be having trouble making ends meet. Have you thought about what you can do to improve your financial situation?"

*Andrea:* "I don't know what can be done. I thought about a part-time job, but that would interfere with working overtime here."

*You:* "I guess it might. I really don't know what to say. Is there anything special you wanted to ask me, or did you just want to talk over your financial situation?"

*Andrea:* "Well, to be honest with you, I was wondering what my chances for a pay raise are. I've been here a while and I really try to be a hard worker."

*You:* "As you know Andrea, pay raises are yearly. I'm sure you will be getting one when your review comes around. Do you know when it is? If not, I will check with personnel."

*Andrea:* "It's not until August."

*You:* "That's six months from now, so it isn't going to help you for a while. Do you have any thoughts on what you can do in the meantime?"

*Andrea:* "Actually, I was wondering if I took a part-time job, could my overtime be scheduled on the nights I don't work? That way, I would be able to swing things financially."

*You:* "I'm sure we could work something out on that, Andrea. Let me suggest that you look for a part-time job with flexible hours. That way you can work overtime here, and work the part-time job when overtime isn't scheduled. I don't mind you not working overtime if you have to go to a part-time job, but missing out on the overtime will cost you more than the job will probably pay. That's why I'm suggesting you try to find a part-time job that will give you some flexibility."

COMMENT: There are a couple of points this example illustrates. The first one is the care needed to not cut someone short if you think they're just making conversation. Imagine if in the example the supervisor interrupted and said, "I don't have time to listen to your financial woes." Quite likely that would have ended the conversation, and left a very unhappy worker. There are times when you will have to cut people short if they're just making conversation. However, you will quickly spot the one or two ear-benders who work for you. Other than those folks, when an employee fumbles around, they obviously have something to say. So a little patience is well worth the effort.

A second point demonstrated by the example is how reluctant some workers may be about raising certain subjects. A pay raise wasn't even what Andrea was looking for even though she mentioned it. Her worry about losing overtime was the main concern. There will be times with touchy subjects when you have to do a little coaxing to find out what workers are driving at. The example also shows how arrangements can be made to accommodate workers when they have a problem, if you're willing to give it some thought.

One final point on being a good listener concerns keeping in mind what someone *doesn't* say when they're talking to you. There are times when people will only tell you what they want you to hear. This means they may either lie to you, or they may not mention something you should be aware of. This is worth keeping in mind, since a subordinate or employee in another department may try to slip something by you without being totally open and honest. For example, a worker may neglect to tell you about an error that has been made even though you are discussing the job it was done on. In these circumstances, if you sense something is out of whack, ask any questions necessary to satisfy yourself that you have been told everything you need to know. Of course, someone may still not tell you the truth, but you have them dead to rights if what they're covering up is discovered later.

## THE RIGHT WAY TO GIVE PRAISE TO WORKERS

With rare exceptions, you can find someone who will disagree with almost anything. One of those exceptions is praise, since it's pretty hard to find anyone who won't accept a boost to their ego now and then— including those who already have an inflated ego. It's a given that praise is a valued tool in the arsenal of a supervisor who is trying to keep employees motivated. What can be overlooked is *how* you go about praising people is almost as important as the praise itself. In fact, if it's not done right, giving praise can even be damaging to morale.

For example, if you arbitrarily praise every worker for doing a good job, then the praise becomes meaningless to those who truly deserve it. So let's look at a few examples of how praise can be used effectively.

First of all, try to relate the praise to a specific accomplishment of the worker:

*Good:*    "Helen, you did a great job showing everyone how to use that new software package."

*Bad:*    "You're doing a great job, Helen."

Be timely when you give praise. Otherwise, in the meantime the employee will think you didn't notice. When you finally get around to it, the impact will be weakened.

*Good:*    "Nice job getting that rush shipment out yesterday, Henry."

*Bad:*    "Hey, Henry, I've been meaning to tell you for two weeks what a great job you did in getting that shipment out." (Henry wonders what the boss is talking about, since he spent the last week on vacation.)

Don't praise routine efforts, since they only serve to make you look foolish:

*Good:*     "That McNally proposal was first-rate, Jim."

*Bad:*      "You sure write great memos, Jim."

Don't neglect to praise your entire unit if the opportunity arises, but refrain if there hasn't been any accomplishment to warrant it:

*Good:*     (At a regular group meeting) "Congratulations every-one. We had the lowest absentee rate of any depart-ment for the past three months."

*Bad:*      "Even though I'm new here, I want you to know you're doing a great job." (If they sense you don't know what you're talking about, you will never be able to develop any credibility with your subordi-nates.)

You can use praise in combination with constructive criticism to encourage a worker to improve a subpar aspect of performance. But only do this if there is something positive to praise:

*Good:*     "Alice, you're faster than anyone else in filling orders, so I know you can cure your habit of being late for work."

Even though you are good at giving praise, workers also like to know their efforts are recognized by others. So whenever possible, let workers know you have told your boss about one of their accomplishments. It's even better if the person you told lets the worker know about it.

Beyond doing it the right way, many bosses have difficulty giving praise for fear of not having it seen as sincere. Don't worry about this, since people are pretty good at recognizing sincerity when they see it. Workers know when they have done a good job, so they are only looking for recognition of it on your part. This just requires honest and sincere statements, not a lot of elegant speechmaking.

## HOW TO ASK QUESTIONS SO YOU DON'T GET EVASIVE ANSWERS

If you want to know what's going on, you have to ask questions. However, that alone won't always get you the information you're looking for. This is especially true if there are problems with something that someone doesn't want to tell you about. Perhaps a worker is trying to cover for something he did wrong, or maybe an employee fears being criticized. Whatever the reason, on occasion you will get evasive answers when you ask a question. When this happens, you have to know how to keep asking until you get the information you need.

The foremost requirement in getting the answers you seek is to be persistent. If a response doesn't satisfy you, keep asking questions until you are satisfied with the answers. In doing this, don't get angry or frustrated, since it will only put the other person on the defensive. This makes it even more difficult to find out what you want to know.

If you ask a question and receive a confusing answer in reply, it might be the worker doesn't understand the question. So for starters, always try to ask specific questions if you're looking for specific answers. For example, if you want to know if an employee has finished an assignment, don't ask a vague question such as, "How's the work going, Joe?" Unless Joe has a specific problem to discuss with you the answer is almost always going to be a terse "Good," or something similar. Instead, target the subject you want a response to in your question. In this example it might be something such as, "Have you finished the Doheny assignment I gave you this morning?" If you receive a no answer, then follow up with another question to find out why the work isn't finished.

In general, workers aren't going to lay problems and mistakes out for you—at least not until they get to know you better. And in addition, workers may be making assumptions as to what you know and don't know about the operation when you're new on the job. Furthermore, since you are new, you will need to ask more questions than if you were a more experienced department head. Don't let this deter you, since the only way you will learn what's going on is by asking plenty of questions and making certain they are answered to your satisfaction.

When you're looking for information, one of the common traps you can fall into is asking questions that can be answered with a yes or no. For instance, if you're looking for an employee to give an assignment to and you start asking around with the question, "Are you busy?" the odds are you will hear a yes from every worker you approach. Of course, when this happens you will pursue the matter further by asking specifics about what each employee is working on. Then, when you find someone who apparently is doing "looking busy" work, you will hand them the assignment. Therefore, unless you specifically want a yes or no answer, phrase your questions to get the answer you're looking for the first time around.

Another problem you will frequently encounter is a vague answer which skirts the issue you're trying to address. This type of response is likely when you're trying to pinpoint the cause of an error or some other work-related difficulty. Many workers will waltz around these issues, so you have to pin them down. Although vague answers can take many forms, one or more of the following tactics will assist you in getting the needed information.

- ✏ Ask follow-up questions which zero in on the issue. Keep asking questions, all the while becoming more specific as you go along.

- ✏ Repeat the answer and ask for greater detail. For instance, "As I understand it, you're telling me you have other work to do when you finish this job. I didn't realize that. What is the other work you have?"

- ✏ Sometimes you can ignore the vague answer, go on to discuss something else, and then come back and ask your initial question all over again. You might be surprised at how effective this can be in getting a better response. One reason is that a worker may be cautious the first time the question is asked, and then relax when it's realized you're not on a search-and-destroy mission because someone made an error.

- ✏ Ask the question in an entirely different way. Sometimes a question can be misunderstood because the person wasn't paying attention when it was asked. Alternatively, maybe it was just misinterpreted. In either case, asking it differently may get you a better answer.

One other common problem you may encounter is when you're questioning an employee about something that went wrong. This is one instance where you don't want your initial question to be too specific. If it is, the worker may well get defensive which will make it that much more difficult to get the facts. Instead, try to ease into the matter slowly with some general conversation, and when you do inquire about the mistake don't be accusatory or argumentative. This approach works well, since once a worker sees you're not about to lower the boom, there's less hesitancy in leveling about what went wrong.

Since this is one of the trickier aspects of asking questions let's look at an example.

## Background

Anna, a new supervisor in the billing department of a large store, has been on the job for two weeks. She is made aware of a number of complaints from customers that their change of address hasn't been made in the company records, so the billings are going out to the wrong address. In her research she discovers that every complaint involves an account which is handled by Marcy, a long-time employee. She decides to see what the problem is.

*Anna:* "How is everything going, Marcy? You look like you're pretty busy."

*Marcy:* "Good, Anna. How about yourself?"

*Anna:* "Not bad, Marcy. I'm still trying to learn the ropes, but some of this stuff is pretty complicated."

*Marcy:* "Well, if I can help you out, let me know."

*Anna:* "Perhaps you can. I'm still trying to figure out how customer address changes are plugged into the computer system. Can you show me how it's done?"

*Marcy:* "Nothing to it. Everyone does their own. It's just a question of entering the correct data. The only problem in that area is that due to the billing cycle and processing lead-time, customers sometimes get one more bill mailed to their old address. Once in a while, they complain because they don't think the change was made."

*Anna:* "Well, I know they complain, because I have a bunch on my desk now, but I wasn't sure how to go about tracking them down."

*Marcy:* "Find the billing rep who handles the account and check with them. If they received the change and entered it, the complaints are only because of the lag time. See if you have any for me, and I'll go over them with you."

*Anna:* (Goes to her desk and comes back with the complaints on Marcy's accounts.) "Here are some that belong to you."

*Marcy:* "Let's check them out." She calls up each file and in every instance the address has been changed. "Look at these dates, Anna. On every one you'll notice the time lag accounts for the last billing being sent to the old address."

*Anna:* "You're right, Marcy. Thanks for helping me with these."

COMMENT: There are a couple of points to be noted about the example given. It would have been easy for Anna to assume from the complaints she had that Marcy was doing something wrong. This would have been disastrous if she had gone to Marcy and started off by asking a question such as, "Why aren't you entering changes of address in the computer?" By easing into the subject, she was able to discover there was no internal error being made by Marcy or anyone else. This example demonstrates one good reason why charges shouldn't be leveled without first getting the facts.

In addition, if Anna had opened with an accusatory question such as, "Why haven't you made these address changes?" Marcy would rightly claim she had. This would have led to unnecessary tension and further questions until Anna was assured Marcy hadn't made the errors. But it's highly unlikely Marcy would have gone to the lengths she did to explain the procedure to Anna.

This is especially important when you're a new supervisor, since things aren't always what appearances would indicate. Therefore, until you know the operation completely, you have to be careful about how you approach workers when it appears errors have been made.

## WHY IT'S CRUCIAL TO ANSWER EMPLOYEES' QUESTIONS

As if it isn't hard enough to learn your job, right from the beginning you will start getting questions from those who work for you. You may feel tempted to beg off by making an excuse about being new to the job. Compounding the problem is that even without time constraints, you haven't been around long enough to know the answers for the questions coming your way. Despite these handicaps, it's essential to your future success to answer employee questions.

Right from the day you start, you are the management link between those you supervise and the company. You *are* the company in the eyes of your subordinates. It's your responsibility in this regard to deal with the wide range of questions employees bring to you. Those that are work-related can have an impact upon your group's performance, while questions concerning personnel issues may affect the worker individually. In either case, answers must be forthcoming.

Of course, all questions won't have the same significance, so how you deal with them will vary. Furthermore, there is assistance available in several forms to help alleviate your burden. Let's look at how you can dispose of typical types of questions.

### 1. Routine Work-Related Questions

Most of these you can dispose of on the spot by making a decision alone or in conjunction with the employee who poses the question. If it's something of a routine nature you can ask the employee how it was handled in the past, and then tell the worker to continue to do it the same way. Sometimes workers will ask a new boss these questions if they're not certain whether the new supervisor wants to continue a past practice.

## 2. Operational Issues that Haven't Been Dealt with Before

You might be faced with a question on work procedure that involves something new or unusual for the workers in your group. Here, it's best to consult your boss or someone else who would have the proper answer.

## 3. Questions on New Personnel Policies

A change in pay practices, benefits, vacation procedures, and similar issues will find most of your workers seeking answers if they don't understand the change. Here, as with other matters that affect the entire unit, get any answers you need and then hold a meeting with the entire group to answer the questions for everyone at once. Otherwise, you will have people popping into your office one at a time seeking the same answer.

## 4. Complicated Questions of a Technical Nature

When you get a complex question that is best answered by someone in the company who is an expert on the subject, find out first who can answer the question, and then refer the worker to them. Ask the employee to let you know the results. If it appears to be an issue that will come up again, you may want to accompany the worker so you know what to do the next time. This is a judgment call depending upon the specifics of the question which needs answering.

## 5. Questions on Issues of Importance to Individual Workers

This category will consist of inquiries such as requests for time off, leaving early to handle a personal emergency, and other matters of this nature. You can pretty much play most of these by ear and make your own decision with due consideration to personnel policies covering the matter.

Sometimes you will get questions that can't be answered immediately. In such cases, let workers know you will find the answer and get back to them. Employees don't expect you to have all of the answers, but their confidence in you will be shaken if you promise answers and then don't follow through. If you run into a situation where you can't get an answer to an employee question, let them know you made the effort but were unsuccessful in getting a satisfactory response.

# HOW TO HANDLE LOADED QUESTIONS

Aside from answering valid questions, you may on occasion have to deal with loaded questions that attempt to put you in a bad light. Alternatively, misleading questions may be used to get you to agree to something without realizing what you have done. There are two broad forms of leading questions you should know how to deal with. The first type seeks a yes-or-no answer and is accusatory in nature, for example, "Have you cured your quality problem?" The assertion is made that you have a quality problem when that may not even be true.

One of the best ways to deal with this sort of question is to combine denial with a question of your own which puts the burden of proof on the person asking the question. For instance, your response to the previous question might be, "We didn't have any quality problem that needed curing. What are you talking about?" This forces the person to either be specific or to backtrack by saying something such as, "Just kidding," or denying what was said.

Frequently, when assertions of this nature are challenged, the person will respond by saying, "I didn't say that. All I wanted to know was..." Whether they handle it this way, or try to justify the accusation, the discussion is now open to the point where you can offer information to refute the claim.

The second type of loaded question you may get attempts to mislead you into answering without realizing what you're committing yourself to. For example, an employee may say, "What happens if we don't finish the Trimex job today?" If you're busy thinking about something else you may respond by saying, "We'll have to work overtime." This, of course, may be a possibility, but the worker takes it as a definitive answer and then spreads the word that there's overtime that night. Never give speculative answers to direct questions, because, as in this example, they can be easily misinterpreted.

There are all kinds of variations to tricky questions, whether intentional or not, that can cause you difficulty if they are not handled with care. Here are a few tips on how to handle questions so you don't get inadvertently trapped into conveying the wrong impression.

✏ Always take the time to think before answering questions. This can be overlooked when you're busy.

✏ Never feel obliged to answer a question right away. If you're not sure about the answer tell the person you will get back to them with a reply. If you're pressed for an immediate response (say, by your boss) give a qualified answer, and promise to follow up with a more detailed reply. (For example, "I think the supplies are due in tomorrow, but I'll check to be certain and let you know.")

✏ If you're asked a confusing question, get clarification before you answer it.

✏ If you feel someone is testing you because you're new, put the ball back in their court by responding to their question with a question of your own. (For example, a supervisor says, "Do you know how to handle a crisis?" Respond by saying, "You're an experienced boss. How do you handle a crisis?"

Fielding tricky questions becomes easier with practice, but don't let anyone get the better of you because of your inexperience. Whenever you find it necessary, you can use your newness as a valid excuse for not having a ready answer. The biggest trap you can fall into is feeling you have to immediately give a response just because someone asked you a question. If you avoid this pitfall, tricky questions won't pose a problem for you.

## TEN WAYS TO BUILD TRUST WITH YOUR SUBORDINATES

A crucial ingredient to your long-term success as a boss is the ability to build a foundation of trust with your subordinates. There can be little doubt that people will do a lot more for someone they trust. Unfortunately, inspiring trust isn't something that can be accomplished overnight. It arises gradually from your interaction with workers starting with your first day on the job.

This is why it's necessary to perform your duties in such a manner that the trust-building process starts right away. Remember, you may be the nicest and most considerate person in the world, but as a new supervisor you're a blank sheet of paper in the eyes of those who work for you.

How you handle your duties will determine the picture that's painted. You will be seen either as a boss who workers can trust and respect or a supervisor employees don't have any confidence in.

Poor morale, low productivity, and workers leaving for other jobs are just a few of the possibilities that can develop when workers don't trust a boss. Incidentally, trusting and respecting a boss shouldn't be confused with popularity. A boss can be trusted and respected without being popular. At the other extreme, a boss may be likeable but not respected. The key difference is in the ability to be a good manager who can make unpopular decisions but is always fair. Sometimes a popular boss is liked, not so much because of job performance, but simply because the individual can't or won't make tough decisions when they're called for. This is the type of person people are inclined to say "...is a nice person, but he doesn't know how to supervise."

On the other hand, to earn trust and respect doesn't mean that a boss can't also be well liked. The difference is that when push comes to shove in terms of taking disciplinary action, or some other distasteful duty, this sort of boss won't avoid the responsibility for fear of becoming unpopular. With these thoughts in mind, let's look at some ways of performing your duties that will eventually earn you the trust and respect of those you supervise.

## 1. Accept the Responsibility when Something Goes Wrong

It's your department for better or worse from the moment you begin your supervisory duties. One of the keys to earning the respect of your subordinates is being willing to personally accept the responsibility when mistakes are made. Some supervisors operate by acting as a conduit for blame by openly pointing the finger of guilt at a subordinate for every mistake that's made. They fail to accept the responsibility for any error originating in their department. Yet they readily accept recognition and compliments from superiors when their unit achieves success. This sort of hypocrisy turns workers off.

Sure, if a worker makes a mistake it should be pointed out and corrected. However, this should be done in a constructive way. Furthermore, in most cases, it should be a private issue between the supervisor and the worker. That's a far cry from openly pinning the blame on a worker when someone outside the department makes a complaint. When a pattern of blaming workers when something goes wrong is practiced by a supervisor, there are inevitable consequences. These include hiding errors from a boss, low morale and productivity, and a total lack of respect for a boss.

Therefore, the first step in building trust with your subordinates is a willingness to take the heat when mistakes are made. Accept the responsibility openly when your boss or others complain to you. Reassure them the situation will be corrected and leave it at that. Then privately assess what went wrong within your group, and take whatever corrective action is needed.

Once workers see you are a stand-up boss who accepts responsibility for the performance of the unit, they will be encouraged to level with you about mistakes. This will go a long way toward establishing a relationship of trust and respect.

## 2. Battle to Get Workers the Recognition They Deserve

Some supervisors do a better job than others in gaining recognition for the efforts of outstanding workers. Top-notch workers become embittered if they see co-workers in other departments continually receiving awards and other recognition for their achievements while their accomplishments go unnoticed. It's only natural this will lead to an attitude of "Why work hard when it isn't even noticed." Therefore, it's worth the effort to do the paperwork and legwork necessary to guarantee your workers will get their fair share of recognition for their efforts.

This can be a time-consuming process and you obviously can't start handing out awards the day you arrive on the scene. But as soon as you have been supervising long enough to know individuals deserving of recognition, make the effort to put them in for cash and other awards. Even before then, if the prior supervisor had awards in process, follow up to make sure they don't fall through the cracks.

## 3. Show You're a Boss Who Cares about People

It's a given that you can't earn the respect of others unless you show them respect in return. A boss who treats workers as little more than a resource necessary to get the work out the door won't be able to establish an effective working relationship with subordinates. Workers don't have to be—nor do they expect to be—coddled, but they should be treated with dignity and respect.

From the beginning you can demonstrate your concern for those who work for you by your actions. There are many ways to do this, which separately aren't of great significance, but taken together they show a pattern of concern for both the work-related and personal aspects of people's lives. It can start with nothing more substantial than greeting workers with a pleasant "good morning" on a daily basis.

This seems like such a small thing, but more than one employee has soured on a supervisor for no greater reason than being greeted with a grunt or being totally ignored, when the worker said "good morning." So showing you care about people can begin with nothing more difficult than being pleasant. And even though you're busy concentrating on learning your new job, make it a daily goal to squeeze in a few minutes for casual conversation with subordinates.

From another standpoint, you can get off to a fast start in showing respect for subordinates by solving the personal difficulties they bring to you for resolution. Such matters as straightening out an error in a worker's paycheck or explaining why vacations have to be scheduled ahead of time mean a lot to the individual with the problem.

It also helps to give a high priority to personnel-related issues that employees talk to you about. When you're busy, it's difficult to find the time to seek answers to such questions. But for the employee involved, a question on health benefit coverage is far more important than exceeding the production goal for the month. So even when you can't immediately get an answer to these types of questions, make it as high a priority as possible—and let the worker know you consider it to be important. In the final analysis, the best way to think about showing concern for employees is to treat them the way you want to be treated by your own boss.

## 4. Don't Overload Your Workers with Other People's Burdens

It's certainly admirable to cooperate with other supervisors, since teamwork is one of the traits that makes any good organization tick. However, as a new supervisor you have to resist the urge to be too helpful at the risk of alienating your workers. You also have to be on the lookout for supervisors who try to take advantage of your status as a new boss. For these reasons, you should exercise caution in volunteering your workers to help out in other departments or take over chores from a group that's allegedly overloaded.

If your employees feel you are being too casual about volunteering them to do work they feel is someone else's responsibility, they may attribute it to your inability to stand up to other managers. Attitudes such as this are hard to shake once they start to develop. So think twice before you do any volunteering, at least until you're settled in enough to make judgments about who is busy and who isn't.

Even if another supervisor should make a formal request to you for help, you're in a good position to claim your group isn't able to offer assistance. Simply say that until you have a firm rein on what needs to be done in your own department, it wouldn't be practical to have your people doing other work.

Of course, if the request comes from your boss you pretty much have to rely on his or her assessment of relative necessity. But if there are later problems with meeting goals in your own group, don't forget to mention you had people doing someone else's work instead of their own.

None of this is meant to imply that supervisors shouldn't cooperate with one another when the need arises. Until you become experienced, however, you have to be aware of being taken advantage of, as well as the negative reaction of workers to helping others if they have work of their own.

## 5. Don't Let Your Workers Be Used as Scapegoats

Occasionally, supervisors or workers in other departments may try to unfairly pin the blame for mistakes on someone who works for you. When this happens, don't accept these claims at face value. Instead, go about finding out exactly what happened. If it turns out the mistake wasn't made by one of your workers, go back to the buck-passer and let it be known you don't appreciate your workers being unfairly blamed for errors made by others. When you stick up for your employees in this manner, their faith in you will rapidly rise. As a bonus, others in the company will realize you're not someone who will sit back and be a scapegoat for other departments.

## 6. Be Consistent in Your Dealings with Subordinates

Most people if they had to choose between a boss who is a consistent S.O.B., and one who ranges from being a tyrant one moment to an insincere flatterer the next would rather work for the former. People can deal with someone unpleasant and consistent far easier than with a boss they don't know what to expect from. So although you certainly don't want to be an S.O.B., neither do you want to be inconsistent in dealing with your subordinates. For example, if you tend to be lenient if workers are a few minutes late, do so on a consistent basis.

Workers will pretty much adapt to the management style of a boss as long as they are able to recognize it. It's when a boss keeps flip-flopping that confusion sets in. And when workers can't figure out what a boss expects, they will become wary in their dealings with the boss. When this happens, two-way communication suffers, morale declines, and the boss wonders what he or she is doing wrong. Therefore, it's important to be consistent in how you handle similar problems.

*Caution:* Being consistent doesn't mean you can't be flexible in dealing with one-of-a-kind situations that arise. For example, you may have a policy of not granting time off without two days prior notice. This doesn't mean you shouldn't grant an occasional exception if an employee has a personal emergency. The same holds true for other policies. The difference is you are consistent under routine circumstances, but yet are able to be flexible and make exceptions if the circumstances warrant it. Workers both recognize and appreciate a boss who operates in this fashion. In a nutshell, just because you're consistent doesn't mean you can't be flexible when it's justified.

## 7. Make Your Expectations Known to Your Subordinates

Along with being consistent in dealing with workers, it's also imperative that workers understand what you expect from them. There's probably nothing that can cause greater friction between a boss and a worker than an unsatisfactory performance evaluation when the worker assumed he was doing a good job. This, in fact, is a reasonable assumption if the worker had never been told otherwise. Yet time and again in the workplace, employees leave performance evaluation meetings bewildered by the discovery they had been doing everything wrong for the past six months.

If you want to earn the respect and loyalty of employees it's essential to make them aware of what you expect from them in their job performance. This also applies to rules on attendance, work and lunch breaks, and other job-related activities. You obviously can't fully establish your expectations until you have been on the job a reasonable length of time. But as times passes, be sure you let workers know the standards you want met, and ask for their feedback in terms of both understanding and agreeing with these fundamentals. Doing this lets employees know what you want and what they have to do to comply.

## 8. Encourage Worker Participation in Job Decisions

There is no one better positioned to know how to do a particular job than the person doing it. Yet all too often there is little or no worker input into how a job can be done better. This also applies to the equipment and machinery which workers use to do their jobs. When worker participation is lacking, employees are likely to respond with a "Don't blame me, I didn't decide to do it that way," when something goes wrong.

You can counteract this attitude by actively consulting with workers on how they can best do their jobs. Making them participants in the decision-making process will give workers a vested interest in doing the job right. It will also encourage them to make suggestions on their own as to how improvements can be made. Therefore, as you ask questions and listen to what employees tell you when you're first learning who does what in your new assignment, express an interest in their ideas. Then, continue to seek their suggestions on how work methods can be improved. Once workers recognize that you take their contributions seriously, they will take a greater interest in doing a good job. And as a side benefit, it will increase their respect for you as a boss.

## 9. Treat Everyone Fairly

This seems to be a no-brainer, since most bosses attempt to be fair in their treatment of employees. However, many an employee would think otherwise. This difference in opinion can often be accounted for by the unintentional actions taken by a boss which are unfair, or are at least construed that way by workers. Another factor is the subconscious tendency to treat those we like more favorably than others.

There are a couple of particulars you have to be on guard against which can create a perception of unfairness in the minds of workers. The first ties in with the prior discussion on the need to be consistent. Everyone has their good moods and bad. Added to this is the fact that some days at work will be more trying than others. Either of these factors can easily lead to making a decision one way today, then taking the opposite approach tomorrow. For example, let's look at a situation with a new supervisor named Joe. His commute was tough today, it's raining, and he got soaked coming in from the parking lot because he forgot his umbrella. Then, before he can even take his coat off, two workers call in sick. Five minutes later in comes Betty to ask to leave an hour early, and being in a bad mood Joe abruptly says no.

Now fast forward to the next day. It's the first warm, sunny day in a week, it's payday, and Joe's boss has just told him what great progress he's making as a supervisor. Hey, let the good times roll. In comes Charlie, asking to leave early since his son has a baseball game he wants to watch. Joe says, "No problem, Charlie. Hope your boy's team wins."

Now let's eavesdrop on the conversation between Betty and her co-workers at lunch upon hearing Charlie's request was granted, after Betty had been turned down the day before.

| | |
|---|---|
| *Betty:* | "Did you hear what that S.O.B. boss of ours did?" |
| *Peg:* | "No, let's hear it." |
| *Betty:* | Yesterday I asked to leave an hour early, and Joe almost bit my head off. Today, Charlie asks him and it's no problem. Boy, does that guy play favorites." |
| *Art:* | "Maybe he's sexist." |
| *Fran:* | "I don't think so. He was out to lunch for two hours with Marlene last week, and she told me he gave her the rest of the afternoon off with pay." |
| *Art:* | "OK, he's a sexist who is having an affair with one of his workers." |
| *Fran:* | "Come on, Art. No one in their right mind would think those two were having an affair." |
| *Art:* | "Well, how do you explain the fact he takes Marlene to lunch for two hours, gives her the afternoon off, and won't give Betty a lousy hour?" |
| *Peg:* | "Not only that, but Marlene's always absent and nothing is done about it." |

*Betty:*       "I don't know or care about that, but it's obvious he plays favorites."

The conversation continues with further speculation, and after lunch the scuttlebutt circulates through the rest of the workers in the unit. Incidentally, the long lunch the workers mentioned was to have a disciplinary conversation in private with Marlene, since she had received prior warnings for her excessive absences. Joe's boss had told him to take her to lunch, explain to her that if her record didn't improve she would have to be terminated. He further instructed Joe to tell Marlene she was being given the rest of the day off with pay so she could decide whether she wanted to continue working for the company. If so, starting the next day she was to turn over a new leaf in terms of her attendance.

What we have here is a typical situation where a thoughtless action sets the rumor mill running rampant. You might tend to think, "Who cares what people think as long as they do their work." The problem is that unhappy workers aren't going to work as hard, and when that little extra effort is needed it won't be forthcoming. Naturally, rumors will always circulate, but there's little to be gained by supplying more grist for the mill.

The essential point is to be on guard against unintentionally taking inconsistent actions because of the mood you're in, or inadvertently playing favorites because you like one person better than another. Being realistic, you can't spend your working day worrying about this, but as long as you're aware of it the occasions when you might slip up will be rare. And unless there's an obvious pattern, even your workers will excuse you for being human once in a while.

## 10. Show Common Courtesy

Whether you're reprimanding someone for disciplinary reasons or just doing routine work, being courteous is a trait that will earn you a great deal of respect. Admittedly, this isn't always easy to do, especially when everything seems to be going wrong or you're in a rush to wrap something up. It's not hard for your blood pressure to soar when workers make careless mistakes, and everyone loses their cool now and then. Nevertheless, under any circumstances always strive to keep your composure. It helps you think better, and beyond that you can look foolish if you blow your stack at someone.

If you do lose your temper and angrily berate a worker, when you calm down, find time to apologize. Everyone gets hot under the collar on occasion, but not everyone has the dignity to recognize their frailty. By letting a worker know you didn't mean to lose your temper, it will keep the employee from silently stewing over the incident. On a broader scale, it will demonstrate to everyone who works for you that you have a genuine concern for them. This goes a long way toward cementing your goal of being a supervisor who is trusted and respected by employees.

## THE ABC'S OF DELEGATING WORK

One of the hardest elements of supervision to learn is how to effectively delegate work to subordinates. Part of the problem centers around personality. Some people are very reluctant to relinquish control of anything they're working on. They operate on the basic assumption that someone else either can't do the work, or at least can't do it as well as they can. At the other extreme are those who essentially delegate every chore imaginable, including those they should properly do themselves.

Wherever your tendencies lie between these two extremes, it's prudent to know how and when to delegate work, since otherwise you will never be able to maximize either your efficiency, or that of your unit. Of course, until you thoroughly understand the operating details of your department, it is impractical, if not impossible, to decide what should be delegated in any orderly fashion. First, you have to master the details of the work. In addition, you have to learn the capabilities of each of your subordinates. Only then will you be able to make sound decisions on what can be delegated, and which worker should be selected for different assignments.

In the meantime, you still have to get the work out while simultaneously learning your new job. Ironically, it's in the early stages of your new assignment that you have the greatest need to delegate work to others. Of course, this is also when you are least prepared to do so. However, if you do nothing you could be overwhelmed by your workload.

Faced with this prospect, the best approach is to delegate as much as you can even though you don't have enough experience to be fully aware of the capabilities of those you assign tasks to. There are a couple of things you can do to minimize the risks. To start with, ask individuals you want to delegate work to if they know how to handle the assignment. If they respond negatively, or appear unsure, don't delegate the task. You're only taking a chance at having the job botched which would create more work for you than if you did it yourself.

Incidentally, once you learn both the operating practices and worker capabilities within the department you won't want to let people beg off of assignments so easily. But in your first few weeks on the job you're better off doing this, since you have to accept what you're told until you learn otherwise.

You can also shift a lot of the initial work burden to any of your subordinates who display a willingness to pitch in and help. Whatever you do delegate, be sure to follow up closely so nothing falls through the cracks. Closely monitoring the assignment will also allow you to track the steps required to do the task, since at first you may know less about how to do it than the person it was delegated to. Some of the work you initially delegate may not be done as well as you would like. With all you have to learn when you first assume your new job, however, any help you can get is a bonus.

Once you start to get control of your new duties, you can begin to delegate work in a more systematic way. To delegate effectively, there are a few general guidelines which you should always try to follow. These are:

- ✏ Be clear about what you want done when you make an assignment.

- ✏ State specifically when the task is expected to be completed.

- ✏ Delegate any necessary authority required to get the job done.

- ✏ Tell the worker to see you anytime assistance is needed.

- ✏ If the project will cover a rather lengthy time period, provide for checkpoints where the employee can report to you on the progress of the task.

- ✏ When the assignment is completed, provide feedback to the worker on his or her performance.

Let's look at some of the specific considerations involved in each of the preceding steps. There are several pitfalls to avoid when you delegate work. When you assign a task, take the time to explain what you want the employee to do. It's sometimes easy to overlook this, particularly if it's a job that has become second-nature to you. This is especially true if the worker has never handled this particular type of assignment before.

Explain carefully what you want the worker to do, and when you're through giving instructions, ask if there are any questions the worker needs answered. It's helpful to suggest that the worker see you later if questions come up, since once the assignment is started, a worker may find the project to be more difficult than anticipated. In addition, if the instructions are lengthy or confusing it may be worthwhile to put them in writing so the employee has a written game plan to follow.

In terms of who you delegate work to, try to match the work with the capabilities of each individual, but, don't limit yourself to only handing out assignments that don't challenge workers. Instead, try to take some risks in an attempt to encourage workers to stretch their abilities. Workers won't generally object to this, especially if they are comfortable in knowing they won't be criticized for making mistakes.

In terms of what chores should be delegated, there are a couple of general rules you can follow. First of all, always delegate routine work that is properly done by your subordinates. Although you may chip in to help get the work out when it's unusually busy and deadlines must be met, you shouldn't do work normally done by your workers. Incidentally, this is a trap you can fall into when you're starting a new position. You may inadvertently assume duties that were previously performed by a subordinate. In fact, a worker may try to pass along a chore to you on the pretext that it was done by the previous supervisor. This is especially true of routine reports and other paperwork where there may be some question as to whether it's a supervisory responsibility or something that can be delegated. A good policy to follow in this regard is "when in doubt, farm it out."

You should also try to delegate duties that eat up big chunks of time, since your supervisory duties won't give you the luxury of doing much of this sort of work yourself. Good examples in this area include training new employees, and the preparation of lengthy reports. Of course, as far as reports go, if they aren't just routine paperwork, you should thoroughly review them upon completion, since you're ultimately responsible for their accuracy.

The final factor in properly delegating work is to adequately follow up on work you have delegated. This is especially true for anything that the employee hasn't worked on before, as well as projects that must be completed by a certain date. The next section covers the specifics on how to follow up.

## How to Follow Up on Assignments Without Being a Pest

Whenever you assign tasks to employees, you have to follow up to be sure that satisfactory progress is being made in completing the assignment as you directed. Otherwise, you may find to your surprise that assignments are done incorrectly due to a failure to follow your directions. Equally bad, employees may let delegated duties sit on the back burner while they do their other work.

The degree to which you follow up will depend upon a number of factors. When you're learning your new role, you will have to follow up more frequently, since you won't be as certain of what has to be done to complete the task, as well as the capabilities of the individuals doing the work. Later on, as you gain experience, your follow-up efforts can be less intensive.

Never be casual in your approach to following up on an assignment. Simply asking, "How's the job going," may elicit a response such as, "Coming along fine, boss," when in fact the employee is having problems. The reasoning behind this type of evasive response is usually either the worker is afraid to point out the problems, or he or she doesn't want you to think they aren't capable of doing the job. So the first rule of follow-up is to be specific when you ask about the progress of an assignment.

Once you're familiar with the individual capabilities of workers, the extent of follow-up will be influenced by the expertise of the person doing the work, as well as the complexity of the project. Naturally, with newer and less experienced workers, follow-up checks should be made more frequently. The same rule applies with experienced workers if they are handling a difficult assignment which may test the limits of their abilities.

On the other hand, you don't want to be too obtrusive in your follow-up efforts, particularly with seasoned employees, since they may interpret your inquiries as a lack of confidence in their ability. Overall, there's a fine line between legitimate follow-up and needless meddling. Establishing the difference between the two is something that you will learn from experience. It should also be mentioned that your temperament also comes into play. Some supervisors delegate readily and follow up minimally, while others hesitate to delegate and then persistently badger the person doing the work. Needless to say, those in the latter category never seem to get caught up with their work. If you eventually want to see the end of the tunnel in terms of your workload, learn both to delegate effectively and to only follow up when justified.

## What to Do if a Worker Disagrees with what You Want Done

After you have been supervising for a month or two you will seldom find a worker disagreeing with you about how something should be done. About the only time that will happen is when you make a change in how workers do their jobs. The objection isn't really aimed at you, but instead reflects the natural resistance to a new way of doing something. Once you explain the need for the change and the advantages to be gained from it, workers will generally accept it without too much of a fuss.

You're likely to get the greatest amount of resistance to direction from workers in your first weeks on the job. At that time, workers won't have settled into the habit of accepting you as their boss. Furthermore, they won't have seen you in action enough to have confidence in your abilities. As a result, you're likely to find yourself facing objections when you ask a worker to do something.

Don't be rattled by this and resist the urge to assert your supervisory authority and insist on having your way. Instead, discuss the pros and cons with the worker, since it may well be that the worker is right. After all, someone who has been doing a job for a lengthy period of time knows the details of doing the work far better than anyone else. That, of course, doesn't mean they're right, but it does guarantee they won't be easily persuaded there's a better way to do something.

Talking the situation out will give you a great deal of insight into why the worker doesn't agree with you. Take the time to explain why the change is necessary, and if it's feasible show them what you want them to do. Just taking the time to discuss the matter will weaken resistance, since it will be seen that you're not being arbitrary. This means a lot to workers when they get a new boss who is willing to do this, since it tells them their opinion is respected. Once you have thoroughly talked the matter over, assuming you haven't heard anything that would change your mind, end the discussion by asking the employee to "give it a try." This usually resolves these problems.

On the other hand, if during your discussion the worker persuades you that he or she is right, don't hesitate to admit you were wrong. As the boss, you can inevitably get it done your way if you insist. But if you do this, workers will feel they have no voice in how their jobs are done. The end result will be they won't keep you from making mistakes, since it will be assumed you aren't interested in hearing what they have to say. In the end, this will make your job a lot more difficult than it has to be.

Of course, there may be a time or two when even though a worker may have valid arguments about why something shouldn't be done, your hands may be tied by policy or management directives. When that happens, you will have to insist it be done the way you want. However, be sure to let the worker know you appreciate and understand his or her opinions. Workers generally know without you saying so when you are locked into a position, so they aren't likely to harbor any resentment toward you.

# Chapter Five

# DEALING WITH
# EMPLOYEE CONCERNS

*A*s time passes in your new job, you will inevitably have to deal with a variety of employee concerns. These include worker disagreements, various complaints, and subordinates badgering you with all sorts of requests. Many of these issues will be significant to the employees involved, even though you know they are unjustified or foolish. Whatever the case, handling these diplomatically isn't always easy, and at times you may want to simply explode in anger. However, that only serves to make a bad situation worse. Let's look at how you can deal with some of these dilemmas with a minimum of frustration.

## WHAT TO DO WHEN TWO EMPLOYEES DON'T GET ALONG

Some of the most unpleasant moments for any supervisor are having to deal with people problems that aren't directly related to work. One such difficulty is having to get involved when two employees dislike each other. Of course, if it has no impact on their work, it's something you want to steer clear of.

Unfortunately, people who work in close proximity to each other for eight hours a day aren't always able to ignore their differences with other employees. So through one means or another they tend to involve others either directly or indirectly. The result can be a serious setback to your attempts to establish teamwork within your group. This will force you to become involved even though you would prefer to remain on the sidelines.

If you're dealing with two people who are low-key about not liking each other, then you may be able to resolve the situation by using preventive measures. For example, avoid giving them assignments where they will have to work closely together. Or, if it's feasible, you may want to adjust their work locations so they aren't physically near each other.

When there's more open disagreement you may first hear about it from one or the other shortly after your arrival. This may take the form of back-stabbing by one of them telling you about the failings of the other person. It's always a bad sign when you hear this sort of rumbling from workers about their peers. Anytime it happens, you want to emphasize how much value you place upon teamwork, and how difficult it is when people can't work well together. This isn't likely to make much difference in resolving the dispute, but it clearly lets workers know your position.

As times passes, if you either notice yourself or receive complaints from other workers that the feuding of two workers is being disruptive, you will have little choice but to take action. The best approach is to call each worker into your office individually and tell them in no uncertain terms that their bickering has to stop since it's interfering with their work. Don't waste time listening to one complain about the other. State emphatically that you're not interested in why they don't get along, but you do insist that it not affect either their work or that of their co-workers.

If these individual meetings don't resolve matters quickly, then call both parties back in together. Tell them they have been told once to knock off the nonsense at work. Advise them that this will be the last time they will be told and that if their disruptive actions continue, you will have to do something about it. Let them know that if it becomes necessary, one or both of them could be terminated.

Both employees have essentially had two bites at the apple to get things squared away. So if they continue their negative activities you will have to take formal action. The form this takes will depend on a number of factors including the extent to which they are a disruptive influence, the impact on their work, and whether they're equally to blame.

The quickest and simplest remedy is to transfer one or both of the culprits out of your department. However, don't ship them elsewhere unless they are good workers. If this tactic isn't feasible, then you may want to initiate formal disciplinary action. The steps you take will depend upon the specific policies of your company. Of course, before you do anything formally, consult with both your boss and the personnel department for advice. Incidentally, if it turns out that disciplinary action is necessary, you may find them getting along better—or at least ignoring one another—once they realize you're not going to put up with their nonsense.

## SOME BASIC WAYS TO RESOLVE EMPLOYEE SQUABBLES

Although the most serious form of employee bickering is when two workers don't like each other, there can also be lesser disagreements of a one-time nature related to some aspect of work. These can arise from almost anything, from disagreements over who should be doing a particular task to arguments about who broke the office copier. Most of these usually resolve themselves rather quickly. However, in some cases one of the participants will bring the dispute to you for resolution. It's times like these that may make you wish you had found another line of work. Be that as it may, you should call both parties into your office to iron out the difficulty.

What you want to do is sit them down and find out precisely what the problem is. Whenever possible, try to finalize the matter by making a decision which everyone accepts as reasonable. If necessary, you may even try to embarrass the two individuals into recognizing how foolish their behavior is. If this sounds a lot like dealing with kids in kindergarten, rest assured it is. After all, some people never grow up, they just get older.

Although how you deal with a particular problem will vary to fit the specific situation, it's useful to look at an example, since this will give you a general idea of the process involved.

## Background

Betty and Peggy sit at adjacent desks and both have phones which can answer any line in the department. They are responsible for answering all phones if someone hasn't picked up their line by the fourth ring. There are ten employees in the department who sit in adjoining cubicles, with two employees per cubicle. Sandy, the supervisor has a separate office. All told there are eleven incoming extensions, so Betty and Peggy are responsible for ten phones besides their own. The department's function is basically a customer-service operation serving business customers.

Betty and Peggy perform clerical duties, while the other eight workers are customer-service representatives. Sandy, the supervisor has been on the job only three weeks but has already received several complaints from other workers that their phones aren't being answered. Following these complaints up, Sandy has essentially had both Peggy and Betty point fingers at each other. Having just received the latest complaint, Sandy decides it's time to settle this problem and calls both workers into her office.

| | |
|---|---|
| *Sandy:* | "There have been a number of complaints about phones not being answered. Can you two tell me what the problem is?" |
| *Betty:* | "Well, it's not me, I answer them unless I'm away from my desk." |
| *Peggy:* | "Don't try to put the blame on me, Betty, I always answer the phone, including yours when you're not at your desk." |
| *Betty:* | "I didn't say it was you." |
| *Peggy:* | "You certainly implied as much. I don't have a problem answering phones, but you have to carry your share of the load." |
| *Betty:* | (Looking mad) "Are you saying I don't?" |
| *Sandy:* | (Quickly interrupting) "Wait a minute you two. I'm not interested in who is or isn't to blame. What I want to know is what we can do to make sure the phones get answered. Do you have any suggestions?" |

| | |
|---|---|
| *Betty:* | "Why not just make everyone responsible for answering their own phones?" |
| *Sandy:* | "That isn't practical. Furthermore, one of the duties you two have is to answer the phones. That shouldn't be difficult to do if we all work together at coming up with a solution." |
| *Peggy:* | "Frank (the previous supervisor) never had a problem with this. I think some of the reps are just trying to get even with us by complaining to you." |
| *Betty:* | "Yea, you're right Peggy. Those people should spend more time at their desks, rather than complaining about phones not being answered." |

COMMENT: Notice how quickly the two workers went from blaming each other to joining forces in blaming someone else? This isn't unusual when two workers are confronted about something going wrong. Once they discover pointing the finger at each other won't work, they join forces to find a common enemy. In these situations, you have to refuse to be diverted from the subject at hand.

| | |
|---|---|
| *Sandy:* | "I'll worry about other people. Right now, we're dealing with getting the phones answered which is the responsibility of you two. Do you have any ideas on what changes can be made so there aren't any more complaints?" |
| *Betty:* | "We'll just have to work harder at it, I guess." |
| *Sandy:* | "Do you have any suggestions, Peggy?" |
| *Peggy:* | "No." |
| *Sandy:* | (Having thought about the problem before calling the meeting.) "Well, here's what we're going to do. First of all, I don't want you both away from your desks at the same time. If you have to leave your desk when you're alone, I want to be notified first. As for lunch, do either of you have a time preference? (Both answer no.) Good, then Peggy, you go eleven to twelve, and Betty, you can go from twelve to one. For |

now, I'm not going to schedule break times, but if I
have to I will. Is this arrangement satisfactory to both
of you?"

*Betty:*   "It's fine with me."

*Peggy:*   "I have no problems with it."

*Sandy:*   "OK, let's do it."

COMMENTS: This example illustrates several useful pointers that can
be applied in resolving many types of squabbles over assignments.
First, never assess blame. Notice that Sandy didn't blame either of
the workers herself and refused to let them blame each other. If you
start to blame people, they will only get defensive, which makes it
even harder to resolve problems.

It's also important not to be drawn off the topic by side issues. Even
if a worker raises what appears to be a valid issue, if it's not related to the
topic, deal with it later. The more issues there are, the harder it is to resolve
any one of them. So handle problems one by one for faster resolution.

When conflicts exist between employees, they are going to be more
willing to accept your decision on resolving the matter, rather than their
co-workers' suggestion. Therefore, always try to have possible solutions
worked out in your mind before meeting with the workers.

Incidentally, although it wasn't an issue in the example, don't inadvertently cause this sort of conflict by being unclear when you make
assignments. In the example, the previous supervisor apparently never
laid down any ground rules on going to lunch, or both employees not
being away from their desks at the same time. This oversight may well
have been what caused this problem in the first place. Whenever you
assign duties, try to mentally work through any problems that may arise.
Naturally, it's not possible to foresee everything. But the minute you
notice anything going awry, make adjustments to get it back on track.

## HOW TO DEAL WITH THE RUMOR MILL

One of the minor irritants you will encounter is having to knock down
rumors that are brought to your attention. However, you're far better off

hearing about rumors than having them run rampant without your knowledge. At least, if you hear a rumor you have a chance to rebut it. Alternatively, if you don't hear about rumors, workers will spend an untold amount of time discussing them. For the sake of efficiency alone, you want to stay tuned to the news from the rumor mill.

There's another aspect of rumors that can be advantageous. Sometimes workers hear rumors that turn out to be fact, even though you have heard nothing from official channels. This is because workers may hear things from a union representative or someone else they know who is in a position to have access to information which top management hasn't announced. So keeping abreast of the rumor mill can sometimes put you a step ahead in receiving valuable information.

However, for the most part your major duty in the area of rumors will be as the sounding board for workers trying to confirm or deny rumors they have heard. Of course, in your early days in your new position, you won't have the knowledge base or contacts to verify the accuracy of rumors you hear. For the most part, you will be limited to controlling the amount of time spent discussing rumors and other gossip. The simplest way to do this is by circulating throughout the work area. When a supervisor is on the scene, employees won't congregate at the water cooler, office copier, or other gossip gathering point. So just walking around and being seen is a practice you should start right away and continue even when there is less of a need for you to be in the working area.

Most rumors and office gossip tend to be of the harmless variety and can be ignored. But, on occasion you may have to deal with a worker who is spreading harmful rumors about a co-worker. This often results from personality conflicts or jealousy. However, once you are convinced someone is doing this, you have to deal with it before it gets out of hand.

Talk to the culprit in private, and without being confrontational mention that someone is spreading malicious rumors. State emphatically that you won't tolerate this sort of behavior within your department, and ask the person if he or she knows anything about it. Most likely, you will get a denial, but rather than challenge the person, simply ask if they will let you know if they hear anything.

Doing it this way sends the message you want without directly accusing the individual. Most likely the practice will cease, since it's now known that you're aware of the rumors. Furthermore, even though you didn't say so directly, the culprit will likely assume he or she is a suspect. This is a less messy way than directly charging the worker with spreading rumors. When you have been supervising the group longer and know the workers better, you might want to be more direct. But being new, you can accomplish the same result indirectly without alienating the worker, since this makes things easier for you.

The last point about rumors is to always be careful about inadvertently starting them. One way this sometimes happens is when a worker asks a supervisor a question which results in speculation on the part of the boss. For example, "Everyone else is laying people off, so I wouldn't be surprised if it happens here," is the type of speculative statement that starts rumors. An employee hears this and before you know it the word is out that you said layoffs are scheduled. Of course, that wasn't what you actually said, but by the time a rumor gets to the fourth or fifth person in the chain, it seldom resembles the information it was originally based upon. So to prevent yourself from being a source for rumors, don't voice opinions on work-related matters that can provide fuel for the rumor mill.

## THE RIGHT WAY TO HANDLE A PAY RAISE OR PROMOTION REQUEST

A new supervisor faces many first-time challenges that more experienced bosses know how to cope with. However, as a new boss there's at least one advantage you have when it comes to dealing with worker pay raise and promotion requests. You can justifiably say that you haven't had sufficient opportunity to observe the person, and until you do it's impossible for you to make any decision on their request. Of course, that excuse can only be used in limited instances, such as with workers who don't deserve pay raises or promotions under any circumstances. Nevertheless, when it comes to countering the inflated opinions some workers have of their performance, anything that helps is a bonus.

For the most part, when workers come looking for advancement, the approaches for dealing with it are the same for new bosses and seasoned pros alike. The greatest added burden you have is a need to rely on performance ratings that were prepared by the prior boss. As a new boss, the first action you should take in this area is to make sure that any personnel actions in process for promotions or pay raises when you take over aren't neglected.

Your own boss will usually let you know if there's anything in the works, but if not, rest assured that the worker affected will be asking you about it. Your job here is simply to expedite actions initiated by others, so there's not a lot to do except for checking on the status of the paperwork and keeping workers apprised of when the personnel action will be finalized.

Whether you're talking a promotion or a pay raise, it's a money issue and nothing could be more important to an employee. So even when you have workers approach you whose prospects for more money are dubious at best, give them an opportunity to express themselves and try to couch your refusal in a positive light. After all, if someone's still on the payroll they must be doing something right, even if it's only meeting the minimum standards necessary to keep their job. Besides, if their desire for advancement is great enough, this is a good time to encourage them to improve their performance.

The most common complaint you will hear about money from workers is some variation of they are not being paid enough. That's not exactly news, since when is the last time you ran into someone who thought they were overpaid? This then is an area where you might like to simply say, "I'm not paid enough either. Don't bother me with nonsense."

Unfortunately, most people take both themselves and money seriously, which means you have to let them down lightly. Another unusual aspect of pay raise requests is that you're likely to find the workers who badger you the most about this topic are generally the ones least deserving of a raise. There's an obvious reason for this: workers who truly deserve raises tend to get them, while mediocre performers don't. So right from the start you might as well condition yourself to learn how to tactfully turn down pay raise requests without actually being as forthright as you might like to be.

In other words, you have to know how to say, "If you work up to your potential in the future, anything is possible," instead of bluntly stating the truth, "You don't deserve a raise." After all, the latter reply may shorten the discussion, but it certainly isn't motivational. And if you want workers to be productive, you have to keep them motivated—which for starters means not insulting them.

In terms of specifics, most of your efforts in this area will center around workers coming to you because they are unhappy with their latest raise. Since you're a recent arrival, a few subordinates may approach you to pitch their case for a future raise. Even though workers can be quite inventive in coming up with reasons to justify why they are worth more money, most of the pitches will rely on some minor variation of a few common themes. Let's look at some of the typical reasons workers give for why they deserve more money and how you can respond.

### 1. "Agnes Got a Bigger Raise than I Did."

Comparisons with other workers are a standard argument used to justify a raise. Don't get caught in a trap here. What someone else is earning is irrelevant. If a worker wants to discuss why they deserve a raise based on their own performance, that's one thing. It has nothing to do with what someone else is earning. In fact, many times workers don't even know what the other person's salary is, but are just using this as a ploy. When you get a comparison argument, halt it by saying, "Look, Debbie, what someone else is or isn't making has no bearing on your performance. If you want to discuss your own performance, that's fine. What would you say if I said your salary is going to be lowered because you're making more than someone else?"

Then go on to discuss the worker's request based upon the merits. Obviously, being new, most of what you will know about the worker's past performance will be from evaluations performed by the prior supervisor. Let the worker know what has to be done to improve job performance from what was said in past performance evaluations. If the worker disputes these statements say something such as, "I wasn't here, Debbie, so all I can do is rely on what Ms. Dunbar (the prior boss) said in your evaluation. I can tell you that my future assessments will be based on my own observations. So let's see how things go between now and your next evaluation. In the meantime, I suggest you think about addressing the comments made in your last evaluation if you think they will help you improve your performance."

### 2. "I've Got Ten Years Experience and I Only Got a 3-Percent Raise."

Raises are based on performance, not on seniority. This is fairly easy to dispose of. Point out that years of service are not what determines the size of a pay raise. If the employee continues to argue that experience should count, point out that it does to the extent that the worker performs at a higher level based upon the experience. Then, refer to the salary range for the job. Obviously, anyone with a lot of service will be much higher up the range. Point this out to the worker by saying something such as, "As you can see, Franco, you're in the top quartile of the salary range for your job. Someone new starts at the bottom figure. So you are making significantly more money because of your experience."

### 3. "I Work Harder than Everyone Else, so I Deserve More Money."

This is the generic argument used by workers who don't perform quite as well as they think they do. Here you should start off by pinning them down to specifics. Take a couple of notes on key points if necessary, since the justification may be long and rambling. Then, point out the weak areas as indicated in the person's prior evaluation as evidence of where they need to improve. Again, as in the salary comparison example, if the worker persists, you can fall back on being new and therefore having to rely on the prior boss's evaluation.

### 4. "I Received a Very Good Performance Rating and I only Got a 5-Percent Raise."

This is the unreasonable expectations argument. Some workers think their raise is too low even when it was on the high end of the scale compared to their peers. All you can do here is point out that the raise exceeded the norm. If the worker isn't satisfied with that explanation, you might say, "Well, perhaps the guidelines will be higher in the future," and leave it at that. Sometimes workers hear rumors of people getting large raises and get upset without knowing the rumors are false. Other people are never satisfied, so there's little point in prolonging these discussions once you give them the facts.

### 5. "I've Got Three Kids and Elderly Parents to Support, Which I Can't Do on a 4-Percent Pay Raise."

This represents the personal circumstances appeal, which may be compelling from an emotional standpoint, but has no bearing on what the person gets for a raise. The best approach here is to show under-standing for the worker's situation, while explaining there's nothing you can do about it. About all you can accomplish here is to lend a willing ear in listening to the worker's plight. If it's feasible, you can also suggest some measures the employee can take to cope with the problem, such as part-time work, schooling to qualify for better paying positions, and so forth.

### 6. *"All the Help-Wanted Ads in the Paper Show a Much Higher Salary for this Position than I'm Making Here."*

This is tilting at windmills, since someone that upset about this would be looking for a job somewhere else. In fact, perhaps they have been, but haven't met with any success. Even more likely, the figures they see are generalized and may not be representative of what someone such as the worker would earn elsewhere. For example, the salary shown may represent the top of the scale, or it may be an exaggeration in an employ-ment agency ad. For the most part, companies try to be competitive with other businesses in the same field. Even when one pays higher rates than another, there are usually offsetting factors. For instance, a company may not offer much in the way of fringe benefits, or perhaps the company's location makes it difficult to attract workers. Naturally, if a worker cites a particular company and you're familiar with the fact that they pay more and are aware of the reason, point this out to the employee. However, for the most part the way to deal with this argument is simply to state, "Our company is very competitive in terms of wages, so I can't really specu-late about what you have seen in the newspaper. However, if you look into the matter carefully, I don't think they pay more than we do for the same job."

The above examples cover most of the general areas you will find workers using to justify why they should be making more money than they are. For the most part, workers will accept your reasoning when you explain the facts to them. In essence, the bottom line is that whatever raise they received conforms to company policy on pay raises. If some-one is adamant and wants to pursue the matter further, then refer them to someone in the personnel office.

In terms of workers hitting you up for promotions, it should be fair-ly rare since you're new on the job. However, one or two opportunistic individuals may decide a new boss might be an easy sell. If people do come to you, go over their file and point out what they have to do to be considered for future promotions. Some may lack qualifications, while others will have to improve their performance. Whatever you do, when it comes to discussing future pay raises or promotions, never make promises to workers.

No matter how clear-cut the situation is, and despite the fact the employee may be truly deserving, future circumstances beyond your control may prevent you from carrying out a promise. If that happens, the worker will blame you. Never promise what you can't deliver. If you want to hold out hope for workers, say something such as, "Keep up the good work, and let's see what happens down the road." That may not leave a worker jumping for joy, but over the long-term, being straightforward with workers will earn you a good deal of respect.

## HOW TO SKILLFULLY TURN DOWN REQUESTS FOR TIME OFF

One of the routine duties you have to perform is making certain enough workers are available to handle the workload assigned to your group. This can be quite a juggling act when you have employees on vacation or out sick, since if your staffing situation is typical, you probably don't have enough workers to give you much flexibility. But, scheduled vacations can be planned for, and illness is unavoidable. What really can give you a headache are the unscheduled requests for time off, whether it's a day or even a couple of hours.

Most of the time workers will give you fairly legitimate reasons for needing time off without prior notice. That's to be expected, since even if they're going fishing, workers aren't going to say so. This puts you in somewhat of a bind. You hate to turn someone down who has a valid need for a day off to deal with a personal problem. On the other hand, you have a responsibility to get the work out on schedule. As a result, even though you want to be flexible in granting time off, there will be many occasions when you have to turn people down.

Another aspect of this dilemma is that some of your subordinates may seek to take advantage of your status as a new boss, hoping you're a soft touch for any sort of excuse. This increases the need for you to be willing to say no when it's necessary, since how you react when workers initially test you will influence the number of requests you get in the future. What it all boils down to is being able to refuse requests without appearing to be unreasonable. A few of the justifications you can use to legitimately deny any request that doesn't represent a genuine emergency include the following:

### An urgent need prevents granting the request.

*Example:* "I can't give time off to anyone until we finish the end-of-year inventory."

### Worker has too many previous requests.

*Example:* "I've already given you unscheduled time off twice in the four weeks I've been here."

### Your group is shorthanded.

*Example:* "I know it's only four hours, but I have two people out sick today."

### Failure to follow vacation policy.

*Example:* "Vacation requests are supposed to be submitted at least two weeks in advance. I can't juggle your workload on two days' notice."

### Prior requests take priority.

*Example:* "You can't have the first week in April off, since someone has already put in for it and I can't have two people on vacation at the same time."

### Worker has no time on the books.

*Example:* "I checked with payroll and you don't have any vacation time left, so I can't approve your request."

### Pass the buck to your boss if a worker is insistent.

*Example:* "I don't see how I can let you go, but since I've only been here two weeks, I'll check with Mr. Osborne."

**Put the burden for refusal on the worker.**

*Example:* "Look, Charlie, if you knew three weeks ago about your appointment, I should have been told then. I can't spare you this afternoon."

These are just a few of the many reasons for rejecting requests for time off. Naturally, the specifics of your job will determine other valid reasons. For instance, in some jobs other workers can cover when someone is unexpectedly absent, while in others there is less flexibility in granting requests. Once employees recognize you aren't going to be a sucker for any old excuse, the number of frivolous requests should decline.

## SIMPLE STRATEGIES FOR DEALING WITH COMPLAINTS ABOUT THE WORK AREA

One of the nuisance issues you have to contend with are complaints about working conditions. Often, these are petty gripes, although the employee who is complaining doesn't think so. On other occasions, there may be a legitimate problem that has to be acted upon. The most vexing situations will be those which may represent a genuine complaint, but for one reason or another there's nothing that you can do to resolve it. This is most likely to happen where older facilities and equipment make for less-than-ideal conditions.

Whenever you receive a complaint about working conditions, a good starting point in dealing with it is to address these questions:

- Is the complaint valid?

- Can an adjustment be made to satisfy the worker?

- Is it a legitimate complaint about the work area, or is the problem something else?

- Have recent changes been made that are causing the complaint?

You may find yourself having to deal with gripes about working conditions shortly after starting your new job. The odds are that any workers who have been complaining without success to the prior supervisor will see your arrival as a fresh chance to voice their complaints. You will be able to easily recognize the validity—or lack thereof—of some of the complaints. In other situations, you will need to have the worker show you what the problem is. This applies particularly when the worker is complaining about either machinery or a piece of office equipment not functioning properly.

Many complaints will center around nothing more significant than a worker's desire to update equipment to the latest configuration, even though what's being used is perfectly adequate. Another fertile area for gripes are general working conditions such as lighting, air conditioning, and so forth.

Once you clearly establish what the specific complaint is, you have to decide whether it's legitimate or just a worker quibbling about some aspect of his or her job. Once you do this, the next step is to determine whether something can be done to satisfy the worker. Even if you decide the employee is grumbling about something meaningless, you should explain why nothing can be done. Complaints in this area will usually involve either general working conditions or the worker's desire for newer equipment.

General work area complaints would include gripes such as the temperature being too hot or cold, inadequate lighting, and the like. Of course, in a rare case the employee may be right. Perhaps the lighting in the worker's area isn't sufficient. If this is true, then take the necessary action to see if something can be done to improve conditions.

Even if the complaint doesn't have any real validity, explain to the worker why it's impossible to do anything about it. Attempt to do so in such a way that the worker will sense your understanding of the problem. Sometimes workers with this sort of beef will be satisfied just knowing you were willing to listen to their gripes. This is especially true if the prior supervisor wasn't too sympathetic to these complaints.

The other type of griping where you have to explain that nothing can be done is when workers want the latest version of the equipment they use. When there's nothing wrong with the equipment from a productivity standpoint, you can tell them there is no money budgeted to replace the item in the current fiscal year. Suggest they check with you in a few months and if it's feasible, perhaps replacement items can be budgeted for at that time. Holding out hope for the future should put this sort of gripe to rest—at least temporarily. When you handle a problem this way, be sure not to make any definite commitment for future replacement; you may forget about it, but the employee won't.

On occasion, you may be able to take some form of action to pacify a worker who has a continuing gripe about working conditions. For example, if a worker complains about poor lighting, perhaps the employee's work station can be moved near a window. Naturally, if you investigate a worker's complaint and you decide it's a legitimate problem, take whatever action is necessary to resolve the matter. This is especially important when the problem is something that hinders the worker's productivity, such as a piece of equipment that isn't working properly.

*Tip:* Early on in your new job, it's very helpful to get to know the maintenance and repair people where you work. These folks can make your job a lot easier when you have a wide variety of problems in your area. Depending on the structure of your company, these people can be charged with a range of duties, from repairing broken equipment to correcting heating, ventilating, and air conditioning problems.

You definitely want to keep on the good side of these people, since they can be very helpful in a number of ways. For instance, if you're looking to replace a piece of office furniture or have another electrical outlet installed, being on friendly terms with these folks can get it done a lot more quickly. However, if you have ever given them a hard time in the past, you can find yourself waiting forever to get work done. The people in these jobs are generally overworked, so who gets the best service is often dictated by whom they like or dislike.

On occasion, you may have a worker making a complaint about some aspect of working conditions that is really only being used to mask some other problem. For example, an employee may come to you complaining about too much noise in and around his work area. This may make little sense, since the worker is experiencing the same noise levels as everyone else.

When someone comes to you with a problem that doesn't make sense on the surface, talk it out with the worker, since the true complaint may be of an entirely different nature. Perhaps the employee just doesn't get along with the person working next to him, or maybe he is located in an area where workers tend to congregate to gossip, such as the water cooler. Some workers may like to be near the center of such activity, while others may find it distracting.

In situations such as these, sometimes you can make a simple adjustment such as moving the employee's work station to alleviate the problem. In any event, don't casually disregard complaints as being the creation of a worker's imagination. Of course, you may have a chronic complainer or two working for you, but after you're on the job for a while, you will get to know who they are. And if a complaint is coming from someone else, the chances are there's something behind it, even though at first glance it doesn't appear to be a legitimate grievance.

There's one additional area which can frequently cause a large number of complaints relating to the work area. This is where recent changes either have been made or are about to be implemented, which rearrange the location of one or more workers. People become familiar with their surroundings, and attempts to move them around are often met with resistance. Something as simple as putting up or taking down cubicles can cause more rumbling than a major earthquake. Needless to say, don't start to move people around without first persuading them of the wisdom of the move.

This, of course, isn't something you're likely to do soon after assuming your new assignment. Even if you see possibilities for improving productivity by making such changes, wait until you have been there long enough to fairly assess the pros and cons. On the other hand, if there has been a recent shuffling of people and their locations shortly before you arrive on the scene, you may be the one to hear a lot of griping about it. It suffices to say that if you do, simply respond by saying something such as, "Let's try it for a while and see what happens." Usually, this sort of griping fades with time as employees adjust to their new surroundings.

Of all the complaints you may get concerning the work area, the one topic that should receive your immediate attention is anything to do with safety. Not only can serious injury result if a safety complaint is ignored, but the company could also be exposed to legal liability. Therefore, once you investigate a complaint in this area and determine its validity, bring the matter to your boss's attention so that immediate action can be taken to resolve the problem. Otherwise, you run the risk of being fingered as the cause of an accident for failing to take the necessary corrective action.

## WHAT TO SAY WHEN A WORKER COMPLAINS ABOUT COMPANY POLICY

One tricky problem you may have to contend with is fielding worker complaints about some aspect of company rules and regulations. It's tempting to dismiss these gripes with a simple response such as, "Those are the rules, and there's nothing I can do about it." Unfortunately, that's essentially the truth, but it does nothing to satisfy the employee's complaint. Furthermore, workers—especially from their viewpoint—may have legitimate gripes. After all, policies are based on meeting the overall needs of the company, and in so doing may not be particularly satisfactory when applied to individual cases. Therefore, workers may rightly feel that a particular policy is detrimental when applied to them. Be that as it may, you're stuck with enforcing the rules, so you have to defend them even if you find them to be unpalatable.

Most of the complaints about policy will focus on issues such as pay guidelines, working hours, vacation policy, and related topics of more than passing interest to the average worker. It's hard enough rationalizing rules and regulations on these topics to workers when you have been on the job for years. When you're new, it's even more of a challenge, since the rationale behind some policies may be as foreign to you as it is to the worker with the grievance.

Nevertheless, you have to take a swing at persuading the worker of the validity of the rule in question. How you go about doing this will vary with the nature of the complaint, but generally you want to explain the need for the policy as well as the fact that any policy doesn't always meet everyone's needs. Let's explore a couple of the more common complaints you may encounter and look at a sampling of responses you can give.

*2:* "Why doesn't the policy on parking provide for assigned parking spaces? I can never get a parking space."

*A:* "The company only has a limited parking area available, so the fair way to do it is by providing for first come, first served. If you come in a little earlier, you won't have any problem."

COMMENT: Sometimes you can turn a question on rules and regulations around to your advantage, such as here where an employee is always late, and tries to blame it on not being able to get a parking space.

**Q:**     "Why are parking spaces assigned? I come in early and can't get a space because I don't have a sticker. Why should the big wheels be able to roll in at the last minute just because they have an assigned space?"

**A:**     "The spaces are generally assigned based upon seniority, with the exception of a few senior executives. Since they are the ones who make the decisions that determine how profitable the company is, I don't have a problem with them having a parking spot. After all, if the company doesn't make money, we don't have a job. As for most of the spaces, once you have enough time in on the job, you will qualify for a space."

COMMENT: As you can see, this is the flip side of the previous question, which isn't as easy to deal with, since perks given to managers are a common source of irritation with workers. However, as here, you can waltz around this issue by emphasizing the importance of these people to the well-being of the company. You won't win any converts, but this approach is preferable to shrugging and essentially agreeing with the worker by saying something like "Rank has its privileges."

**Q:**     "Why do I have to put in my vacation request for the year in January? I don't know what my plans are going to be this summer."

**A:**     "Vacations have to be scheduled so there's coverage during the summer months, since everyone can't be out at the same time. Since you don't have plans yet, when you do make them, this way you will know when your vacation is. That's a lot better than putting a deposit down at a resort next month, and then finding out this summer you can't take vacation those two weeks."

**COMMENT:** No matter what a vacation policy is, some workers will complain about it. The fact is, many people want the same time periods off, which is impossible to do. But as long as a vacation policy is fair and consistent, it's easy enough to defend.

*2:* "What's with this memo on pay raises? It says all raises will be in a range of from 0 percent to 4 percent. That's not fair."

*A:* "The ranges are adjusted every year to take into account the company's profitability, economic conditions, and competitor pay rates. They're not just figures pulled from a hat."

**COMMENT:** Any policy on pay always draws more criticism than most anything else. The simplest line of defense is to emphasize the policies were prepared after carefully considering all relevant factors. What you want to avoid is being drawn into endless arguments as to what is fair and what is unfair. Anyone unhappy over pay policy isn't likely to be dissuaded by the arguments of a prize-winning economist, much less their boss, so arguing the issue is worse than trying to roll boulders up a hill.

*2:* "The safety policy says food and beverages aren't allowed in the working area. Does this mean I can't have coffee at my bench before I start work in the morning? The machines aren't even running then.

*A:* "That's exactly what it means. There should be no food or drinks in the work area at any time. I know that may seem unreasonable before work, but once any exceptions are made abuses start to occur. And when that happens, accidents will follow."

**COMMENT:** Whether it's safety or something else, rules and regulations have to be broad enough to be all-encompassing; when exceptions start to be made, the particular rule soon becomes meaningless.

In the example, it's easy enough to visualize how some workers would continue to drink their coffee after the machines had started up, or perhaps coffee would be spilled causing someone to slip and fall. With many policies, when employees question them, you can defend them by explaining the possible problems caused by making exceptions to the rules.

**2:**               "This new policy on overtime means I can't work more than eight hours of overtime a week. That stinks."

**A:**               "Neither you nor anyone else has worked more than eight hours of overtime since I've been here, and according to Mr. Hoyle (your boss), no one in the company has in at least two years. This policy is designed to prevent fatigue, which can result in both defective work and injuries."

COMMENT: New policies always come in for more than their fair share of criticism. Frequently, workers start griping about a policy when it doesn't even affect them. Whenever you're able to point this out, the arguments cease.

Although it's impossible to cover every conceivable complaint workers may have about a company policy, the examples should give you a general idea on how to respond to many situations. As a general rule, always try to point out the validity of the policy on an overall basis, without getting drawn into an argument on specifics. Incidentally, from time to time there may be policies that you don't agree with, but always be careful to avoid criticizing them in front of your subordinates. As a member of management, it's your responsibility to uphold the rules and regulations—not lobby against them.

This is especially true in your early days on the job, since workers may view your disagreement with a policy as justification for them to ignore rules and regulations they don't like. You can rest assured that the first time you call someone on breaking a rule they are likely to say, "Well, you said yourself it was a stupid regulation."

## HOW TO TACTFULLY TELL AN EMPLOYEE
## TO GET LOST

As has been mentioned before, you want to listen to what workers have to say, since it helps immeasurably in learning the details of your new job. Therefore, you don't want to casually give a worker the brush-off even when you're busy. However, after you have been on the job for a few weeks you will pretty much be able to pinpoint a couple of workers who consistently interrupt you for little or no reason. There also may be one or two employees who even though they have a valid reason for seeing you, don't have the sense to recognize when you're too busy to be interrupted with matters that can wait for another time.

For these reasons, there are occasions when you will have to tell subordinates to see you later. There's nothing remarkable about that as a general rule, but with the aforementioned pests, persistence is one of their specialties. In other words, they won't always accept a simple "I'll see you later" for an answer. As a result, you have to employ some subtle—and some not so subtle—tactics to get rid of them. Of course, you could just tell them to get lost, but this runs the risk that you might unintentionally deter other workers from approaching you. Since one of your goals is to have an open line of communication with your subordinates, it pays to be cautious in this area.

Another facet of this problem involves people who see you for a legitimate purpose, but overstay their welcome after business is concluded. You certainly don't want to be antisocial, but neither do you want to be subjected to a blow-by-blow account of someone's latest fishing trip or shopping spree. Here too, you have to know how to edge people along.

Incidentally, your problems with pests won't be limited to those who work for you. Every company has their collection of employees who seemingly have no mission other than to wander around and keep other people from pursuing their work. Being new to your position makes you a tempting target for these people, since those who know them better have long since learned to send them quickly on their way.

Given the need to get your work done, people who create unnecessary distractions have to be sent on their way. Here are a variety of ways to do that.

## 1. What to Say to Workers Who Interrupt for No Valid Reason

✏ "Are you looking for work to do, Cathy?"

✏ "I thought you said you were busy."

✏ "While you're here, will you run this down to purchasing?"

COMMENTS: The specifics of what you say aren't important, as long as you imply the employee should be working rather than bothering you. You can also discourage them from interrupting you by sending them on any errands you need to have done. This practice may not work on more persistent types, or those who have a limited capability to grasp the subtlety of what you're doing. As a result, they may run the errand and then come back to haunt you, which may force you to bluntly advise them to get busy before you find something else for them to do.

## 2. How to Edge People Out of Your Office

✏ Pick up the phone and start to make a call while saying, "Excuse me, I have a call to return."

✏ Get up and start to leave your office while dismissing the person by saying something such as, "I've got to see someone. Will you excuse me?"

✏ Pick up a memo and start to read it, or start to write something down while saying, "Thanks for dropping by." Starting to do something else will send a message the meeting is at an end to most people.

COMMENTS: There are any number of things you can do to signal a discussion is at an end. Don't hesitate to do this for fear of being rude. Those who recognize someone is busy won't see it that way, while those who linger everywhere they go are probably used to being given hints.

### 3. Use Your Position as a New Supervisor as an Excuse

✎ "I'd like to talk longer, but I have to get this new job under control."

✎ "You'll have to excuse me, but this new job doesn't allow me to spend as much time as I would like with people."

✎ "If that's all you have to discuss Maria, I have to see about catching up on this paperwork, since it's all new to me."

COMMENTS: The beauty of using your new job as an excuse is that it has a sincere ring to it. Therefore, no one is likely to be offended, if that's something of concern to you. In addition, only a real jerk would ignore the plea of someone trying to learn a new job.

### 4. Use Pass-the-Buck Techniques

✎ "I don't know much about that. Why don't you see Fred?"

✎ "I'm too new to know the details. Check it out with personnel and let me know what you find out."

✎ "You know what, Carla? Tom had a similar problem this morning. Why don't you ask him what to do?"

COMMENTS: This is especially useful in getting rid of subordinates who are badgering you with questions. It's also practical, since you may not know the answer and would only have to chase it down yourself.

### 5. The "Tell It Like It Is" Approach

✎ "I'm just too busy to talk now, Mimi. I'll see you when I get a chance."

✎ "That will have to wait, Peter. I can't see you now."

COMMENTS: If at all possible, you want to avoid being blunt. However, some people just don't take hints, and you just have to spell it out for them.

## A Basic Roadmap for Resolving Any Kind of Grievance

One unpleasant task you have to contend with as a supervisor is the resolution of grievances brought to you by employees. If the subject matter is of a serious nature, you should seek the counsel of your boss at the outset. This holds true particularly for union-related grievances, since there are set procedures to be followed in dealing with them.

You will be able to handle yourself those of a less serious nature, perhaps with a bit of advice from your boss. No matter what the subject of the grievance is, there is a more-or-less standard procedure you can follow to reach a satisfactory result. The steps to follow are:

1. Listen carefully to the complaint. Sometimes people are visibly angry or upset, so strive to calm them down before you proceed. Once you have heard the employee's complaint, ask any questions you feel are necessary to help you fully understand the problem.

2. If the grievance is of such a nature that you have to obtain information from others, tell the employee you will look into the matter and get back to them promptly. Then go about gathering all the relevant facts.

3. Once you have assembled all of the information you need, take the time to explore your possible options for resolving the problem. If the cooperation of anyone else will be needed for any of the options to be implemented, be sure you get at least tentative approval before proposing any solution to the employee. For example, if a transfer to another unit appears to be the most viable option, explore this with your boss, and then get any necessary approvals from others who will be affected.

4. Select the best of the available options, although many times there won't be more than one option available. Then discuss your proposed suggestion for resolving the difficulty with the employee. It also helps to solicit any suggestions the employee may have for resolving the matter. The more you're able to make the employee an active participant in devising a solution, the better the chance of a satisfactory resolution being reached. However, you have to steer the

employee away from solutions that are either impractical or impossible to implement. But attempt to do so without presenting the choice in terms of "this-or-nothing."

5. Once you have the agreement of the employee, make any decisions necessary to implement it. Furthermore, don't neglect to follow up to see if the problem has been satisfactorily resolved. Otherwise, you will soon find yourself starting out all over again with the employee even more unhappy than on the first go-around.

You may on occasion feel that an employee would prefer to discuss a grievance with someone other than yourself. This may be particularly true when you're new, since the worker doesn't have any feel for how you will react to the complaint. If you sense this, suggest to the worker that perhaps someone else would be more suitable to talk with. If you do this, be sure to discuss with the employee possible alternatives, so the employee will feel comfortable with the person chosen.

Another tricky aspect of some grievances is when the employee doing the complaining is actually part of the problem. This is frequently the situation when the grievance involves two or more workers. There may be enough guilt to go around, so don't blithely assume the person bringing the grievance is the innocent victim. They may just be smart enough to get to you first in the hopes of projecting an image of innocence. In any event, when this happens, deal with the one making the complaint as part of the solution.

## WHAT TO DO WHEN AN EMPLOYEE COMPLAINS ABOUT HAVING TOO MUCH WORK

One of the joys of being a first-time boss is being able to delegate work to subordinates. However, everything comes with a price. Although you're now in a position where you can assign work to others, those same people have a right to complain to you about being overworked— and complain they will. In fact, you have to be on guard against workers who try to take advantage of your recent arrival to unload some of their chores. The reasons for this vary from being lazy to seeing an opportunity to unload an unpleasant duty they have been saddled with by their previous boss.

Worker complaints about having too much work are far more likely in your early days on the job. Once you get to know individual capabilities—as well as tendencies for goofing off—employees know they aren't going to be able to make phony claims of being overloaded with work. Consequently, anyone who is going to try this ploy will do so shortly after you become their boss.

These pleas about having too much work are hard to rebut, since you're too new to easily assess the validity of every claim. As a result, you have to do some digging before you can reject a worker's assertions. A good place to start is by placing the burden of proof on the worker by asking some pointed questions about the employee's workload. Let's look at how you can do this:

### The confrontation

John M., a first-time supervisor who has been on the job a week is approached by Pete, who is one of his workers.

*Pete:* "John, you're going to have to take that rush job away from me. I've got too much work and I won't be able to finish it on time."

*John:* "What rush job are you talking about, Pete?"

*Pete:* "The order for that hospital in New Jersey."

*John:* (Looks at the work schedule and then says,) "That was assigned to you by Procter (the prior supervisor) a week before I got here. It's due out in four days and it only takes two days to work on it. Why is it a rush job?"

*Pete:* "Well, it's because by the time I finish the orders that came in before it, I won't be able to complete it by the due date."

*John:* "Why are you so far behind, Pete?"

*Pete:* "I'm carrying too much work compared to everyone else."

*John:* "Why do you say that?"

*Pete:* "Because I'm working my butt off and I'm behind while everyone else is ahead of schedule."

*John:* "I don't know who else I could give anything to right now. Let me check things out and get back to you after lunch."

(After Pete leaves, John starts checking work schedules for the past month. They reveal a balanced workload for everyone in the unit. He also looks at Pete's last performance evaluation and notices a comment about excessive absences. He then checks timesheets for the past two weeks and discovers Pete was absent three days without prior approval the week before John started the job. This was the same week Pete was assigned the order he claims can't be finished on time. John then checks with customer service on Pete's other outstanding orders and is informed that one customer has asked for later delivery than is currently scheduled. The customer service representative states the paperwork changing the delivery date will be sent to John in a day or two. John now knows that Pete can work on the New Jersey hospital order without jeopardizing any other delivery dates. Armed with this knowledge, John calls Pete into his office after lunch.)

*John:* "Pete, I checked work schedules for the last month and it seems the work was distributed pretty evenly. What I want you to do is work exclusively on the New Jersey order. It will only take two days, so there's no problem meeting the delivery date."

*Pete:* "Who should I give my other work to?"

*John:* "No one. Go back to work on it in two days when you finish the New Jersey job."

*Pete:* "Well the delivery dates won't be met on all of them. Being new, you may not realize it, but hell breaks loose around here when delivery dates aren't met."

*John:* "I recognize the importance of delivery dates. I also know that it would be unfair for me to reassign work to someone else because you're not able to handle it."

*Pete:*   "Hey, I can handle my fair share, but I can't do every-thing."

*John:*   "I'm certain you can handle your work if you're here, Pete, but you can't keep up if you are constantly tak-ing off. I want to get off to a fresh start with every-one, Pete, so I'm not going to make an issue of it this time. But your previous performance evaluation shows you were absent a number of times without approval. You were also out three days after you received the New Jersey job. If you had been here, you wouldn't be in a bind now. I intend to level with everyone, and I expect them to do the same with me. So I want you to know that continued absences without approval won't be accepted. As for your cur-rent workload, do the New Jersey order as I said, then start your other work. I'll take care of the deliv-ery dates. Do we understand each other?"

*Pete:*   "Yes."

**Note:** John could have let Pete know about the revised delivery date that was forthcoming, but chose not to do so, since that would only give Pete an excuse to take his time with the orders. This way Pete is more likely to work harder, since he doesn't know the date has been changed.

COMMENTS: There are a number of points worth noting about this example. First of all, be alert for phony claims. For the most part, you aren't going to have your best workers coming to you with complaints about too much work. This is especially true when you're new, since they will recognize you aren't yet in a position to make that determi-nation. Therefore, it's more likely to be goof-offs like Pete who voice complaints.

If you receive complaints of overwork, don't accept what the work-er says as fact. Ask plenty of questions, and if you get general answers, keep probing until you get to the specifics. If you still don't have enough information, withhold any decision until you do some further checking, as John did here.

Finally, especially since you're new to the job, try to avoid reassigning work when someone complains about having too much work. Even if the claim appears to be true, look for ways to solve the problem short of giving some of the work to other people. If you start to shuffle work around, those on the receiving end are going to be upset with you.

Of course, if a special situation comes up, such as a priority project, then reassignments are legitimate. But for the run-of-the-mill case where a worker is overloaded, find other alternatives or tell the worker to do his or her best to handle the current assignments. If you take this latter approach, reassure the employee that you will lighten the load in the future.

Incidentally, when you're trying to determine whether someone has too much work, don't rely strictly on making comparisons by some form of quantitative measure, such as the number of units, dollar value of work, and so forth. You also have to take into account the difficulty of the work. But even when there's little variance in complexity, other factors such as individual capabilities and training can't be ignored.

# Chapter Six

# Managing Worker Job Performance Issues

*T*here are a number of different aspects of employee performance you have to handle in your supervisory role. One of these is performance evaluations, which you will be looking at from an entirely different perspective now that you're a boss. You may have been less than satisfied with one or more of your own evaluations before you were appointed to a supervisory position. Now, of course, you will be the one doing the evaluating. This chapter contains tips to help you do this, as well as how to handle a worker who is dissatisfied with an evaluation.

There are other work-related issues such as tardiness, absenteeism, and endless excuses to be dealt with. Along with this you may have to encourage a goof-off or two to pick up the pace. These and other related issues are covered in this chapter.

## THE NECESSARY STEPS FOR CONDUCTING PERFORMANCE EVALUATIONS

Performance evaluations are always difficult to do, since no matter how good a company's formal procedure may be, the end result is basically the subjective opinion of the evaluator. Being new to the job makes the process harder because you have little knowledge of the past performance of the workers you have to evaluate. As a result, your first few evaluations will essentially be a learning experience.

Adding to the burden are the typical reactions of workers, who always think they should be rated more highly than they are. Although many times workers will suffer in silence rather than openly complain about a performance rating, they are more apt to react with a new boss. In fact, one or more workers may decide their ratings weren't higher because you're new to the job and not fully aware of their capabilities. As a result, they may protest to you and your boss. All of these factors combine to make your first few performance evaluations a real challenge.

Despite all of the obstacles, for the most part your first few evaluations can be completed with few hassles if you do your homework beforehand. The procedure will vary from company to company, but generally the personnel office, or your boss, will notify you when an employee's evaluation is due. The first time this happens, take the worker's evaluation form to your boss, and ask for guidance. If you have only been on the job for a few weeks, the boss may decide to do the evaluation for you. This would certainly make sense, since you will not have been around long enough to make a fair assessment of the employee's performance.

However, your boss may tell you to dig out the worker's last evaluation and use that as a basis for rating the employee. If you do use this approach, note on the form that your evaluation is based on direct observation of the employee for whatever amount of time you have been supervising the worker.

In general terms, evaluations fall into three broad categories. There are the superior evaluations which often form the basis for employee awards and above average pay raises. You will never get an argument from an employee when you do one of these. Of course, until you have been on the job a sufficient length of time, there's no basis for you to initiate such an evaluation. It's also highly unlikely that the prior supervisor would have left such an evaluation in limbo, since it's only the problems that seem to get left behind.

At the other end of the scale are poor performers who are the toughest to evaluate, since you will have to be quite pointed about what the employee has to do to improve his or her performance. Here too, until you have more experience on the job, you can't be expected to give someone a poor performance rating. Incidentally, if your boss has told you to give an evaluation using the prior evaluation as a guideline, consult with your boss if the evaluation was very poor. Chances are the boss will either do the evaluation himself, or will make arrangements to postpone the evaluation. The latter action will give you a chance to observe the employee under your supervision before you do any evaluating.

Fortunately—or unfortunately, depending upon which end of the scale they're on—there are very few superior or inferior ratings given out. Most evaluations fall somewhere in the average range, and it's this type of evaluation you're likely to do early in your new supervisory role. A quick checklist to prepare for such an evaluation will require you to do the following:

- Let the employee know a few days before the evaluation is scheduled.

- Study the form so you understand it.

- Look over the evaluation done by the previous supervisor.

- If the evaluation requires performance goals for the next period to be established, try to expand on what the previous supervisor did.

- For your first evaluation or two, see if you can run through it beforehand with your boss.

- Meet with the employee and explain that you have only had a short period of time to observe his or her performance.

- Discuss any areas of performance that are above or below average.

- Jointly establish with the employee performance goals for the next rating period.

- If you get any disagreement from the employee, emphasize your need to rely on the prior evaluation and state that future evaluations will more closely reflect your assessment. This will encourage the employee to improve poorer aspects of his or her performance.

✒ After the evaluation is completed, give the employee time to look it over and make any comments before it is signed.

There are other aspects of conducting performance evaluations which aren't relevant to your early days on the job. These include rating the employee on the overall period of performance, and not just the days and weeks leading up to the evaluation, as well as not rating employees against the standards set by a superior performer. However, these and other issues don't come into play until you have been on the job long enough to observe your subordinates in action for an extended period of time.

*Tip:* There is one technique you can start using right from the start to simplify the process for future evaluations: Start keeping notes when workers do something exceptionally well, or alternatively when they do anything wrong. Otherwise, when performance evaluation time arrives, you'll be scratching your head trying to remember what a worker did or didn't do in the past six months or a year.

## HOW TO HANDLE WORKERS WHO DISAGREE WITH YOUR EVALUATION

Most employees are savvy enough to want to get off on the right foot with a new boss. So for the most part you shouldn't have too much trouble getting through your first few performance evaluations. But you may have a worker or two who decide to take exception to one or more of the ratings on their performance evaluation. Usually, it's either a borderline dud or someone who thrives on being argumentative. Whatever the reason, there's nothing to be gained by having a prolonged debate over why any one factor was rated average instead of good. So the approach to take is basically, "I hear what you're saying, but I don't agree with you." Let's look at how a typical situation can be handled.

### Background

Carol, a newly-appointed supervisor, has been on the job one month and has just given Jennifer her performance evaluation. It is average overall and is comparable to the evaluation done by the previous boss. Carol also considers it to be fair, considering the limited time she has had to observe Jennifer.

*Jennifer:* "Oh, you have me rated 'needs improvement' on the 'Attendance/Punctuality' factor. I don't understand that at all."

*Carol:* "It's the overall rating, which is satisfactory, that matters, Jennifer, not each individual element."

*Jennifer:* "Well, it's certainly not fair to say something needs improvement when it doesn't."

*Carol:* "As I mentioned to you when we had our meeting on your evaluation, you need to do a better job of being on time for work."

*Jennifer:* "I didn't get the impression it was such a big deal that I would get a 'needs improvement' rating."

*Carol:* "Jennifer, you're making too big an issue out of one element on the entire appraisal. When we talked about this, you agreed you had to do better about being on time for work."

*Jennifer:* "I may be late once in a while, but so are other people. Are they getting a bad rating too?"

*Carol:* "You didn't get a bad rating. Furthermore, on that one element you agreed you are sometimes late for work. As for other people, we are discussing your performance, not anyone else's."

*Jennifer:* "I explained that I was only late when my bus was late."

*Carol:* "Yes, and I told you if that was the problem to take an earlier bus."

*Jennifer:* "Well I am now, and I'm not late anymore."

*Carol:* "I'm glad to hear that, Jennifer, and if that continues, you won't have this problem on your next evaluation. But our discussion only took place two days ago, and this evaluation covers the year prior to that."

*Jennifer:*  "If I have corrected the problem, why does it have to be mentioned in my evaluation?"

*Carol:*  (Doing her utmost to retain her composure) "As I just said, the evaluation covers the period when you were late. I can't see where we're getting anywhere with this discussion. I'm glad you're now making an effort, Jennifer, to be on time. But as for this evaluation the rating is not going to be changed. As you know, you have the right to add your own comments on this subject to the evaluation. Then, if need be, I will add to the form the specific dates you were late over the past year, so the record will be complete. Do you want to add anything? If not, please sign it so we can both get back to work."

*Jennifer:*  "I'll just sign it, but I hope this rating is better on my next evaluation."

*Carol:*  "That is entirely within your control Jennifer, but I'm fully confident you can do it."

COMMENTS: There are a number of points illustrated in this example to keep in mind when a worker disagrees with your evaluation. Briefly, these are:

1. When an employee takes exception to one or two of the rating factors, emphasize the importance of the employee's overall rating and try to downplay the individual components. This keeps you from getting bogged down in an extended debate over every single element on the evaluation form. Carol tried this but wasn't successful. However, if an employee has general objections, rather than being upset over a single item, this tactic will usually work.

2. Employees don't always listen carefully when you're going over an evaluation with them. Then, when they see a rating or a comment they don't like when it's time to sign the form, they raise objections, as Jennifer did here. To avoid this, be certain workers understand any criti-

cal comments you have on their performance. It can be helpful, after discussing the issue, to summarize what you said and add, "Do you understand what needs to be improved?" This helps to prevent later disagreements such as happened with Jennifer.

**3.** When you specifically point out the area of performance that needs improvement, you will often find an employee starts to make excuses of one form or another. Don't get bogged down in discussing these, since they only serve as a smokescreen to divert your attention from the real issue.

**4.** Listen to what workers have to say when they voice objections to their evaluations, but don't overdo it. Once you have heard enough to determine there is no merit in the rebuttal, bring the discussion to an end. Let the employee know they can object in writing if they so desire. However, as in the example, reserve your right to add additional comments. This is necessary to prevent a worker from distorting the facts.

For instance, in the example, Jennifer might have chosen to add a comment saying she was never tardy. You then would have an evaluation with a block checked for attendance/punctuality showing "needs improvement," and a comment by Jennifer stating she was never late for work. Naturally, anyone who subsequently looked at the review might not place much credibility in Jennifer's comment. However, if Carol then added the specific dates from attendance records showing the late arrivals, there would be no room for doubt about who was correct.

It may not always be necessary to do this, but you should be clear about having the right to do so when you're discussing the matter with an employee. In fact, just pointing this out may dissuade an employee from adding comments.

## The Best Way to Assign Undesirable Tasks

In your role as a supervisor, you may from time to time have to assign undesirable tasks to subordinates. This is never easy to do, but it can have even greater implications when you're a new boss. Workers may feel they're being unfairly targeted or wonder how they got on your wrong side so soon. Others may try to talk their way out of getting the assignment by concocting some excuse on the assumption you haven't been around long enough to see through the charade. As for volunteers, don't hold your breathe waiting for anyone to step forward.

Faced with these prospects, just how should you go about handing out a thankless job? There are several possible approaches you can take. The first, of course, is to ask the group as a whole if anyone is willing to take the assignment on. That's unlikely, but you can't lose anything by trying. If you're lucky, you may have a consummate office politician working for you who decides this may be a great way to gain favor with a new boss.

Another logical approach is to alternate assigning unpleasant tasks to workers. There are a couple of pitfalls here. One is that such tasks may be a rarity so there's little likelihood of everyone having to take a turn. A second problem is that what is and isn't an undesirable job can vary in the eyes of the beholder—what one worker sees as undesirable might not be an opinion shared by others. As a result, the equity which alternating assignments would achieve then becomes a topic of controversy.

Faced with these dilemmas, some supervisors take the easy road and ask one of their best workers to handle the task. Some workers don't quibble over what they have to do, and without a fuss just go about getting the job done. It's inherently unfair to take advantage of these people, however, because those less conscientious are let off the hook.

At the other extreme—and the choice of preference for many a savvy supervisor—is to dish out the dirty jobs to the duds and malcontents within the group. The problem for you is that you may not have been on the job a sufficient length of time to be able to identify the duds. It's always easier when you start a new job to get a handle on who the good workers are, since the duds will try to disguise their weaknesses. So until you have been on the job a month or two, finding a dud to dump on may not be possible.

Given these circumstances, we're now back at square one. The logical choice then is to assign the undesirable jobs at random, until you have the opportunity to pinpoint a troublemaker or two who justly deserve this kind of work. However, be sure to qualify these assignments so the worker knows you're not singling him or her out for any unrevealed reason. Here's how to do it:

## Background

Robert is the newly-appointed supervisor of the deli department of a large supermarket. One task that everyone dislikes is having to wash out the deli case. Because of the large number of part-time employees working varying schedules, it's not possible to assign tasks on a rotating basis. Therefore, Robert decides it has to be done at random, at least until he gets to know the employees better.

*Robert:*   "Adam, I want you to clean the deli case tonight. Incidentally, I don't want you to think I'm sticking you with this permanently. I'll give it to someone else the next time. Until I get a handle on things, I need to assign it to someone I can count on."

*Adam:*   "No problem."

COMMENTS: With few words, Robert did three things:

- He made the assignment;
- He reassured the worker it wasn't a permanent assignment; and
- He praised the worker for being reliable.

Although they may seem insignificant, each of these elements is important.

When you make an undesirable assignment, don't be wishy-washy about it, since it gives the worker an opening to object. Make it clear the task is assigned, and avoid phrasing it as a question such as, "Adam, would you clean the deli case tonight?" A sharp worker will have a quick rebuttal such as, "I'll be busy cleaning the slicers until closing." Of course, you can still direct the employee to do the job, but it becomes more confrontational and it gives the worker an opportunity to grumble to others about how unreasonable you are. Being direct when assigning undesirable jobs doesn't leave room for argument.

Everyone hates the dirty jobs, but it's at least acceptable if they know it's a one-shot deal. Therefore, reassure people the job isn't permanent when you give them unpleasant tasks to do. Finally, offering encouragement in the form of praise takes the sting out of being handed an undesirable assignment. Sure, a worker might think to himself, "Yea,

I'm so reliable he gives me the lousy jobs." But beneath that thinking, everyone likes to feel needed, even if it isn't always under the best of circumstances.

Incidentally, as the final touch in making undesirable assignments, take the time to thank the person for doing the job after it is finished. This too helps to alleviate any brewing resentment.

## A FEW TECHNIQUES FOR TELLING A WORKER TO SHAPE UP

You won't be on the job too long before you notice signs of workers who aren't doing their share of the work. It stands to reason that any employee who strives to do as little work as possible will look upon the arrival of a new boss as a golden opportunity to goof off. They will continue to avoid work until such time as you force them to pick up the pace. In the meantime, more conscientious workers will resent this and wonder when you're going to get around to doing something about it. For these reasons, you have to move swiftly once you are sure a worker isn't doing his or her job. Otherwise, the tendency to slack off will spread to other workers.

There are a number of ways you can go about sending a message to anyone who hasn't been working at a reasonable pace. The following are among the approaches you can try:

**1.** Ask the worker if there's a problem you can help with. The worker is more than likely going to respond by saying no. You can reply to this by saying, "Oh I thought something was wrong, since it looks like you may be having some trouble getting your work done." This should get the point across that you recognize the worker has been goofing off. Alternatively, the worker might actually have a problem you were unaware of. Although it's unlikely, if this is the case then see what can be done to resolve the difficulty. This is a good first approach to nudging the worker into action.

**2.** Another nonconfrontational tactic is to make frequent visits to the work area of anyone not doing their job. Your presence should serve as a motivator. The downside to this is you can't be spending all of your time doing this. In addition, the minute you leave the work will grind to a halt again. Therefore, you're better off combining this approach with others, rather than relying on it alone to do the trick.

**3.** A more direct approach to solving the problem is to ask the employee specific questions about the progress of his or her assigned work. If you use this tactic, make note of what you're told and be sure to follow up. Otherwise, an employee may try to sell you a bill of goods and hope you don't come back to check.

**4.** The most direct way to get things moving is to confront workers with evidence they aren't doing their jobs. This works especially well where the worker's output is quantitative and easily measured. Simply show them a record of their output and specifically ask why they're not producing the amount of work they should be. Usually you will get a wide variety of excuses in response, but don't accept them. Instead, clearly state that in the future you expect to see output, rather than hear reasons for a lack of it.

Although it's nice if one of the less confrontational approaches succeeds in getting workers off their butts, if it becomes necessary, don't hesitate to be direct in telling a worker to pick up the pace. When you're new on the job, all of your subordinates are watching to see how you react to different situations. Therefore, it's important to establish at the outset that you won't tolerate people goofing off.

## THE HASSLE-FREE WAY TO PUT GOOF-OFFS TO WORK

Aside from workers who intentionally try to avoid doing any work, you may have a couple of workers who for one reason or another can't keep up the pace. With many of these people, simply telling them to get busy doesn't always solve the problem. Fortunately, there are alternatives which can be tried to keep them productively engaged.

The most effective way to deal with laggards is to put them on a short leash. You have to supervise them much more closely than other people. Therefore, the more of them you have working for you, the harder your job will be.

One good way to encourage lackluster workers to speed it up is to give them assignments tied to specific completion dates. Be careful here though, since if you assign something with a completion date far into the future, the worker may putter along until it's too late to get the job done on time. Therefore, it's preferable to assign tasks that have to be finished within a short period of time.

Keeping goof-offs busy can be time-consuming for you, since constant follow-up is needed to prod them into getting things done. You want to be sure they are making progress on any assignment you give them. Beyond that, periodic checking will prevent them from finishing a task and then hanging around without letting you know it has been completed. It's admittedly a hassle to be constantly monitoring someone's performance, but if you don't, their work won't get done.

If you show goof-offs you aren't about to sit back and let them coast through the day, even though they will never become top producers eventually they should be working at an acceptable level. Then again, if over a period of time your efforts to keep them busy aren't succeeding, you may have to consider disciplinary action. However, that's something best left for after you have sufficiently mastered your job. Getting involved with serious disciplinary matters is something best avoided during your first month or two. You have enough to do without the added burden of learning the company procedure on disciplinary actions.

*Caution:* Shortly after you begin your new supervisory duties, you will start to form opinions about who works hard and who doesn't. This may lead to targeting a few plodders as goof-offs. Be careful in doing this, since there may be valid reasons as to why someone isn't working very hard. Therefore, before you begin to prod a perceived goof-off into doing more work, take a close look at the situation. You may discover any one of several factors that contribute to people not performing up to their capabilities.

For example, has the employee been adequately trained for the job? A lack of training might force a conscientious employee to work slowly rather than risk making mistakes. However, if you're not looking for this, it's easy to assume someone is goofing-off. Another possibility is the employee doesn't have adequate skills to perform the assigned job. Abilities differ, and it's not uncommon for workers to be mismatched with a job. Whatever the reason, take the time to analyze the cause of an employee's ineptness. Otherwise, a worker may be unfairly labeled as a goof-off.

# FOUR EASY METHODS FOR CONTROLLING TARDINESS

One of the difficult issues you will have to deal with at the beginning of your career as a supervisor is tardiness. Naturally enough, the first step in discouraging workers from showing up late for work is to set a good example. So even if you're a slow starter in the morning, try to get to work well ahead of the starting time. You may wonder what's wrong with planning to arrive a few minutes early, rather than being at your desk about thirty minutes before the official start of the workday.

For one thing, if you cut your arrival time too close, something such as heavy traffic will mean you're a few minutes late. If this happens a couple of times it can cause problems. First of all, your boss isn't going to be impressed with a new supervisor not being on time. Beyond that, if your employees notice you come in late—and rest assured they will—it encourages them to do the same. And once your subordinates see you being late for work, it becomes more difficult to tell them to be on time. One of the basics of controlling tardiness is to practice what you preach.

Another practical reason for arriving at work early is to get a running start on the day's chores. A little quiet time in the morning allows you to catch up on paperwork or plan the day's schedule without being interrupted. Even if you're the type of person who starts slowly in the morning, you can use the extra time to have coffee or otherwise pull yourself together for the day ahead.

Of course, reality can't be ignored, and commuting arrangements may be such that you're not able to arrive much before the starting bell. If at all possible, however, try to arrive early for at least the first month or two. Initial impressions are very important in establishing expectations, and if you're early for work, your subordinates know you expect them to be on time. Once everything settles down, there's less of a problem with arriving at the last minute, as long as you're not consistently late.

In terms of enforcing the rules on tardiness, you want to comply not only with the formal company procedure, but also with the unspoken rules of enforcement. The two may very well not be the same. For instance, the written procedure may require disciplinary action be taken for repeated instances of tardiness, while in practice the rules may be virtually ignored. If the latter is true, then it's hard to admonish workers for being late.

Even when company procedures are generally enforced, the previous supervisor may have set a bad precedent by being lax in following the rules. This makes it extremely difficult for you to turn things around when you take over. Nevertheless, do it you must, or you are likely to find people consistently late for work.

The best approach when you are succeeding someone who has been lax in this area is to tell your subordinates as a group what you expect in terms of being on time. If you get any arguments, explain the rules. If an employee points out that their former boss didn't mind people being a few minutes late, simply state the rules are what count, not what someone else chose to do.

This isn't a typical problem, since generally the level of enforcement is pretty standard company-wide. However, there are situations where the supervisor you're replacing may have been careless in controlling tardiness. Perhaps the previous boss was coasting toward retirement and had become casual about enforcing the rules. An even more common problem is when the former boss leaves the company for employment elsewhere and eases off on enforcing the rules during his last few weeks on the job.

In any event, when you arrive on the job, take your clues from other supervisors as to the general level of enforcement regarding tardiness. If you notice inconsistency or are otherwise unsure of what to do, consult your boss for guidance. Usually, there is some leeway for a supervisor to excuse lateness if it's justified. This makes sense, since even punctual people will be late on occasion because of some unforeseen event such as a traffic accident or a detour caused by road repair crews.

There are four basic steps you can take that will establish the ground rules for dealing with tardiness within your group. These are:

1. Let your subordinates know you expect them to be on time. Do this in a meeting, so everyone gets the same message at once.

2. Explain the basic rules you will follow, and clearly state how exceptions will be handled. Don't let employees pin you down as to what constitutes a justifiable excuse for being late. First of all, it's impossible to identify every conceivable situation that might come up. On top of that, if you give employees various examples of justifiable excuses, you can expect to hear them used time and time again.

3. Once everyone knows your expectations, don't ignore it when someone is late. If they don't come to you with an explanation, go to them and ask for one.

4. If it becomes necessary, take remedial action once someone becomes a chronic offender. The measures you take can range from having the worker make the time up to disciplinary action if the problem continues.

*Note:* It's important to start implementing these practices within your first couple of weeks on the job. The longer you wait, the more difficult it will become to control the problem.

Probably the biggest headache in controlling tardiness is the variety of excuses you will hear. This is something you have to learn to deal with, since the alternative is not to consider any tardiness as justifiable. That's impractical, since causes beyond someone's control can cause them to be late for work. Therefore, some flexibility in excusing tardiness is necessary, which makes you the judge and jury in rendering the verdict as to whether the excuse is a valid one.

Since dealing with tardiness issues can get tricky, the following dialogue explores some of the approaches you can take in discussions with subordinates.

## 1. The Worker with a One-Time Excuse

*Worker:* "Sorry I'm late, boss, but the train was late this morning."

*You:* "Don't worry about it, Joe. These things happen once in a while."

COMMENT: When a worker who is seldom late runs into a problem, all you have to do is acknowledge the fact. However, if someone is late and they don't come to you with a reason, go to them and ask for one. Say something such as, "What happened to you this morning?" Also let them know they should see you when they're late. It's easy to assume that when someone is late without letting you know, it's because they don't have a valid excuse. This isn't necessarily true, since some workers may be too embarrassed to approach you. So don't rush to judgment when this happens. Once you're on the job long enough for subordinates to know you're reasonable in listening to their reasons for being late, only chronic offenders will avoid you.

## 2. The Worker Who Is Tardy Because of a Recurring Problem

*Worker:* "I hit traffic after dropping my daughter off at day-care."

*You:* "This has happened a couple of times since I've been here, Phil. Why don't you just leave a little earlier in the morning?"

*Worker:* "That's not my problem. The daycare center doesn't open until seven o'clock, so that only leaves me fifteen minutes to get here. If I hit any traffic, I can't help being late."

*You:* "You're on a pretty tight schedule. Are there any other places open any earlier near where you live?"

*Worker:* "No, I looked into that before, since Fred (the prior supervisor) was always on me about being late. He even docked my pay a couple of times. It isn't that I'm goofing off or something. I just don't know what I can do."

*You:* "Could you work a half-hour later at night without any problem?

*Worker:* "Sure, I could just pick Julie up later. The center doesn't close until six."

*You:* "Here's what I'll do. I'm going to talk to Bill Rowen, the department head, about shifting your schedule thirty minutes. That way, you won't have to worry about being late, and it will make it easier for you in the morning."

*Worker:* "Thanks a lot. I'm driving too fast as it is to get here in the morning."

COMMENT: When you have a situation where an employee is repeatedly late because of a difficulty such as this one, try to adjust their schedule if it's feasible to do so. If this isn't possible try to work out some arrangement for them to make up the time. Obviously, the ultimate responsibility for being on time rests with the employee. However, being flexible about making adjustments to accommodate a worker with a legitimate problem is beneficial to an employer. A supervisor who goes out of his or her way to help an employee out reaps the benefits of a grateful worker. This pays dividends when you need workers to put forth a little extra effort on the job. The caring boss has workers produce in the clutch, and the boss who takes the easy way out by going by the book doesn't.

## 3. The Worker with an Alibi

*Worker:*　"I carpool, and my driver was late this morning."

*You:*　"That can happen once in a while, Chris, but this is the second time in two weeks. If it continues, you had better make other arrangements for getting to work."

COMMENT: Frequently, workers will use a third-party defense, which may be true. However, it's up to the individual to straighten the matter out, rather than continue to be late for work. It's important to distinguish between this and the previous situation. Here, the worker has other options, such as driving to work himself or forming another carpool without the person who is making him late. Furthermore, with the carpool, the worker can't make the time up on the other end.

In the situation with the daycare center, the worker had no viable morning alternatives, but there was the chance to adjust the schedule on the back end. These are the judgment areas where you have to decide whether the worker's problems justify trying to make some sort of accommodation. Of course, you also have to take into account whether any adjustment is possible or practical from the company's standpoint. Be careful when doing this, since you don't want to appear to be showing favoritism. Nevertheless, don't let that worry discourage you from doing what you feel is right.

## 4. The Worker Doesn't Get the Picture

*You:*　(A worker is late but doesn't come to you with any excuse.) "What happened to you this morning?"

*Worker:*   "What do you mean?"

*You:*   "You were twenty minutes late."

*Worker:*   "Oh, I just overslept. I was tired after working over-time last night."

*You:*   "Working overtime isn't an excuse for being late."

*Worker:*   "Oh, if I'd known that, I would have rushed to get here this morning. I figured since I worked last night, you wouldn't object if I was a couple of minutes late. Carl, our previous boss, never said anything."

*You:*   "I'm not interested in what Carl did. I expect every-one to be on time for work. You'll have to make up the twenty minutes tonight. In the future, when you work overtime please get here on time the next morning."

COMMENT: This example shows exactly why you should have a meet-ing at the outset to let employees know you don't condone tardiness. Otherwise, they will follow the lead of what their previous boss did in dealing with the issue. And beyond that, if that supervisor isn't with the company any longer, an employee or two may falsely state that tardiness was tolerated when it wasn't. Some workers think being late isn't any big deal. This is especially true of younger employees who haven't yet learned the ways of the working world. Other employees are by nature slow starters in the morning, and although their intentions may be good, their physiological time clock may have them strolling in late. These folks also need the motivation of a boss who takes tardiness seriously.

## 5. The Worker Who Is Consistently Late

Despite your best efforts, you may have a worker who continues to be consistently late. Once you're satisfied someone has used up their quota of excuses, you have to take some action.

*You:*   "Jason, you've been late five times in four weeks with little or no justification. I'm giving you a formal verbal warning as of now. If you continue to be late, I'll have to give you a written warning the next time. If you can't cure this tardiness problem, you could end up losing your job."

COMMENT: Once you have given persistent abusers of working hours a chance to cure the problem, initiate disciplinary action. This may motivate the person to finally get to work on time. After all, they really haven't had anything to lose up until the point where you take formal action. If you continue to tolerate someone being late indefinitely, other workers will become resentful. In addition, those with the inclination to do so will start to ignore the starting time. The longer you let someone with a tardiness problem get away with it, the harder it will be to straighten things out.

## HOW TO PUT THE LID ON ABSENTEEISM

As a new boss, you have to watch for workers who abuse leave privileges by taking unscheduled days off. Anyone who does this is, of course, hoping you will be too busy with other matters to concentrate your attention on absenteeism. Furthermore, workers know that being new on the job, you're less likely to question them when they call in sick.

In fact, canny workers will call and leave a message rather than talk to you at all. If you later speak to them about this, they're apt to plead they didn't know who to contact. Others will watch to see what time you arrive in order to call before then, so they can leave a message rather than have to talk with you. Incidentally, this is one more reason for you to arrive early at work.

For the most part, your problems with absenteeism in your early days on the job will be limited to making sure everyone follows the established procedures for taking time off. It won't be until after you have been on the job for an extended period that long-term abuses of leave by individuals become an issue. Your first chores in this area will be to learn the company policy on unscheduled absence and then follow the rules in dealing with this problem.

Since you may have people try to skirt the rules at the beginning, let's look at how you should confront workers who do this.

## Background

You find a message on your desk that Cindy called in and said she had to take the day off to care for her son who was ill.

### The next day

*You:* "How's your boy feeling, Cindy? I hope he's alright."

*Cindy:* "He's feeling better, boss. Just a case of the flu. I have my mother taking care of him today."

*You:* "Glad to hear it's nothing more serious. Oh, by the way Cindy, I know when parents are worried about their kids, it's sometimes hard to think straight. But the next time you have to call in, please make sure you talk to me directly. I'm not trying to be picky just because that's the rule. From a practical standpoint, if someone forgets to relay a message, you would be listed as an unauthorized absence and might not get paid for the day."

*Cindy:* "Oh sure, boss. I guess I just forgot."

COMMENT: The worker's reason for being absent was justifiable, so all you want to do here is let her know you should be the one called. Incidentally, this situation also shows how you can show concern for employees while at the same time letting them know a mistake was made. It also presented an opportunity to give the worker an incentive to call you.

## Background

Two days after you start work Joe is absent, but you haven't heard from him. You ask around and Ted says, "Oh, I meant to tell you, he called in sick this morning." You say, (for Ted's benefit) "Doesn't he know I'm supposed to be notified?"

### The next day

*You:* "Glad to see you're feeling better, Joe. By the way, the next time you're going to be out suddenly, make sure you call me directly."

*Joe:* "Oh sure, boss. To tell you the truth, I had forgotten your name, so I just left a message."

*You:* (chuckling) "OK, Joe, I can buy that, since I'm having my own problem remembering names."

**COMMENT:** Whether it's true or not, these are the sort of excuses you may get in your early days on the job. You don't want to make an issue of it at this stage of the game. Those who abuse leave will give you plenty of opportunity at a later date. Right now, all you want to do is let employees know you expect them to follow the rules.

## Background

Early on a Friday morning, your second week on the job, you receive back-to-back calls from Hector and Harold telling you they are sick and won't be in. You essentially tell them to take care of themselves, and that you will see them on Monday.

### The following Monday

*You:* (approaching Hector early in the morning) "Hey, I'm glad to see you're in, Hector. You do a good job, and something's missing when you're absent."

*Hector:* "Thanks boss, I'm glad to be back." (You say essentially the same thing to Harold, a short time later.)

**COMMENT:** There are three points to mention here. The first is when people call in sick, be solicitous of their condition. Assuming it's nothing serious, let them know you're looking forward to seeing them the next workday. This sends a subtle message you expect to see them back at work soon. This discourages workers from stretching a one-day absence into two.

The second point is when workers return, take a minute to ask how they feel and let them know you're glad to see them back. If workers feel they're needed, this helps to reduce unnecessary absences.

The final point is that Friday (the day of absence here) along with Monday are typical days for abuse of leave, as workers make themselves a three-day weekend. The day before and after holidays are other prime days for skipping work. There's not a lot you can do to control this, but when your department is particularly busy, it does help to inquire if everyone is going to be in the day before a holiday or on a Monday or Friday. This is especially true during the summer when employees are more likely to plan a long weekend. Doing this gently reminds workers you need them on the job and won't appreciate people being absent.

## How to Make Criticism Stick Without Making Workers Angry

As you may know from personal experience, it's no fun to be criticized by someone. Yet one of the requirements of your new supervisory role will be to provide constructive criticism when workers make mistakes. If you aren't already aware of it, you will soon discover that giving criticism is only slightly preferable to receiving it.

Because it is such an unpleasant task, you don't want to have to dispense criticism any more than is necessary. For this reason alone, it's worthwhile to do it right the first time. Having to criticize someone more than once for the same mistake is doubly painful.

Always keep in mind the goal of criticism is to correct mistakes or behavior so they're not repeated. Its purpose is not to punish or embarrass the person who made the mistake. This is crucial to remember, since most people—yourself included—have been the victim at one time or another of the wrong approach to criticism.

The wrong way to do it is to rant and rave at people and imply they're stupid because of an error that was made. Ironically, often the error wasn't even the fault of the person being blamed. For example, mistakes can be made because of a lack of training or any of a number of other reasons beyond the control of the worker.

Belittling people when they make mistakes can have a number of negative consequences. For one thing, it's inclined to put workers on the defensive. This can lead to potential problems going undetected because workers won't report problems for fear of being criticized. Negative criticism can also lead workers to be so cautious about making mistakes that their work output is reduced. Perhaps most important of all, a negative style of criticism which points the finger of blame at workers is going to destroy morale.

A worker subjected to abusive criticism isn't going to work any harder than the minimum necessary to avoid the wrath of a boss. There's also the very real possibility of workers doing what they can to undermine their boss in the eyes of others. Another adverse result is workers leaving for other jobs, since no one wants to work for this type of boss.

For criticism to be effective, the key is to focus on the mistake and not on the worker. This means identifying what went wrong and why, and then making a decision as to how it can be avoided in the future. Since it's so important to give constructive rather than destructive criticism, let's look at an example of the right and wrong way to go about it.

*Bad:* A supervisor, beet-red with anger, shouts at a worker in front of co-workers, "Look at this report. There's a dozen errors in it. What are you, illiterate?"

### Problems:

1. The supervisor is angry. One of the keys to giving effective criticism is to keep control of your emotions.

2. The supervisor insults the worker by calling him illiterate. This is a personal attack on the individual rather than the problem itself.

3. The supervisor criticizes the worker in front of others. A good rule is to criticize in private and praise in public.

*The right way:* The supervisor calls the worker into his office and says, "Paul, I just wanted to go over this report with you. It looks pretty good, and I can tell you spent a lot of time putting it together. There are just a few errors to be corrected before I sign off on it. Nothing significant, just the inevitable mistakes that occur with a report of this length. I've marked them off. Will you correct them and give it back to me when you finish?"

COMMENT: Unlike the previous example, the supervisor remained calm, didn't launch a personal attack, and discussed the matter in private with the worker. What's more, this boss softened the reference to the mistakes by complimenting the overall report.

If there's one major distinction between good and bad criticism, it's the attitude of the person giving the criticism. Two people can criticize the same thing in totally different ways. While one will succeed in correcting the cause of the mistake, the other person will only incur the dislike of the individual being criticized. The fundamental difference between the two approaches is nothing more than the ability to remain calm, rather than reacting angrily toward the worker.

Although keeping your emotions under control is the primary key in learning how to criticize constructively, there are several additional ingredients for criticism to be successful. These are:

- ✆ Be specific about identifying what has to be corrected.

- ✆ When giving criticism, avoid embarrassing a worker in front of other people.

- ✆ Listen to what the worker has to say about what went wrong.

- ✆ Determine whether it's a one-time error or whether there's an underlying factor which will result in a continuing problem. If there is a basic problem, take whatever action is necessary to correct it.

- ✆ Make the worker a participant in developing proposed solutions to prevent repeated errors.

- ✆ Be certain the worker understands what has to be done to correct the problem.

- ✆ If necessary, follow up to be sure the corrective action has been taken.

## HOW TO PUT EXCUSES TO BED

If you have a good sense of humor, it might be worthwhile to keep a record of the various excuses you hear during your career as a boss. Such a collection might make for enjoyable reading during your retirement. Being a first-time boss, you may think that sooner or later you will hear every excuse there is. Although it may someday seem that way, chances are you will still be listening to new and creative excuses right up until your retirement party.

Even though you know little about the capabilities of your subordinates as you start your new job, you can rest assured several of them excel at making excuses. Of course, the excuse-makers will take full advantage of the fact that you're new on the job. This can present some problems for you if the excuses relate to work procedures, since it will take some time for you to learn the details of everyone's job. Until you do, it will be difficult to separate fact from fiction when a subordinate gives you a work-related excuse.

However, you don't want to start your new job by grilling employees whenever they give you an excuse. Until you learn the operating procedures, you're better off taking it slowly in challenging excuses. The risk of looking foolish by questioning excuses which would be taken for granted if you had more experience outweighs any benefits to be achieved. After all, you won't have to be on the job too long to figure out who the chronic excuse-makers are. These are the people you will have to contend with over the long haul. With them, there's no rush to make an immediate issue of their excuses, since they will give you plenty of opportunities after you have settled into your job.

For the most part, the best way to deal with excuses is to ignore them. What you want to do is focus on what went wrong and how it can be corrected. Here's an example of how to practice excuse avoidance.

*Worker:* "I would have finished this job today except people kept interrupting me."

*You:* "What is the status of the project right now?" (After getting an answer to your question, follow up.) "When will you be finished?"

COMMENT: When the worker uses interruptions as an excuse, it would be easy to get drawn into a discussion of who interrupted and why. This does nothing to solve the problem, which is to get the job finished. As a general rule, you should attack the problem and ignore the excuse.

If the person in the example was a habitual excuse-maker, you could have started the discussion by saying something such as, "You're responsible for getting the job finished, which means you shouldn't have let people interfere with doing that." This would send a message that you're not interested in hearing excuses. However, with workers who don't ordinarily make excuses, there's little reason to be critical, since very few people will ignore the chance to use an alibi if they can think of one.

There is one particular type of excuse-maker you have to rebuke about the excuse game. This is the individual who uses different excuses for the same offense. For instance, an employee may continually come back late from lunch, each time with a new excuse for being late. Here, you have to be pretty blunt about letting the worker know you're not interested in excuses. Say something such as, "Carlos, I'm not interested in excuses. You're the one responsible for being back here on time. If it happens again, I'll have to give you a formal reprimand."

Opposed to the individual who dredges up new excuses for the same problem is the worker who uses the same excuse repetitively for a continuing problem. For example, a worker who constantly blames a machine for jamming as the reason for low production, or an employee who is always late claiming it's because he has to drop his kids off at school. In these types of situations, frequently the employee has a real difficulty that has to be solved. Then, and only then, will the problem be straightened out.

## WHY IT'S VITAL TO RECOGNIZE INDIVIDUAL CAPABILITIES

When mistakes are made or workers appear to be goofing off, the natural assumption is to blame the worker. However, there are many other possibilities that can't be ignored. These can range from a lack of necessary training to unreasonable expectations in terms of the quality and quantity of work an employee is capable of doing. This tendency can only be overcome by learning the individual capabilities of everyone who works for you. Being new on the job, this will take some time. Meanwhile, don't draw hasty assumptions about someone's work ethic.

The benefits of recognizing each employee's capabilities are numerous, and the following are particularly significant.

1. You can assign work according to employee strengths and weaknesses instead of making assignments on a random basis. This is especially important when you have difficult or priority jobs to be done that require assignment to someone you have confidence in.

2.  The overall productivity of your group will increase if you're able to parcel work out to take advantage of individual strengths. For instance, some workers will be better than others on jobs that require a greater attention to detail. Others may be best at getting things done fast.

3.  Assigning work on the basis of individual talents won't discourage workers who can't meet the skill levels of some of their peers. When someone is assigned a task beyond their capabilities, errors are made and the employee becomes discouraged.

4.  Knowing exactly what each worker is capable of doing allows you to plan your group's training needs more effectively. In this way, you can continually strive to raise the skill levels of everyone working for you.

5.  When individual talents are ignored, someone may work slowly or make mistakes. As a result workers may be labeled as lazy or careless when actually they were a poor choice for the particular assignment. Once you know the abilities of each worker, you're able to avoid these misconceptions.

6.  By assigning jobs based on individual skills, worker boredom is avoided. This is especially true in the case of highly skilled employees who are easily bored when assigned routine tasks that don't challenge their capabilities.

7.  You can do a better job of assigning employees to work in teams by pairing a person with a particular skill with someone else who may not have the same level of expertise.

Of course, if everyone in your group performs the same tasks on a daily basis there's less to be gained by knowing individual capabilities. But even here there are advantages in terms of knowing who needs training and who is more likely to meet rigid deadlines. Whatever the nature of the work performed by the unit you supervise, make it a priority to learn what each employee does best.

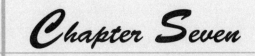

*Chapter Seven*

# DISCIPLINE AND OTHER DISTASTEFUL DUTIES

$S$ome of the most unpleasant moments you have as a supervisor will be those spent dealing with disciplinary matters. You can only hope that not too many of these will occur early in your tenure as a new boss. It's difficult enough to learn everything else without the added strain of serious personnel problems. Nevertheless, whenever they happen, you have to be prepared to cope with them. This chapter focuses on many of the major problem areas you may have to confront, including alcohol and drugs, theft, sexual harassment, and employee termination.

Beyond disciplinary matters, there are other troubling aspects of a supervisory position that are headache inducing. These include how to react when the crisis button is pushed, along with handling a wide assortment of difficult people. If those problems aren't enough, you may eventually have the misfortune of coping with laying off people who work for you. This chapter explores your options in all of these areas.

# How to Handle All Kinds of
# Difficult People

You will run into all sorts of difficult people on your job. Some of them will work directly for you, while others will be employed elsewhere within the company. If your job requires outside contact with customers or suppliers, you will have an additional source of unpleasant people to deal with. The extent to which these people cause you problems will vary. In many instances, they will be personally aggravating but won't affect your work. Others will create work-related difficulties for you and their co-workers.

Of course, your own personality will influence the extent to which some of these people get under your skin. Some bothersome people who don't trouble you directly will be the source of complaints from their co-workers. The list of categories of personality quirks you may encounter on the job is lengthy. Fortunately, you're not going to have the misfortune of having every type of misfit working for you.

On the other hand, anyone with a tendency to be troublesome may take advantage of your status as a new supervisor. Therefore, it's worthwhile to explore some of the possible types of pests you may have to deal with. The following list represents the more common kinds of irritating people you may encounter and includes a few pointers on dealing with them.

## *Intimidators*

These are the classic bullies who try to get their way with bluster and bravado. The biggest work-related difficulty you will have here is with people your department does work for. Intimidators will try bullying tactics to get top priority for their work, or otherwise attempt to make your life uncomfortable. Although you should always try to remain calm when dealing with these people, don't let them buffalo you into giving in to their demands.

If you have a situation where a staff person or the supervisor of another group simply refuses to discuss matters reasonably, you may want to call the problem to your boss's attention. Most bullies will back off when someone stands their ground. However, a particularly persistent type may go over the line with you, since you haven't been around long enough to establish a reputation for not being intimidated.

By getting your boss involved, the troublemaker will realize you're not about to give in to his unreasonable demands. In addition, it will put the bully in a bad light, since your boss will undoubtedly be aware of the tendencies of the individual to try and push people around. Bullies usually have far-flung reputations, so they try to avoid encounters with higher-level managers who won't tolerate their nonsense.

Don't be surprised if you have a bully working for you. Otherwise, you will be in for a shock when they blatantly try to intimidate you. Of course, when a bully works for you, the situation is a lot easier to handle since you're the boss. Nevertheless, try to put the person in place without having to exert your supervisory authority. For one thing, the bully may be trying to make you issue a direct order, so he can complain to others that you're acting like a big shot. Therefore, keep your composure while still standing your ground.

Of course, if someone who works for you pushes it a little too far, talk to him or her privately and state clearly that you won't tolerate insubordination. Let them know if they want to be unreasonable with you, they can expect to face disciplinary action. It's rare that a run-of-the-mill intimidator will go this far, since their survival at work rests upon a keen ability to sense when they have pushed an issue as far as it will go.

## Procrastinators

You may find you have workers who are habitual procrastinators. They always finish a rush job at the last minute, arrive at meetings just as they are about to start, and have a sixth sense that gets them to work at precisely the starting time. This is the nature of certain people and you're not about to change it. In fact, other than being aggravating, these people usually won't cause you any great difficulties. So don't waste any time trying to reform them.

Of course, where procrastinators run into problems is by pushing their time limits to the edge. For example, this can result in them being late on occasion. When someone with this type of personality only does this infrequently, you don't want to make a major issue of it. However, you can at least get some personal satisfaction out of it by saying something such as "You wouldn't be late if you didn't leave everything until the last minute."

Once you recognize a procrastinator as such, it's easy enough to have confidence they will finish jobs on time. However, until you get to know them, you may refrain from assigning them urgent tasks, assuming they aren't motivated to finish them on schedule. This is something you will learn as you go along.

## Practical Jokers

A little bit of humor can certainly brighten a busy day, but practical jokers can cause problems. Sometimes they overdo it with their gags, and on other occasions they bother people who don't appreciate it. If you have a practical joker who goes a little too far, you may have to rein the person in. This also applies if you get complaints about them from other workers. When this happens, let the person know by saying something such as "Joe, let's lay off the practical jokes for a while. I'm getting complaints about you getting under someone's skin."

There are a couple of instances where a practical joker can cause trouble. One is when they refuse to heed your initial admonishment to knock it off. When this happens, you may be forced to tell them you don't want to see any more practical jokes taking place. Sometimes practical jokers aren't too savvy about where they practice their brand of humor. This can lead to you being embarrassed by your boss or someone outside your department. If this happens, put a quick halt to the clowning around. Otherwise, the word may spread about you not having enough control over the people you supervise.

Naturally, since you're new on the scene, a particularly venturesome practical joker may decide to play a prank on you. If this should happen to you, take it in stride and laugh about it. This can go a long way toward letting your subordinates feel comfortable with you. It will also break the initial tension and feeling-out process that occur whenever a new boss assumes command.

## Know-It-Alls

You may have the misfortune to have a know-it-all working for you. This type of individual will start giving you advice on how to do your job from day one. Aside from getting on your nerves, you may get resistance from someone like this when you give instructions on how something should be done. The first time or two this happens, hear them out, and then tell them why you want it done your way. Once you have someone firmly pegged as a know-it-all, don't waste any more of your time in humoring them.

Over the long haul, a good way to tone these people down is to give them the most boring jobs you can find. Naturally, they will consider these tasks to be beneath their dignity. If they complain to you about it, you will know you have succeeded in getting the best of them.

## Sneaks and Liars

If you have any deceitful people in your group, they can cause real headaches until you recognize what they're up to. These types will go to any length to blame others for their mistakes. Once you suspect someone is operating in this manner, be sure you confirm anything important they tell you. Otherwise, you can be led astray if you accept what they say as fact.

Sooner or later, you will catch these individuals trying to con their way out of trouble. This is the time to confront them directly and let them know you won't tolerate their nonsense. Once they realize you're on to their game, it's unlikely they will risk your wrath by trying to further deceive you.

These people can cause the most trouble for you in your early days on the job. You may luck out here though, since sneaks have usually made enemies along the way. Therefore, either a subordinate or another supervisor may clue you in right at the start. Although as a general rule you don't want to put too much credibility in what someone says about other people, at least you can remain alert for potential problems.

## Flirts

There are two primary problems flirts can create for you. The first is spending time flirting to the extent it disrupts the work within your group. If the individual works for you, make sure he or she is kept too busy to bother other people. If the culprits come from other departments, shoo them on their way whenever you observe them meandering through your work area. If they don't get the message this way, then you may want to let their boss know how much time they're spending away from their work.

A far more serious problem with flirting is it can evolve into sexual harassment. This topic is covered in detail later in this chapter, but keeping a lid on flirting is one way to minimize the opportunity for harassment to take place.

### Gossips

For the most part, gossips are more annoying than harmful, so unless it gets out of hand, don't waste any energy on trying to control gossip. The biggest problem in this area is the damage that rumors can cause on the gossip circuit. This was discussed back in Chapter 5, so there's little additional to cover here. Once you recognize who the one or two confirmed gossips are, just keep a watch on them so they aren't wasting a lot of time gossiping instead of working. If it becomes necessary, you may have to tell them to spend more time working and less talking.

---

## A STEP-BY-STEP APPROACH FOR USING DISCIPLINARY MEASURES

---

If you're fortunate, you won't have to handle any serious disciplinary actions until you have been on the job for a reasonable period of time. When it becomes necessary to take your first disciplinary action, however, it's important to follow the established company procedures. Being a first-time supervisor, your best bet is to seek expert advice from your personnel department on the proper steps to take. Your boss can also be of assistance, as will be discussed later.

The basis for initiating any disciplinary measure is to correct employee behavior or inadequate job performance. Its purpose is not to punish the worker, although employees often see this as the sole goal of the action taken. This is a point worth emphasizing to the employee, since what you want to achieve is getting the worker to turn things around. Otherwise, each step in the disciplinary process will be inevitably leading to the ultimate termination of the employee.

Of course, serious breaches of conduct such as theft may result in immediate action toward terminating a worker. This is covered later in this chapter. Here, the emphasis will be on correcting inadequate behavior or job performance, so the employee can be retained as a worthwhile contributor within your department. On this basis, let's look at the steps you should take in disciplining a worker.

First and foremost, before any formal disciplinary action is contemplated, make sure the employee has had ample warning of what is being done wrong and how it can be corrected. This will take the form of sitting down with the employee and talking the problem over. Be careful at this time to listen to what the worker has to say. Perhaps the poor performance results from factors beyond the control of the employee. If this is true, then action to correct the problem is needed, instead of disciplining the worker.

Any number of things beyond the worker's control may be contributing to the substandard performance. A lack of training, inadequate equipment, or even a lack of necessary support from other people within or outside your department, are all possibilities to explore. Naturally, an employee accused of doing inferior work will have a laundry list of excuses as to why the problem isn't his or her fault.

Normally, you might ignore this rationalizing, and get right to what has to be done to correct the situation. However, when you get to the point where disciplinary action will be the next step if this meeting doesn't straighten things out, you have to proceed carefully. At this stage, be sure to do any checking necessary to verify the truth or falsehood of any remotely valid excuses the employee gives you.

In practical terms, this will probably be your second or subsequent go-around with the worker on the same problem. It will also be your last discussion of the subject prior to taking formal disciplinary measures. For this reason, you want to verify that you're on firm ground and that no mitigating circumstances exist to excuse the worker's inadequate performance.

Once you have assured yourself the problem is the employee's and no contributing factors exist, then disciplinary action will be the next step. At this time, you should make yourself fully informed of the specifics of your company's disciplinary procedures. Although they vary from business to business, most procedures provide for progressive discipline starting with a verbal warning, written warnings, and finally firing the worker.

Whatever the specific procedure is, be certain to follow it carefully. It's also useful to give some thought to what you intend to say to the employee, as well as what sort of reaction you might expect. The better prepared you are beforehand, the smoother the disciplinary session will go. Needless to say, the meeting should be held in private. Try to arrange it in a location where you won't be interrupted, for this reason, your own office may not be a good choice. With preparations out of the way, it's time to sit down with the employee and take action. Let's look at an example of how this might play out.

## Background

Jake, who is one of your workers, has been consistently violating working hours. He comes in late, leaves early, and takes extended breaks and lunch hours. You have admonished him on three separate occasions about straightening this problem out. At your last meeting on the subject, you told him if his disregard for working hours continued, you would have to take disciplinary action. This was one week ago, and since that time you have directly observed three occasions when he broke the rules. Even other workers have complained about his being missing when he was needed. You are now about to give him a formal warning.

**You:** "Jake, as you know, I've discussed your lack of observance of working hours with you on three prior occasions. The last time we met, I told you disciplinary action would be taken if your conduct didn't improve. As of now Jake, I'm giving you a formal verbal warning that you must as of now fully observe the rules on time and attendance. If you don't, then my next action will be to give you a written warning. As you may know, the inevitable result if you don't take corrective action will be termination."

**Jake:** "Does that mean, if I'm a couple of minutes late coming back from lunch, I will get a written warning?"

**You:** "Yes, Jake. As of now, you are required to be on time for everything, whether it's going or coming from lunch, arriving in the morning, or leaving in the evening. Oh, and let's not forget coffee breaks. You get two fifteen minute breaks a day, not twenty or twenty-five minutes."

**Jake:** "It seems pretty unfair to me. After all, anyone can be a few minutes late on occasion. Heck, this means if my bus is late a couple of times, I can be fired."

**You:** "I've been extremely fair with you before on this, Jake, and have accepted a number of excuses in the past. I've also told you three different times to get it together. You didn't do that. As a result, the responsibility is yours to be punctual. It's not the bus driver, the slow cook where you eat, or anything else. The responsibility is yours. If you have a problem with the bus, take an earlier one or make other arrangements. If the service is slow where you eat, then find someplace else. These things are your responsibility, not someone else's."

*Jake:* "Well, I still think it's unfair."

*You:* "There's nothing I can say, Jake, that will change your opinion. All I can do is emphasize the need for you to abide by the rules in terms of being on the job when you're supposed to be there. I would suggest you take this warning seriously if you value your job. I feel you have the ability to abide by the rules if you want to, Jake, but it's up to you."

COMMENTS: One point to note in the example is how the supervisor refused to express any willingness to accept future excuses for being late. This may seem unfair, since valid reasons can occur. When you get to the disciplinary stage, however, it's important not to leave any loopholes open. If it was done here, the first time Jake is late again, he would have some form of allegedly valid excuse to cover himself. Therefore, you would in effect be right back at the beginning in terms of taking disciplinary action. Once you get to the stage of taking disciplinary action, you can't be flexible about making exceptions. Furthermore, assuming the employee straightens out, there's nothing preventing you from accepting a valid excuse two months down the road. What you don't want to do is convey an impression you're not serious about having the worker abide by the rules.

It's also worth noting that you shouldn't drag a disciplinary meeting out any longer than is necessary to say what has to be said. The more conversation that takes place, the greater the opportunity for something to be misinterpreted.

Disciplinary actions aren't something even a veteran boss likes to handle, and as a first-time supervisor, you may be understandably reluctant to initiate such actions. Nevertheless, if the situation calls for it, and every other avenue to resolve the problem has been explored, don't hesitate to act. The longer matters requiring disciplinary action drag on without anything being done, the harder it becomes to straighten them out.

**Note:** If you supervise union workers, the provisions of the labor agreement may influence the procedures for handling disciplinary actions. In these circumstances, consult with your industrial relations people or other in-house experts on union relations before undertaking any action.

## HOW TO GET YOUR BOSS INVOLVED WHEN YOU TAKE DISCIPLINARY ACTION

Given the serious nature of disciplinary actions, you should always keep your boss briefed as the situation develops. If a serious infraction requiring disciplinary action is needed shortly after your arrival, it's reasonable to expect your boss will handle it. Such matters as theft of company property or physical assaults require immediate action. Furthermore, there's a greater likelihood of potential legal action with these types of offenses. Therefore, in the event something such as this comes up while you're new on the job, you may be fortunate enough to be nothing more than an interested observer as your boss handles the matter.

Even with less severe problems requiring possible disciplinary action, it's smart to talk these over with your boss. There are any number of reasons for this, besides the obvious one of you having no prior experience in handling disciplinary actions. For one thing, not every company deals with disciplinary actions in the same fashion. In some companies there's a greater tendency to work things out before taking disciplinary action. Others require a more rigid adherence to the rules. This isn't something you can learn from reading procedures or policy statements.

In fact, even managers differ in their attitudes toward disciplinary procedures. Within the same company, you may find one boss who has never taken disciplinary action, while another may have done it often enough to wallpaper a good-sized room with the forms. So aside from learning how to proceed, talking with your boss will fill you in on his or her thoughts, as well as company practices.

Beyond this, there are reasons you may be unaware of for not taking a disciplinary action you're about to proceed on. Perhaps the employee in question has some form of protected status, such as a friend in top management. These political reasons for tolerating infractions may not sit well with you, but if they exist, you have to live with them. So for these reasons, along with any practical guidance you may get, always seek the counsel of your boss before proceeding down the disciplinary path.

If you catch a bad break in terms of your new boss, you may discover to your surprise a complete unwillingness to help. This might be because your boss doesn't know anything about handling these situations. On the other hand, he or she may simply not want to get involved. If you find yourself caught in this bind, then seek out the expert in your personnel office who can help you. Here you may find the staff person is helpful and knowledgeable about the regulations, but isn't up to speed on the practical steps to take. Your best bet under these circumstances would be to seek guidance from a veteran supervisor who has handled disciplinary actions before.

## WHAT TO DO IF YOU HAVE TO FIRE SOMEONE

You may not think much about it at the time, but your first disciplinary action may ultimately lead to having to fire someone. Some employees turn things around once they are given a formal disciplinary action. Others either don't try, don't care, or are incapable of doing their job. With these people, giving them a termination notice is inevitable.

Firing someone isn't pleasant, but the alternative of keeping a nonperformer on the job can be even more trying. It makes it difficult for you and the person's co-workers, and it isn't doing the worker much good to be kept dangling waiting for the axe to fall. Therefore, despite any misgivings you might have, when it becomes necessary to fire someone, put your qualms aside and move forward. You will never be able to concentrate on the other aspects of your job, while this sort of problem is hanging in the balance.

When you get to the point where firing an employee becomes a consideration, talk it over with both your boss and with people in the personnel office. Review the prior documentation on disciplinary actions to make certain everything has been handled properly. You, as the worker's boss, should be the person to deliver the termination decision to the employee. However, if you haven't been supervising the unit for any length of time, your boss may accompany you.

As for the mechanics of notifying the employee, it should be done in private, but not in your office. There are two reasons for this. One, the person may get emotional and start to rant and rave at you. This is an unpleasant prospect which can be avoided by holding the meeting somewhere other than your office. Then if things get out of hand, you can get up and walk out. Once you have told the employee of the dismissal, someone from the personnel office will take over and explain the worker's rights and benefits. By holding it elsewhere, you are able to depart and go back to work.

One of the main concerns you may have is the impact of the firing on your other workers. Don't spend time worrying about this. The people who work for you know why the person was fired. In fact, most of them may be relieved, especially if the individual was a disruptive influence within the group. There's also a potential benefit to you, as unpleasant as the task may have been. If you have other workers who aren't doing their jobs, they may shape up quickly as they realize you will make difficult decisions if you have to.

## THE BEST WAY TO DEAL WITH LAYOFFS

In the sometimes wacky world of business, many decisions are made which can leave you shaking your head in amazement. One such instance is being hired for a new supervisory position, only to shortly thereafter have to deal with a workforce reduction. Didn't they tell you when you were interviewed for the job about the great growth prospects for the company? And weren't you reassured when you asked about job stability? Sure you were, and here you are maybe two months later having to pick two people as pink-slip candidates.

More than one supervisor has found themselves facing such a scenario. Of course, you may have already been working for the company when you received your supervisory appointment. Even then, there may have been no inklings circulating about the possibility of layoffs. On the other hand, perhaps there were rumblings afloat about future layoffs being considered by top management. After all, in companies where people seem to be coming and going on a shuttle bus, such rumors are part of the daily ritual.

You can only hope that layoffs won't be an issue you have to deal with too soon in your first supervisory job. But given the competitive nature of the business world, whether you were promoted from within or hired from outside, you have to be prepared to oversee layoffs. There are three major considerations involved in doing this:

- fielding questions about layoff rumors,

- selecting and notifying workers who are terminated, and

- managing your department effectively after layoffs.

The greatest chance of you having to take any action concerning layoffs will be in the area of workers speculating about workforce reductions. This is always a topic of conversation for employees which can be triggered by events totally unrelated to the company you work for. Business may be booming for your employer, but media reports of a slumping economy or industry problems can start layoff talk by your workers. Any sort of comment overheard by a confirmed gossip can kindle rumors. Of course, if business has been slow, nothing else is needed to start workers worrying about their jobs.

There are practical reasons for making a concerted effort to knock down any layoff rumors brought to your attention. First off, if your subordinates are busily engaged in gossiping about rumors, there won't be much work done. Beyond that, it shows a genuine concern for those who work for you when you try to keep them fully informed as to what's going on.

It's admittedly difficult for you to be able to obtain anything factual about potential workforce reductions. For starters, if anything is in the works, it's usually closely guarded information available only to top executives. Therefore, the only possibility for learning anything is through contacts who may be positioned to have overheard discussions or who were privy to information by virtue of knowing one of the company's senior managers. Being new to your position, it's unlikely you have been able to establish these sources of information.

This handicap doesn't prevent you from listening to what a subordinate tells you is the latest rumor making the rounds. For starters, you can reassure the worker you have no knowledge of any basis for the rumor.

On the other hand, don't idly speculate and make statements such as, "Business is great, so there's no conceivable reason the company would be planning layoffs." As fate would have it, two days after you say something like this, a workforce reduction will be announced. The problem you avoid by refusing to speculate is being proved wrong and thereby losing credibility with your subordinates as a source of reliable information.

The one positive action you can take in this area is to talk with your boss about the rumors. However, don't do this unless they appear to have some grounding in reality and are so widespread as to be affecting people's work. Let the boss know the extent to which productivity is suffering and how low morale is among your workers. Other supervisors reporting to your boss are probably experiencing similar difficulties. Therefore, if this information is ultimately relayed to top management, a denial may be forthcoming if the rumors are false.

The hardest task to tackle in this area will be if an actual workforce reduction takes place. If you will lose someone to the layoff axe, either you will be asked to select people to be terminated, or it will be done without consulting you. The latter possibility is likely, especially if the layoffs take place shortly after you have taken over as the supervisor of the group. That's a blessing for you, since it's a lot easier to tell people they're terminated if you weren't the person who made the selection.

Of course, the procedures for targeting positions to be eliminated within a workforce reduction will vary from company to company. If the workforce is unionized, the provisions of the labor agreement will determine who gets laid off.

In any event, if anyone within your group is being let go, you should try to do what you can to help them adjust to the realities. In this regard, people from your personnel office will likely inform the people to be terminated of their rights and benefits. From your standpoint, do what you can to help with any requests you may get from a terminated worker.

After layoffs take place, your immediate goal is to keep your department running smoothly. You may have some initial problems with this if you're left shorthanded by a layoff. If this is the case, look for any adjustments in workload that can be made to lighten everyone's load. You may find some people are left with more work than others. If so, make any adjustments needed to bring about a more equitable distribution of work.

Be sure to keep your boss posted on problems arising from a workforce reduction. This is important, since as a recent arrival, you're the new supervisor on the block. As a result, if you don't speak up, you may get the short end of the stick in terms of the resources needed to do your job.

*Note:* Even if layoffs don't directly affect your group, you may experience difficulties caused by losses in departments you do business with. Here too, be aggressive in letting your boss know about it. If you're not able to get timely support from other groups, the productivity of your group may suffer. If you don't point out the causes, the failure may be attributed to you.

To the extent you can, try to offer reassurance to your people after a layoff takes place. The sooner everyone stops dwelling on what happened, the quicker things will return to normal. However, be realistic about people adjusting, since both the layoffs and any changes resulting from them aren't easy for people to cope with.

## SIMPLE MEASURES TO PREVENT SEXUAL HARASSMENT OR DISCRIMINATION

Undoubtedly your company has policies and procedures dealing with sexual harassment and other forms of discrimination. In addition, your company may hold training classes for employees on these topics. But no matter how much support you may have from upper management, as a supervisor you hold the leading role in controlling these abusive and illegal practices.

Employees take their cues from their immediate supervisor. If a boss has a no-nonsense attitude about wanting everyone to be treated with respect and dignity, then workers will be more cautious in what they say or do. As you are a new boss, workers will watch carefully to see what you will or won't tolerate. From your first day on the job, you can set the tone for how you want people to treat their co-workers.

At the first opportunity, which should be one of your first meetings, make your thoughts on sexual harassment and discrimination known. Point out the fact everyone should be treated with respect and dignity and emphasize the importance of not doing anything to violate that principle. Ask if anyone has any questions in this area. If you get any questions you can't answer, then seek out the company experts to get the information you need. Make sure the answers are then relayed to your entire group. Doing this will prevent someone from later pleading, "I didn't know you couldn't do that."

The most common problems you will have to contend with are workers who don't have the savvy to realize their conduct is unacceptable. Then again, they might sense it is wrong and not want to admit it. Whichever it is, when workers exhibit unacceptable conduct, you should immediately call it to their attention.

Where things can get out of hand is when workers casually joke or kid around with one another. Sometimes even the person being kidded may not find the conduct improper. Yet this very conduct may be highly offensive to someone else. For this reason, you want to discourage any sort of bantering that has sexual or discriminatory undertones.

Obvious remarks are easy to recognize, but where supervisors have difficulty is when comments are open to interpretation. As a result, it's these casual comments that often lead to trouble. Many companies have training programs for employees in this area. But whether your employer does or doesn't, you have to recognize there's no magic quick-fix in this area. Effective prevention of sexual harassment and other discriminatory behavior still comes down to what you will or won't tolerate within your group.

Of course, the million-dollar question is, what specifically constitutes offensive behavior? This isn't something that can be easily pinpointed by a list of rules stating precisely what is prohibited, and leaving the erroneous assumption that anything else is acceptable. For one thing, the law is constantly evolving in the area of sexual harassment. From a practical standpoint, what's offensive to one person may not be to another. Conduct that's obviously offensive is easy to identify; it's the gray area that causes confusion. As an example, let's look at a typical workplace example:

### *To Compliment or Not to Compliment*

John and Julie both work in the same group. Julie always dresses well and wears expensive clothes. This is commonly known and recognized by everyone. Almost every day, John will greet Julie when she arrives for work and say something such as, "That's a pretty dress," or "I like your jacket." Julie smiles and says, "Thanks, John," and then usually proceeds to tell him how much it cost and where she bought it. This appears to be pretty harmless and probably not offensive. But let's just change the facts a bit.

Suppose John never says anything to Julie about being a good dresser, but Fridays in the summer are casual dress days and on the first such day, Julie wears shorts and a low-cut blouse. John says, "Looking good today, Julie." She blushes, says, "Knock it off, John," and continues on her way. This remark has sexual innuendo attached to it and is a potential problem, because:

- ✏ Julie has indicated it's offensive to her by blushing and telling John to knock it off;

- ✏ John has never before remarked about how Julie dresses; and

- ✏ if John persists, Julie may well complain about sexual harassment.

***Comment:*** Compliments are one area where the possibility for problems is always present. Of course, you have to look at the entire context of a situation to determine whether there is a problem. Although it's not readily admitted, people usually are aware of their intent when they make remarks. Of course, this is sometimes the result of someone putting their mouth in drive before they put their brain in gear. But for the most part, offensive remarks of a sexual nature are avoidable.

Obviously, in many of these gray-area situations it's not easy to distinguish between acceptable and unacceptable conduct. Therefore, to practice sexual harassment prevention effectively you are better off adopting a conservative posture in terms of the conduct you expect on the job. How do you do that?

- ✏ Let your workers know offensive conduct won't be tolerated.

- ✏ Remind them that what one person finds acceptable, another may find objectionable.

- ✏ Suggest they practice a policy of "when in doubt, don't do it."

- ✏ Tell everyone you want to hear about anything said or done which bothers them. If your workers know they can confide in you, it will be easier to nip these problems in the bud.

✏ When anyone brings a complaint, act on it promptly.

✏ Let employees know they can complain to someone in the personnel office if they don't feel comfortable about discussing the matter with you.

Beyond anything else, immediately tell employees to stop anytime you hear them making remarks you consider to be uncalled for. Inevitably, employees will ask the question as to what can't be said. You can't be vague here and say, "Use your best judgment." The fact is, some folks don't have very good judgment. Instead, give them a standard, such as, "If you wouldn't say or do it in your house of worship, don't do it here." Another possibility is to say, "If you wouldn't treat your mother, sister, or daughter that way, then don't do it at work." This at least gives employees a handle on deciding what you will and won't tolerate. Of course, just as they didn't always listen to their mother, they may not heed what you're saying. If that happens, and they subsequently get in trouble, it won't be because you didn't set the standards.

## WHAT TO DO IN ANY KIND OF CRISIS

One of the first tests of your ability to withstand pressure as a boss will be when the panic button is pushed and your boss comes running with an urgent edict such as, "Drop everything and get this job done in three days. Our executive vice-president made a promise to a customer." It suddenly becomes crunch time as you discover the three-day job normally takes two weeks.

This is the sort of work-related crisis you will have to deal with from time to time. How you react is significant in determining whether you can succeed in accomplishing seemingly impossible tasks. First of all, in any pressure situation always remain calm. It's easy enough to say but not always easy to do, especially if everyone else appears to be running around in circles. In order to think straight and make the right decisions you have to control your emotions.

Although there will be variations in how you respond to any specific top-priority project, the basic guidelines are:

## 1. Identify the Assignment

Being relatively new on the job, you don't want to mistakenly go off on a tangent because you misinterpreted what someone said. Furthermore, when upper-level management takes an interest in having something done, the request can come down the line misinterpreted.

The primary reason for this is that when senior managers make requests, those reporting to them rush to follow orders without bothering to ask any questions about the specifics. These directives then get passed down the line without any elaboration on what is required. When the assignment reaches the working level, any questions raised are answered with a shrug, since the intermediate manager isn't about to pursue questions with upper-level bosses. As a result, the assignment is completed on a "best-guess" basis and goes back up the line. Panic then sets in when the executive says, "That wasn't what I wanted." When someone starts pointing fingers, the blame generally gets placed on those at the bottom of the ladder.

To cover yourself in these situations, when your boss comes to you with a top-priority task, ask all the questions you need to fully understand what has to be done. Even if you don't get the answers you're looking for, at least you have asked the questions. Furthermore, once the assignment gets underway give your boss a memo stating what you are going to do and asking for any resources you need to complete the job. By putting it in writing, you accomplish two things: First, you keep the boss informed; second, you protect yourself against subsequent criticism if anything goes wrong.

## 2. Determine Precisely What Has to Be Done

This will include everything from overtime approval to help from other departments. If meeting a completion deadline requires receiving outside support by certain dates, state this in a memo to your boss and whoever is furnishing the support. Also let them know that failure to furnish the necessary assistance on a timely basis will result in the job not being completed on schedule. In addition, ask to be notified immediately if any required support can't be furnished. If this happens, bring it to your boss's attention so adjustments can be made.

### 3. Monitor Progress

As the assignment proceeds stay right on top of its progress. Rest assured, you will be constantly badgered by your boss, and perhaps other managers, if the task is a high-profile job of interest to top management. Therefore, you want to be prepared to give instant status reports at all times.

When a high-priority project is completed, if you are praised for doing an exceptional job, give credit to your workers and to the people in other departments who contributed to the project. People will be willing to pitch in the next time lightning strikes if they see their efforts recognized. Be sure to express your personal appreciation to your subordinates and to the other participants.

**Note:** Most of your crisis situations will be of the kind just described here, where for one reason or another work has to be completed to meet impossible deadlines. Yet there's also a bit of crisis prevention you can practice within your own group. By encouraging your subordinates to keep you posted about potential problems with their work, you can avoid the possibility of a crisis developing.

For example, if a machine starts acting up and a worker doesn't notify you until it breaks down completely, a work stoppage could result. There are any number of other minor matters that, if not dealt with promptly, could result in serious problems. Therefore, good communication with your subordinates will allow these things to be dealt with before they escalate into something more serious.

## WHY TOLERATING MINOR IRRITANTS CAN LEAD TO MAJOR HEADACHES

As you'll discover after a short period of time on the job, there will be a lot of little nuisance items that bother you. The tendency is to ignore them, particularly since you're a new boss and perhaps a bit hesitant about seeming to make waves over insignificant details. Personalities also come into play here, as some people by their nature tend to ignore the little daily irritants that come their way. Other people may go to the other extreme and try to make mountains out of molehills.

Although you certainly don't want to stir people up over every petty problem that comes along, you have to be selective in choosing what you decide to ignore. Otherwise, you may find that big problems can arise from failing to deal with minor annoyances right away. The key to problem prevention is to ask yourself what the potential is for the irritant to escalate into something more serious in the future.

There are a number of considerations to think about before you decide to either act on something or let it slide and see what happens. These include:

- What is the immediate impact of not acting?

- What are the possible long-range consequences if you do nothing?

- Do the advantages of waiting outweigh the disadvantages of taking immediate action?

- Even if you do take action, will it solve the problem?

- Is removing the irritant something that requires support from outside your department?

- Is it your problem to resolve, or is it someone else's responsibility?

Let's look at each of these considerations. First off, if there's nothing to be lost by not acting immediately, then there's little to be gained by doing something about the problem right away. Your time is probably better spent working on something else. An example of an irritant falling in this category would be reports you receive which you have no use for. Nothing happens if you don't act to have your name removed from the distribution list, other than the reports continue to come your way.

On the other hand, getting your name taken off the distribution list might require tracking down the initiator and perhaps having to write a memo requesting your name be removed. That might not take a lot of time, but time is a valuable commodity when you're busily engaged in doing your job. Even more important, minor chores such as this often end up as time traps which take considerably longer to resolve than they should. The simplest matter can sometimes evolve into a series of lengthy meetings, extended phone calls, and long memos. So if you're dealing with a minor irritant of little consequence, ignore it until the day comes when you have time to spare.

The second consideration in deciding whether to take immediate action on a problem is what the long-term consequences will be if you fail to act. Obviously, if not acting won't have any ill effects down the road, there's little urgency attached to tackling the problem. For example, you may have a machine or piece of office equipment that is showing signs of wear. It still functions satisfactorily, but it obviously will have to be replaced in the not-too-distant future. Should you act now or later?

This depends to a large extent on the specifics of the equipment. If there are long lead times involved in replacing the item or time-consuming paperwork to be processed, immediate action is necessary. Conversely, if it's an off-the-shelf item that can be quickly replaced, there's nothing to be gained by acting now. In fact, if you do go about preparing a replacement request, your boss is likely to send it back and tell you to wait until the machine conks out. This example illustrates the value of thinking these things out when you have minor irritants to deal with. Otherwise, you can waste a good deal of time on unnecessary effort.

With some problems, the advantages to waiting and doing nothing may outweigh any benefits to be gained from taking prompt action. For example, you have an employee who is never on time for work. You're now at the stage of deciding whether to take disciplinary action. However, you are aware the employee's request for transfer to the night shift has been approved and will take place in three weeks.

It's to your obvious advantage to wait for three weeks, and see your problem solve itself. Otherwise, you would be spending a great deal of time processing a disciplinary action, only to have the employee transfer out of your unit. There are any number of minor irritants which aren't worth spending the effort on. Some of them may resolve themselves, while others will continue yet not be significant enough to warrant taking action. Learning to recognize and ignore these petty issues can save you a great deal of grief.

Sometimes when you think about an issue, you will decide that even if you do take action, it won't do anything to solve the problem. This is reason alone to justify doing nothing about it. A good example is two workers who don't get along with each other. It doesn't affect their work, and even though you would like to see them stop bickering, you know there's nothing you can do to improve their relationship.

With some problems, outside support is required for resolution. For example, the equipment used by your group is nearing its maximum capacity based on current use levels. Even though you can—and should—let your boss know of this, additional equipment of this nature is a budgetary decision that will be made at higher levels.

The final consideration with many irritants is whether the problem is yours at all. Some matters may be irritating, but they're beyond your control to do anything about. For example, your group may have cramped working quarters. The same conditions pretty much apply to other departments as well. Since it's obvious there's no additional space that can be allocated to your group, the solution to this problem isn't even your responsibility. Of course, you can gripe to your boss, but that's a futile exercise, since the boss would be as well aware of this situation as anyone else. Therefore, why bother to aggravate your boss when there's nothing to be gained by it?

In summary, many of the irritants you will encounter in doing your job require immediate attention before they escalate into something more serious. Other problems can be ignored, at least for the time being. Finally, there may be a few irritating problems that get under your skin which you will just have to learn to live with. The important point is to evaluate the possibilities and then decide what you should or shouldn't do in any given situation.

## WHAT YOU CAN DO TO CONTROL SUBSTANCE ABUSE AT WORK

One of the toughest problems to cope with as a supervisor is dealing with a worker who has a substance abuse problem. It's a touchy area for even veteran bosses, so as a first-time boss it's imperative to pay close attention to company policy for handling these cases. Your company may have a drug-free workplace program and require drug-testing of employees. It also may provide counseling services to substance abusers.

It's certainly beneficial for an employer to offer programs to assist problem substance abusers to recover from their addiction. It demonstrates concern for the well-being of employees which can be a workforce morale booster. In addition, it may also encourage workers to seek assistance voluntarily if they know the company favors rehabilitation over punishment.

There are also benefits for an employer in terms of saving the cost of hiring and training replacements for otherwise valuable employees. In any event, whatever the company's policies and programs are, your first responsibility as a supervisor is to know the rules and regulations currently in effect within your company. Although drug abuse and alcohol abuse will at times be referred to as separate issues in this section, it's worth noting that alcohol is also a drug, with the primary difference being that its use is legalized.

Your main duty in this area will be to detect the presence of drugs within your unit, as well as being able to recognize the symptoms. There are a number of indicators which may signal one of your workers is having a substance-abuse problem. For starters, you may notice diminished performance on the part of one of your workers. In fact, workers abusing alcohol and drugs are major contributors to on-the-job accidents: impaired employees are accident prone. Problem drinkers and drug abusers may also be chronically late for or absent from work.

You also may notice physical symptoms such as irritability, rapid changes in energy levels, or even smell alcohol on the worker's breath. Of course, just because certain symptoms are present doesn't necessarily mean the employee is a substance abuser. Other causes such as personal problems or medication may be the reason for altered behavior. You might even come across physical evidence in the form of liquor bottles, or drug paraphernalia such as roach clips and rolling papers.

***Important Point:*** You should never attempt to act as either an investigator or a substance-abuse counselor. There are experts available to handle these duties. If you find any evidence, bring it to the attention of your boss and the appropriate party in charge of substance abuse within your company. This is also the appropriate approach to take if you suspect one of your workers has a substance-abuse problem.

Since detection is so important, let's look at an example in this area.

## Background

Marcus has been a supervisor in a metal fabricating facility for three months. Angus, one of his subordinates, is an extremely productive worker during Marcus's first month on the job. However, over the last six weeks, both the quality and quantity of his work has diminished. Initially, Marcus didn't think much of it, but the following indicators have Marcus wondering whether Angus has a substance-abuse problem.

March 8 — Angus called in sick and said he had the flu. He returned to work on March 11.

March 15 — Angus was 30 minutes late for work, which he said was caused by a flat tire on his car.

March 17 — After lunch, Marcus goes to see Angus for information he needs, smells liquor and notices Angus, who is usually subdued, is in a jovial mood.

March 21 — Shortly after lunch, Angus accidentally spills coffee on a co-worker's desk. Marcus discovers this when he asks the co-worker what she is cleaning up. She says it is coffee, and when Marcus remarks he thought she was pretty sure-handed, she replies, "It was Angus who spilled the coffee."

March 23 — Marcus receives the production report for the past six months with output broken down by employee. In reviewing it, he notices Angus's output has dropped off sharply in the last two months.

March 24 — Early in the morning, Marcus goes to see Angus about the drop-off in production, but notices he's not at his desk. He asks JoAnn, who works next to Angus, if she has seen him. She says "No" and Marcus asks her to tell Angus to see him when Angus arrives for work.

Ten minutes later, Angus appears in Marcus's office and says, "I'm really sorry I'm late, boss, but the fuel pump went on my car this morning, and I had to take the bus. If you want, I'll make the time up after work."

COMMENT: There are some indications Angus may have a drinking problem, but Marcus isn't about to make accusations. What he does do is ask Angus about the drop-off in production.

*Marcus:* "I was looking for you this morning, Angus, to have a talk with you. Your output has dropped significantly in the past two months. What seems to be the problem?"

*Angus:* (Looking embarrassed) "I knew you would notice that sooner or later boss, but I didn't want to tell you. I've been doubling-up trying to help JoAnn out. She's been having trouble learning the job. She's really a hard worker, and I know she'll pick up the pace in a few more weeks."

*Marcus:* "Why didn't you or JoAnn tell me about this?"

*Angus:* "To be honest boss, being new we didn't think you would notice, and we were also worried about what you would do."

*Marcus:* "I'll talk with JoAnn about this Angus. Incidentally, you've been late a couple of times in the past two weeks. Are you having a problem there?"

*Angus:* "I had a problem which was the junk box I'm driving. That's getting resolved tonight, as I'm getting a new car after work. Those are the first two times I've been late in a couple of years."

*Marcus:* "OK, Angus, I'll get back to you later."

COMMENTS: To make a long story short, Marcus confirms with JoAnn that she is having a problem and Angus has been helping her out. Angus has a new car in a few days, and within a few weeks both his and JoAnn's production improve significantly. So what Angus told Marcus was true. What about the liquor Marcus smelled on Angus's breath one day? The day was March 17, St. Patrick's Day, and Angus went to lunch with several other workers. As Marcus later learned, Angus rarely drinks, and the couple of drinks he had affected him more than would be the case with someone else. As for the spilled coffee, it was just an accident, which wouldn't have been noticed under other circumstances.

A couple of points are demonstrated by the example. First of all, you have to be careful about assuming someone has a substance-abuse problem, since appearances can be deceiving. Additionally, even when you suspect a problem in this area, don't make such an accusation to the employee. When the time comes to talk with the worker, stick to the issue of the worker's performance. You certainly should ask if the employee has any problem that might be contributing to the deteriorating performance. But do it in a general way, such as by saying, "Is there any specific reason you want to talk about that's causing your poor performance?"

Maybe the employee will tell you he or she has a drinking or drug problem. If not, agree on what will be done to improve the worker's performance. If it still doesn't improve in a short period of time, then meet with the worker again. Let them know you will have to take disciplinary action, unless they want to talk with a counselor in the company's employee assistance program. Of course, before this meeting takes place, discuss the matter with the staff person charged with overseeing the program to see how to proceed. Many companies that don't have in-house counseling have provisions to refer workers to outside sources for assistance.

## HOW TO COMBAT PETTY THEFT

Along with substance abuse, another headache you may have to deal with is the problem of theft. The importance of this issue will, of course, vary with the nature of your work. It's a major concern in industries such as retailing and in any jobs where employees handle cash or cash equivalents. But even in other industries, such as manufacturing, there's little limit on the imagination of individuals as to what can be stolen. So even if you think this is a problem you won't have to deal with, you may be unpleasantly surprised.

As a supervisor, your greatest impact in the area of theft will be in the form of prevention. The starting point for this effort is to impress upon your subordinates that theft will not be tolerated. Of course, to a large extent the company policy on theft will influence how much support you get in this area. Some companies, as well as some supervisors, recognize theft exists, but blithely assume it's taking place somewhere else.

As a first-time boss, you can get off to a good start in the area of theft prevention by refusing to draw assumptions. This is dangerous when it comes to theft, since the dishonest worker may be the one you least suspect. So if you do run into problems of theft, don't make assumptions as to who it is—or who it isn't. You may be chagrined to later find out how wrong you were.

It's also important to recognize the impact theft can have on your department. Whether it's tools taken from the factory floor or supplies pilfered from the office, the damage can be far greater than just the dollar value of the missing items. For example, valuable production time can be lost waiting for stolen items to be replaced.

Aside from company-initiated measures to control theft, there are a few practical measures you can take on your own. These include:

- ✆ Keep office supplies in a locked area, and assign a worker to be responsible for the supplies. Have that person keep a sign-out sheet for people to sign when they need anything.

- ✆ Require broken or worn-out tools or other small items of value to be turned in when a replacement is to be issued.

- ✆ Office copiers are best located where you can easily view them. Sheets to sign for usage are of little value, since if someone is using the copier for personal reasons, they're not going to put their name down.

- ✆ Let employees know that taking office supplies or computer software, making personal long-distance phone calls, padding expense accounts, and similar actions are forms of theft.

Above all else, remain aware of the possibilities for theft within your unit. If it's relatively high, then theft prevention should receive a significant amount of attention on your part. On the other hand, if there's little of value to steal, or the opportunity is limited because of stringent company safeguards, then you won't have to focus as much energy on this area.

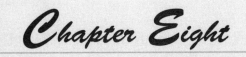

## *Chapter Eight*

# How to Work with People Outside Your Department

*A*s if you didn't have enough problems managing your own group, there are any number of outsiders you have to deal with in doing your job. These include other supervisors, staff personnel, and higher-level managers. You'll find that, just as with your own employees, some of them will be cooperative and others less so. This chapter explores how to work around some of the problems other people can create for you. Included here are people who are critical of your department, as well as bottlenecks who prevent you from getting your job done.

Although you may find it distasteful, you have to know how to cope with office politics. Not knowing how to play the game can cause you plenty of difficulties. In addition, to succeed at your job you need to have the necessary resources. But unfortunately, unless you know how to go about it, you won't succeed in getting your fair share. Furthermore, if you have union employees, it's to your advantage to learn how to gain the cooperation of the union steward. Let's see what you have to do to succeed in these areas.

## How to Accept Responsibility for Your Group's Performance

As a new supervisor, you will be experiencing for the first time the need to accept the responsibility for the performance of other people. Prior to becoming a boss, you were accountable only for your own actions at work. Now, you have to answer for what each and every one of your subordinates does at work on a daily basis. It can be an unsettling feeling knowing you have to answer for the performance of others. This is particularly true if you tend toward being a perfectionist with little patience for those who are casual about their work.

Nevertheless, the overall productivity and performance of your department is your responsibility. There may be any number of factors that make it difficult for your group to perform at a satisfactory level. These include:

- being understaffed,

- not having the proper equipment,

- too heavy a workload,

- inadequately trained workers, and

- mostly inexperienced workers due to a high turnover rate, with few employees staying on the job for long periods of time.

Of course, you can make your thoughts known to your boss about such things as not having enough help or the need to train employees. Other factors will be beyond your control. For example, if you supervise a department which employs a large number of part-time workers, a high labor turnover rate is to be expected. Workers can also come and go in jobs that are essentially dead-end positions or where the company isn't competitive in terms of pay and fringe benefits.

However, despite any built-in obstacles which hinder your group's performance, there are certain standards to adhere to in accepting responsibility as the supervisor of the department. First of all, don't make excuses to your boss or other higher-level managers when something goes wrong in your department. No one wants to hear excuses. If there are valid reasons why your group isn't performing up to par, these should be made known to your boss. But once your boss is made aware of the problem, be it a lack of training or an overload of work, don't continue to use this as an excuse.

For one thing, doing this repetitively will downgrade the importance of the problem. When people have to listen to someone complain about the same thing all of the time, it loses its impact and isn't taken seriously. Furthermore, since your boss is aware of the problem, it aggravates the situation to keep bringing it up. Making your boss mad won't get your problem solved any sooner.

Don't shunt the blame elsewhere if your boss criticizes your department. In the first place, you should already have taken steps to resolve the matter. Second, and of even greater significance, your boss may think you're trying to find a scapegoat rather than accept the responsibility. Finally, don't constantly gripe about existing problems. Your boss is as aware of them as you are, so you'll only be pegged as a constant complainer.

Being a stand-up person in accepting responsibility for your group is crucial to long-term success because of your status as a first-time boss. How you react will set the tone for the future in terms of your relationship with your boss. If you're viewed as someone who isn't always looking for an excuse when something happens, your credibility will be enhanced. Not only that, but when you have legitimate complaints, your boss will take you seriously.

In your first month or two on the job, you may feel on occasion that the boss isn't taking your novice status into account. Some bosses go slowly on a new supervisor, while others essentially adopt an attitude of "sink or swim." Whatever the case, don't feel you have to be defensive and try to rationalize everything that goes wrong. After all, no matter how good you are at your job, even under optimum conditions mistakes will be made. It goes with the territory, so accept the fact and learn to live with it.

## WAYS TO KEEP FROM BEING PUSHED AROUND BY OTHER MANAGERS

Accepting criticism from your boss and other higher-level managers is one thing. It's something else again when one of your supervisory peers tries to belittle your status as a first-time boss. In the first days and weeks of your new assignment, you want to tread carefully in terms of offending anyone. After all, at the beginning it's sometimes hard to know whether you're the target of good-natured ribbing, or unreasonable treatment. However, once you have picked up enough knowledge about the people you deal with, it's time to call a halt to any attempts to make your job more difficult than it already is.

Although it's not likely you will run into any supervisors who are personally offensive, you have to be prepared to respond if you do. Whether or not you encounter anyone who is obnoxious, there's a far better chance of a few of your peers trying to take advantage of your novice status to benefit their own departments at your expense.

How you go about dealing with these people will vary with the situation, but what you want to do is emphasize you're not going to be a patsy for someone else. Incidentally, what we're concerned with here are actions aimed at you personally. Criticism aimed at your department will be covered in the following section. Let's look at a few situations, and how you can put anyone who pulls these stunts in their place.

## *Sarcastic Remarks at Staff Meetings with Your Boss*

You may have a peer who goes out of his or her way at staff meetings to belittle people. As a new addition to the supervisory ranks, you're a prime target for such an individual. The first time or two you're subject to some form of smart remark, it's better to refrain from responding if the nature of the remark is such that a reply isn't required. This gives you an opportunity to observe the reactions of others. You may notice looks of disgust, or someone may make a comment in response.

If the individual is just baiting you, the remarks should cease once they realize you're not biting at the bait. On the other hand, the person may see your failure to reply as a sign of weakness and continue to make disparaging comments whenever the opportunity presents itself. When this happens, it's time to call a halt. The best approach for doing this is to say something in response that makes them look like the fool they are. For example:

> *Remark:* "Why don't we send the rookie for coffee. She's not doing much of anything else around here."

> ***Response:*** "That's a good idea. I'll bring back cake too. With your sharp tongue, we won't need a knife to cut it."

> ***Response:*** "Why don't you worry about yourself, and let Mr. Fahey (your boss) worry about what I'm doing."

COMMENT: How you respond to snide remarks made by another supervisor is dictated by the circumstances, the nature of the remark, and your own personality. You may want to needle them personally as in the first response, or let them know it's not their concern as in the second reply. The only cautions are:

- don't try cute remarks if you're not good at doing it; and
- never show you're angry—even if you are.

## Attempts to Have One of Your Subordinates Reassigned

Veteran supervisors may see an opportunity to take advantage of you by trying to get one of your subordinates assigned to their department. The thinking is you won't protest because you're new. One approach to doing this is to allege it's only on a temporary basis. In reality, once the person is transferred, they're gone forever and you have one person less to handle your department's workload. Frequently, the suggestion will be made in a staff meeting, since you either have to protest then or its a done deal.

So when this happens, you'd better respond both promptly and aggressively.

> ***Remark:*** (Addressed to the boss in a supervisor's meeting) "Jim, (the boss) I'm way behind since Bill Smith left. Arthur, in Fred's group, said he wasn't busy. Why not transfer him temporarily to my department until we get caught up?"

> ***Response:*** "Wait a minute. Even though I may be new, I know when a worker is trying to pull a fast one. Arthur has plenty of work because I gave it to him. He just wants to get out from having to do it. There's no way I could spare him or anyone else right now."

COMMENT: If another supervisor is looking for help—and who isn't?—they may try to make a move to get someone from your department. They probably won't ask you directly, since they know you will refuse. And if they go to your mutual boss, he or she is likely going to consult with you first. This again gives you an opportunity to object. Therefore, they may make the attempt at a supervisor's meeting, hoping to catch you off guard. If any such request should come up suddenly in this fashion, be prepared to protest on the spot.

Of course, your boss might turn them down, but it's more probable he or she will turn to you and say, "What do you think?" This type of ploy is most likely going to take place shortly after your arrival. The perpetrator is, of course, hoping you aren't going to object since you're a new arrival. But even though you haven't been there long enough to assess the situation, state emphatically you can't afford to lend anyone out. Otherwise, you may be saying farewell to one slot in your department for good.

## Attempts to Pawn Assignments off on You

All sorts of one-time assignments are handed out to supervisors. With you being new on the scene, one of your peers may sense an opportunity to unload an undesirable chore on you.

*Remark:* (Made at a supervisor's meeting with your boss.) "Jim, (your boss) instead of me being on the Incentive Awards Committee, why don't we give the assignment to Mary. It's a good opportunity to get to know people."

*Jim:* (turning to you) "What do you think?"

*Mary:* "That's up to you, boss, but I'd rather get a firm grip on my new job before I do anything like that."

COMMENT: These types of assignments are a good way to get to know other people who may be able to help you out down the line. However, when you're first starting out, you want to get control over your workload and learn the operation you supervise. With the type of response above, you're not refusing outright, which might kill your chances for any future assignment such as this which you might want. On the other hand, by emphasizing a desire to master the job first, you're showing the kind of dedication any boss can appreciate. For this reason, your boss will probably agree with you.

The above examples are just a few of the possible ways some of your peers may try to take advantage of your status as a first-time boss. Of course, most of your peers won't operate this way. If you're fortunate enough to be working with a good group of people, you may not have to deal with this type of situation. Furthermore, you always want to be cooperative, since teamwork leads to both personal and professional success. Therefore, cooperate whenever it's feasible to do so, but be prepared to defend your interests when necessary.

## HOW TO DEAL WITH PEOPLE WHO CRITICIZE YOUR DEPARTMENT

Beyond any personal criticism you may receive as a first-time boss, there will be occasions when your department is subjected to criticism. Sometimes the judgments will be valid, while on other occasions they may be an attempt to use your department as a scapegoat for someone else's failures. In fact, someone looking to avert blame may decide your department is a tempting target, since as a new boss, there's less of a chance you will take exception to the finger-pointing.

The criticism may be leveled against the department as a whole or targeted toward one or more of your subordinates. Whichever it is, your goal should be to defend the department as well as you can. Of course, whenever possible, you want to use tact and diplomacy in blunting the criticism. But there may be a time or two, when your group is unfairly targeted, where you have to be assertive.

There are a couple of valid reasons for being aggressive in defending your unit when it's criticized. For one thing, if you don't respond, anyone looking for a future scapegoat will put your group at the top of the list. Beyond that, your subordinates will be watching your reaction when the department comes under attack. If they sense you're not going to come to their defense, it can create several problems for you.

First of all, your workers will be less willing to take risks if they fear it will subject them to unfair criticism. Second, they may also conclude you won't be willing to go to bat for them when their personal interests are at stake on issues such as performance awards, pay raises, and promotions. In addition, it will seriously hamper your ability to create the loyalty you need to successfully manage the group under pressure situations.

Although the specifics of any criticism against your group will vary with the nature of your work, there are a variety of techniques you can use to counter criticism. Of course, your strategy will also hinge upon whether the criticism is valid and whether your group is being used as a scapegoat. First, let's consider some options you can use if your department receives criticism for some work-related deficiency which is fairly attributed to your group.

### 1. Agree Your Department Is to Blame, but Show It Was Due to Circumstances Beyond Your Control

This is usually the easiest tactic to use. However, you have to come up with facts that support your position. For instance, if your department was late in meeting a completion date, perhaps you can show necessary materials weren't received in time to complete the job on schedule. Frequently, you need time to look into the matter before you can prove your point. So when someone makes an accusation, simply say, "I'm not sure what went wrong, but I'll look into it and get back to you."

Incidentally, always keep an open mind about any criticism. If you indicate resentment or hostility, it makes it harder to persuade people your arguments are valid. Always be positive when you respond. If you give every appearance of being convinced what you're saying is true, then other people are more likely to think you're believable.

### 2. Agree Your Department Is Partly to Blame

This is basically a share-the-blame defense. For example, when a department is blamed for having too many defects in items being produced, perhaps it can be shown the material furnished to do the job contributed to the problem. Whatever the circumstances, the approach here is to admit your group goofed, but there were other contributing factors.

### 3. Show Why the Mistake Was Unavoidable

With this approach you're admitting a screw-up by your department, but claiming there were extenuating circumstances that made the

error unavoidable. For example, a new production process was just introduced, or new machinery or office equipment were used for the first
time. The strategy here is the errors were to be expected due to some
new factor being introduced that made the mistake almost inevitable.
This is basically a learning-curve argument, which won't carry any weight
if the same problem keeps happening over an extended period of time.

### 4. Fall Back on Being New to the Job

This is basically an acceptance of the blame with the reasoning
being it only happened because of your inexperience on the job. Say
something such as, "I see what you mean. I didn't realize that before, but
I do now. I'm sure this wouldn't have happened if I was more familiar
with the operation."

It's unfortunate, but you may receive criticism for mistakes being
made which any reasonable person would expect a newcomer to make.
However, there are people who always look for a chance to criticize someone, and they ignore any justification that might take away their opportunity to be critical. When you deal with these characters, it's best to just
take the criticism in stride and forget about it.

If there isn't any basis for the criticism being given to your department then the proper approach is to prove it with the facts. However, you
may find another department head unwilling to listen to your reasoning.
After all, that department might be at fault, so the supervisor certainly
isn't going to casually let you disprove what he or she claimed. Frankly,
if you run into this, don't be argumentative. Instead, let your boss know
the true facts. After all, your boss is the person you answer to.

Needless to say, be careful in any future dealings with anyone who
unfairly tries to pin the blame for errors on your department. Incidentally,
if your workers are aware of the criticism, be sure you let them know your
boss has been told where the blame really belongs. Otherwise, your
workers won't know you went to their defense.

## SEVERAL WAYS TO GET ACTION WITHOUT BEING A NUISANCE

Getting your job done on a daily basis requires the cooperation of many
people in other parts of the company. You will work with some of them

on a regular basis, while you will need others only occasionally. These people will have their own work priorities, and doing something for you may not be at the top of their list. As a result, to meet your own work demands you may have to encourage others to do work for you more quickly than they might want.

This isn't always easy to accomplish, and if people sense you're pestering them, it could move your request farther down on their list of things to do. In fact, if you aggravate someone enough with excessive demands, you may find yourself receiving less service than if you hadn't pursued the matter at all. As a result, the bottom line in getting the assistance you need is to learn how to do so without being perceived as a pest.

One of the keys for getting people to respond to your requests is to adjust your approach when dealing with different people. Some people are always willing to help out, while others do so only grudgingly. Therefore, you will need to have more tact in dealing with some individuals. It will take a while for you to recognize these personality differences, but even in your early days on the job it's useful to recognize you have to use different strokes for different folks.

Most of the time people will do their best to accommodate your needs. But even those who are obliging may resist on occasion because of other work pressures. You have to learn to adjust your tactics when you see this happening. Beyond anything else, how you go about asking for assistance is the most important aspect of getting the results you want from others.

Being new to the supervisory ranks in your company will work both for and against you. On the positive side of the ledger, most people are more willing to help someone who is new. Mostly this is due to a recognition of the difficulties faced by anyone starting a new job. It also doesn't hurt that you haven't been around long enough to wear your welcome out with people.

From a negative standpoint, those who always resist giving assistance may decide that your being new to the job is a good reason to discourage you from seeking help. They may think it's advantageous to prove their unwillingness to help you right from the start. That way, the reasoning goes, you'll learn not to bother them anymore. Alternatively, they may decide you don't have any clout, so there's little to be lost by giving you a hard time. Whatever the basis for this intransigence may be, you have to work around it to get the job done.

Irrespective of the ease or difficulty of dealing with various people, here are a few tactics you can use to gain the assistance you need in doing your job.

**1.** Deal directly with the people who are doing your work. For example, if you're waiting for something being done by another department, try asking the person doing the work to move it along for you, rather than going to the supervisor. For one thing, the department head may give you the brush-off, especially if you have made previous inquiries. Besides that, they will have to check with the person doing the work anyway. If you ask yourself, workers may not feel you're pressuring them by going to their boss. Be careful about doing this though, if the department head objects to people dealing directly with workers.

**2.** Spread your requests for help around if it's feasible. In some situations, you may have a choice of people who can do something for you. If you can, alternate your requests so you're not always going to the same person. There's a tendency to go to those who are most willing to help. This makes sense, but enough requests for assistance can wear a welcome out with anyone. A sensible way to work around this is to ask for assistance from those who don't respond as quickly when you have work which doesn't have a rigid deadline. This way, you can save your rush requests for those people who give you better service.

**3.** Try to make adjustments in what you need to accommodate the person providing assistance. It's not always possible, but when it is, be flexible in what you're asking for. For example, if someone can't give you what you need by a certain date, can you change the date, or perhaps accept part of the job being done on time with the rest being done later? Another possibility may be to adjust your requirements so less work is required to meet your needs. Of course, sometimes flexibility isn't possible, but keep an open mind about it, since it may work in certain situations.

**4.** Don't put unnecessary pressure on people. If a job isn't top priority, don't push other departments or individuals to complete jobs in a hurry just to make your department look good. You're only going to be able to plead priority so many times before people start to ignore you. If anyone senses they're being taken advantage of, rest assured your work will never get done.

**5.** Offer assistance in helping to get something done by another department. If it's both necessary and feasible to do so, look for ways you can provide help to another department in getting your work done to meet a deadline. Perhaps you can lend them a worker, or maybe some of the routine work can be done in your own group. It might also be possible for some of the work of the other group to be done in your department to free up their people to work on your requirement. These measures are sometimes possible where something requiring a certain skill is being done in another area that also has more routine work your people could do.

**6.** Bring top-down pressure into play as a last resort. If you're trying to complete an urgent project and all your efforts at getting cooperation from another group have failed, you have to take action. Bring the matter to the attention of your boss, so he or she can direct the other supervisor to comply with your request. Don't do this routinely though, since it's a sure-fire way to make enemies in a hurry. Usually when this happens, it's the result of dealing with someone who always resists efforts to comply with requests. So it won't be any surprise to your boss when you come calling for assistance.

## TACTICS TO AVOID GETTING STUCK WITH DIRTY JOBS

As a new boss, you may find yourself being assigned all kinds of unpleasant chores. In fact, you may not even realize an assignment is a lousy one until you start to do it. Alternatively, your first indication may be when one of your supervisory peers needles you about getting stuck with a can of worms. In any event, you may soon realize you're receiving more than your fair share of the nasty jobs.

Don't be resentful of this, and above all, don't protest to your boss. After all, the boss made the assignments and isn't going to appreciate a new supervisor implying bad decisions are being made. On a more practical level, it pays to take these assignments in stride. After all, you're the new kid on the block and, from the boss's viewpoint, are paying your initiation dues.

But just because you don't protest doesn't mean you can't try a few ploys to avoid getting stuck with all of the dirty jobs. Besides, you don't want your boss developing any bad habits in terms of giving you thankless tasks to do—and that can happen if you work for someone who always looks for the path of least resistance when handing out work.

Here are a few possibilities to try that may help you avoid being given thankless tasks:

- ✎ Avoid your boss if you know there's a dirty job to be done. First come, first served is the fastest way for a boss to hand out assignments.

- ✎ Plead ignorance. Since you're new, it's not too hard for you to claim you don't know how to handle the assignment.

- ✎ Find a sucker. Always remember that one person's garbage is another person's gold. You may be able to find a peer who likes the kind of assignment you hate.

- ✎ If you get stuck doing the job, pester your boss with questions. Helping you with a dirty job is almost as bad as if your boss had to do it himself. This may prevent future assignments of this nature.

- ✎ If you get a thankless job to do, don't do too good a job or you may become the designated expert for the future.

- ✎ Delegate the task to an unlucky subordinate. Be nice about it and say you're trying to develop his or her management skills. (Some people will believe anything.)

## SOME SMART WAYS TO GET THE RESOURCES YOU NEED

One of the easiest times for you to get any resources you need for your department is when you're just starting out. This is the time when a boss is most likely to be obliging in terms of meeting your requests. In fact, you may be lucky enough on your first day on the job to hear your boss say something such as, "If you need anything, let me know." Of course, this may be uttered with the firm conviction you won't be coming back with any requests. If it is, then this is one of the first surprises you should have in store for your boss.

As soon as you can, preferably within your first few days on the job, assess the situation and see what the department's needs are in the area of supplies and equipment. Incidentally, it's too early at this stage to determine whether you need additional help. That's a tougher nut to crack anyway, and the boss will likely respond by asking, "How can you know you need help until you've been here long enough to see what the workload is, and what your people can handle?" In any event, this topic will be covered in Chapter 10.

To get a quick fix on what you may need in the way of resources, check the equipment throughout your department. Ask your subordinates if there have been problems with equipment breakdowns. They can also be helpful in furnishing a wish list of what they need to do their jobs better. Once this is done, your initial step is complete.

However, you can't just take a list and go in and hand it to your boss. Santa Claus he or she ain't, so don't do any dreaming on that score. The very first thing you can expect from any boss when they see a wish list is for their eyes to glaze over. Then, chances are, they will methodically go through the list with you and ask, "What do you need this for?" If you don't have a good answer, off the list it comes—and sometimes that will happen even when you do have a good answer.

Therefore, before you approach your boss, determine the precise reasons why each item on the list is a necessity. This is where you should have your subordinates work with you. The kind of answers you want to have for your boss are those that show how the equipment will increase productivity, cut costs, or some other valid criterion to justify the expenditure. If all you're doing is updating to the latest "bells and whistles" configuration, rest assured the boss's pencil will be drawn through the item.

Once your initial list is drawn up, if it's lengthy, screen it yourself and eliminate those items that don't stand a chance of being approved. Try to come up with a final list with only the items which you feel will definitely contribute to the increased efficiency of your department. By doing this, your boss will at least give you credit for being sensible.

Of course, you're not likely to get everything on your list, or anything at all for that matter. This may be because of corporate-wide budget constraints, or the timing may be bad in terms of fiscal-year budgeting. If the latter is true, you may at least get a promise to include some of the items in the next budget.

On the other hand, your boss may feel obligated to approve a couple of items. For one thing, she doesn't want you thinking you won't get the necessary resources to do your job. Besides, if she told you to see her if you needed anything, she won't want you thinking she doesn't follow-through on what she says. These are reasons directly linked to your status as a new boss, which is why your chances for success are better now than they will be for some time to come.

*Note:* If you don't get much of what you asked for when you meet with your boss, all is not lost. She may at least feel compelled to hold out hope for the future by saying something such as, "Funds are tight right now, but let's see what we can do six months down the road." Of course, this may be farthest from her thoughts, and she's hoping you will forget all about this promise within a couple of weeks.

Whatever you do, save your list. Even if your boss doesn't make any promises for the future, your list can still come in handy. Perhaps at some future date, you may be under the gun for what higher-level managers consider to be poor productivity. If that happens, it's a nice time to be able to pull out your list and say, "These are the items I've been trying to get to increase efficiency since I started this job."—one more reason for limiting your initial list to items which offer the hope of increased productivity.

## HOW TO WORK AROUND BOTTLENECKS TO GET JOBS DONE FASTER

One frustrating aspect of any job is trying to get something done only to be impeded by someone who throws an unnecessary roadblock in your path. Naturally what's necessary or useless is often a judgment that depends on which side of the desk you're sitting on. But by any standards there are people who can and do slow everyone down. There are many reasons for this, a few of which are:

- ✏ Born procrastinators are born bottlenecks.
- ✏ Anyone who is indecisive is a natural bottleneck.
- ✏ Certain people like to demonstrate their power by showing they have the ability to hold something up.

- If someone opposes something being done, they may slow it up in the hope it will be cancelled.

- Personality clashes can cause work to be held up for spiteful reasons.

- A lack of knowledge may result in something being delayed because of uncertainty on the part of someone in the approval process.

- Career competition among managers can cause delays if someone sees an opportunity to hinder work being done by a competitor's group.

- People trying to make themselves look busy can act as bottlenecks while trying to justify their job.

Whatever the reason, if you have to deal with bottlenecks, you have to learn how to work around them. Otherwise, you will become a victim of missed deadlines, incessant delays, and sooner or later an unhappy boss who wants to know why something is taking forever to get done. When that happens, you can't plead it's being delayed by someone who is a bottleneck.

The first problem you have is to identify potential bottlenecks beforehand, not after they have caused you to slip a scheduled date because of their intransigence. Since you're new, it will be harder to do this at first. Frequently, it takes several unfortunate experiences in being impeded by someone before you conclude the person is a chronic bottleneck.

If you're lucky, you may pick up scuttlebutt from your supervisory peers as to who the bottlenecks are. These people usually have a well-earned reputation for obstructing the work flow and are often discussed in less-than-glowing terms. Even some of your subordinates may make remarks about some of these individuals. Although this information should put you on the alert, don't accept it as fact. In some cases, it may be nothing more than a personality clash between two individuals.

Whether you're fortunate enough to find out beforehand, or learn from experience in dealing with a bottleneck, your ultimate goal is to find ways to prevent them from holding your work up unnecessarily. Here are some of the best alternatives for doing this. Some tactics will be better than others in certain situations. It will largely depend upon what kind of work you're asking the bottleneck to do. This can vary from seeking a signature approving some action you have taken to performing a complex job for your department.

## Be Persistent in Getting Them to Act

Although it's not usually prudent to be a pest, with a bottleneck it becomes a virtual necessity. Otherwise, your work will never get done. If you're not actively encouraging bottlenecks to act, then it's much easier for them to avoid taking any action. Of course, you run the risk of them continually trying to find something wrong with your work or putting you on a endless chase seeking answers to satisfy their questions. But that can't last forever, and at least you're progressing toward getting action from the obstructionist. If you weren't bothering them, their badgering would just start later rather than sooner. When you deal with people who play this sort of game, you're better off dealing with their delaying tactics as soon as possible.

## Avoid Them Completely

This is the easiest way to prevent a bottleneck from holding your work up. It can't always be done, but in certain situations it can be effective. For example, if you need to coordinate something with several different people, just skip the bottleneck completely. This is particularly effective if the process is such that a failure to coordinate with someone isn't apt to be noticed.

Even if your omission is discovered and you have to go through the obstructionist, nothing has been lost. Alternatively, if you get your work through the cycle, and the bottleneck later discovers he or she was left out of the loop, your being new to the job is a handy alibi.

## Go Around Them to Someone Else

If it's feasible, go to someone who works with the bottleneck to get what you want done. Of course, if the person doesn't have authorization to give you what you want, this won't work. The next best bet here is to wait until the bottleneck is out of work for the day. Generally, someone will be responsible for filling in during the absence.

An offshoot of this tactic is to go looking for an approval when the person is at lunch. Then, proceed without seeing them at all. If you're caught, say your project was urgent and they weren't there when you went looking for approval. Of course, this, like many of the other tactics, can't be used on a regular basis.

## Ask for a Commitment in Writing

If the nature of what you want done justifies it, then send the bottleneck a memo asking for a specific date they will finish doing your work. Send a copy to your boss. There's a good chance the bottleneck will give you a date much beyond when you need the work to be completed. If that happens, you may want to get your boss involved to help move things along.

Another tactic you can use with bottlenecks is to give them a completion date which is sooner than what you actually need. This way you can build in a time factor to allow for their procrastination.

## Look for Loopholes to Avoid Dealing with a Bottleneck

Sometimes the nature of what you're working on will provide an opportunity for you to leave the bottleneck out of the process. For example, if you have a complicated company procedure to follow, look for a way of using it to justify not having to deal with the bottleneck. For example, if a procedure requires the approval of this person under certain conditions, see if you can show what you're doing doesn't meet the criteria where the approval will be needed.

## Get Someone Else Involved to Move Things Along

When the person holding things up is basically indecisive, you may want to suggest getting someone else involved in your discussions with the bottleneck. The angle you're looking for here is to bring someone in who will essentially reassure the bottleneck there's no problem with what you're doing. This can be effective, since indecisive people love the chance to have someone else make the decision for them. Then, if something goes wrong, they have someone to blame.

## Bring Management Pressure to Get what You Want

If the stalling becomes totally unacceptable, look for a way to involve higher-level managers in getting the bottleneck to take action. You can't do this with routine actions, but if you're working on something of interest to top management (or will be if it isn't completed on time), get your boss involved. Alternatively, if the manager you're doing the work for has significant clout, clue him in as to what your problem is. Of course, if you have to work regularly with the person you're putting pressure on, this tactic should only be used as a last resort. It's hard enough as it is to get obstructionists to act on anything. If you cause them to hold a grudge against you, in the future you will think their past performance was speedy.

## LEARNING HOW TO DEAL WITH PEOPLE WHO PLAY OFFICE POLITICS

As you start your job as a first-time boss, you won't have the slightest idea as to the role office politics plays within your company. Of course, if you have been working for the company and received a promotion into your new position, you may have some vague knowledge of what transpired. But even here your view was probably limited, since you weren't in a supervisory capacity.

Therefore, whichever route you took to your present job, you're probably dealing with a lot of unfamiliar faces, behind which lurk a wide variety of office politicians. How you deal with them can affect not only your long-term career prospects, but also the ability to get your job done as efficiently as possible on a daily basis. For these reasons, no matter how you play the political game at work, you had better learn the rules and who the players are.

Being new, it's extremely important to avoid criticizing anyone, since you don't know how people interact on or off the job. Even when individuals don't have any business dealings at work, there are other possibilities. They may belong to the same bowling league, health club, or civic organization. Their relationship could be based on car pooling together, or living in the same neighborhood. As a result, it isn't smart to start spouting off about someone, since what you say may get back to the person. And when that happens, you have made an enemy without even knowing it. There's nothing to be gained by being critical of others—a sound rule to follow, not only when you're starting out on the job, but throughout your career.

Beyond being tight-lipped about others, it's advantageous to observe how people interact on the job. Be careful to note the friendships that exist at work, as well as the animosities. This will keep you from inadvertently alienating someone who may be in a position to help you in your job. Don't be hasty about forming your own friendships at work, since they could do you more harm than good. For example, if you start chumming around with a supervisor who isn't liked by your boss, this hostility could carry over to you. You may find such an attitude to be unfair—and it is—but fairness has nothing to do with reality.

Incidentally, don't let your subordinates play office politics by using you as their pawn. One or more of your workers who are office politicians may decide to further their cause by trying to befriend you. Although you don't want to be rude, it's good policy to politely reject any offers to socialize with these people. As you already know, it's crucial to be very careful not to show any indication of favoring one employee over another. However, you may decide you can socialize with someone and still treat everyone in your group equally. Whether that is true or not, your friendship alone carries with it the perception of favoritism. And when it comes to creating morale problems within your unit, it doesn't matter whether they're caused by perception or reality.

One of the tricky aspects of office politics is when people use their close relationship with a higher-level manager to try and influence you into doing what they want. Usually this is done to get priority treatment of one sort or another. Let's look at an example of how you can deal with this type of problem.

## Background

Andy, the supervisor of another department, is looking to get work your group is doing for him pushed ahead of jobs being done for other people. He happens to be a neighbor of Robert A., who is a senior vice-president, a fact Andy makes certain everyone is aware of.

*Andy:*      (Enters your office, sits down, and says,) "Say, old buddy, I need your help."

*You:*       "What can I do for you, Andy?"

*Andy:*      "Well I need the Rapidix order in two days. I know it wasn't scheduled to be finished for another two weeks, but the buyer called me and they need it as soon as possible."

| | |
|---|---|
| *You:* | "I'd sure like to help out, Andy, but we're booked solid." |
| *Andy:* | "Look, this account is Robert A.'s baby, and if we don't get this order out, he'll be plenty ticked off." |
| *You:* | "Hey, I'm sympathetic, Andy, but I don't have the authority to just switch jobs around on a whim. I'm sure everyone else feels their work is just as important." |
| *Andy:* | "Yeah, well everyone else isn't going to have a vice-president of the company on their butt if Rapidix doesn't get their stuff." |
| *You:* | "Just tell him the facts, Andy. I'm sure he's reasonable." |
| *Andy:* | "Like heck he is. Let me tell you something. I play doubles tennis with the guy every Saturday, and I know him real well. He expects action, and he doesn't care how he gets it. I know you're new here, so let me give you some good advice. This is one guy you don't want to have mad at you. I'd suggest you just put my work into the system right now, and push some other job back. That way, we both stay out of trouble." |
| *You:* | "I can't do that Andy, but I would like to help out. Why don't we go see Jim (your boss). I'll see if we can work overtime to finish your job." |
| *Andy:* | "I can't do that. I tried that once before and Jim said it would be OK as long as I was willing to pick up the overtime tab in my budget. I'm not going to foot that bill." |
| *You:* | "Then all I can suggest is that you get Mr. A. to approve shifting jobs. You better have him notify Jim, though, because other departments are involved." |
| *Andy:* | "I'll get back to you." (Nothing more is heard from Andy and the job is completed as regularly scheduled.) |

**COMMENTS:** This example illustrates what frequently happens when office politicians try to intimidate people by referring to their connections in high places—which incidentally, aren't always quite as solid as implied. If you stand your ground, very likely nothing will come of it. Generally, the person making the threat has no intention of getting any higher-level contact involved. Usually it's only a bluff, and the way to deal with bluffs is to call them.

Also, since you're new on the job, it's perfectly valid to suggest your boss be brought in as a participant in the discussion if the person continues to push the issue. This is another quick way to dispose with this sort of intimidation. Someone may think you're easy game for this type of maneuver because you're new, but they know your boss will see right through their charade. So the minute you mention getting your boss into the act, the person will back off. Another typical trait of politicians is to treat you like a buddy at first: if that doesn't get them what they want they will resort to veiled threats as in the example.

Of course, the flip side of office politics, which can't be ignored, is whether you should practice a little politicking of your own. This largely is based on your own personality. If you're good at office politics, it certainly can't hinder your career, and it may help. If you don't feel playing office politics is one of your strong suits, then at least learn how to play the game minimally. Otherwise, you will be hard-pressed to find support at higher levels when you need it. More often than you might think, a little bit of politicking is necessary to get the job done.

Here are a few tactics you may find useful in practicing a little bit of office politics:

### Be a volunteer

There are always a variety of one-shot projects your boss will be looking for someone to do. As a new supervisor, you can gain your boss's attention quickly by taking these tasks on. As you gain a little bit of experience, try to distinguish between thankless tasks, and those that can gain you a bit of visibility through dealing with managers in other areas of the company.

### Be a joiner

Company sponsored activities such as bowling leagues, golf and basketball teams, and similar activities are a quick way to get to know people. Incidentally, it's not only high-level contacts who can help you in your job. If you are on a bowling team with a vice-president and the supervisor of the maintenance department, the latter contact may be of more value to you in the long run.

### Become an expert

If new equipment or procedures are introduced, make the effort to become the person most knowledgeable about them. Then, show a willingness to help others who aren't as informed as you are. This makes you a valuable person to know, and you can use this as a trade-off to get favors you may need in the future.

### Be friendly toward everyone

You never know who may be able to do you a favor in the future, so always be pleasant with people.

### Learn who has influence within the company

Someone can wield a good deal of influence with senior managers without having an impressive title. It may be a respected long-standing employee, or the niece of someone who went to college with the company president. Whatever the connection might be, you can't take advantage of it unless you know it exists. So be on the alert for these informal sources of power within the company.

### Know who to avoid

Some people go to great lengths to figure out who the right people are to cultivate relationships with. Who they neglect to think about are the people who it's wise to avoid. These range from those who are always in conflict with one or more managers to those who for one reason or another are thought of as misfits.

### Look for people who share your interests

Whether it's gardening or the local sports teams, if higher-level managers share these interests, look for opportunities to discuss these topics. This is a great way to get to know senior managers who you might otherwise never meet. Use a little tact in doing this though, since you don't want to be spotlighted as an apple-polisher.

*Note:* No matter what lengths you go to in trying to establish good contacts, always keep the potential reaction of your immediate boss in mind. This is the bread-and-butter person you have to impress. If your boss is the insecure type or senses you're trying to undermine his or her authority, your efforts to cultivate other managers may backfire on you. The end result may be an unhappy boss who isn't about to do you any favors.

Therefore, always stay tuned to your boss's point of view on the issue of office politics. If your boss appears to resent people who do any politicking, be low-key with your approach to building a circle of contacts.

## A Good Way to Get Along with a Union Steward

If your subordinates are union members, you will have added responsibilities in terms of operating within the framework of a union/management agreement. This may mean certain work rules have to be followed in making assignments. There may also be a lengthy formal grievance procedure for disciplinary measures. It will also require you to interact with the union steward who is representing your subordinates in terms of ensuring the labor agreement is carried out.

Being a first-time boss, and therefore unfamiliar with the provisions of the labor agreement, it's imperative to work closely with both your boss and the labor-relations staffers within your company. If you have any questions on any aspect of work rules or other union-related matters, seek advice before proceeding. This is the surest way to avoid unnecessary union grievances being filed.

After you're on the job for a sufficient length of time, you will know how to proceed without having to seek advice so often. But initially at least, abide by the rule of "when in doubt, find out." If you do that, then you shouldn't have any difficulty in getting the job done without a lot of unnecessary hassles.

As a supervisor, your working relationship with the union steward can greatly influence the extent of any union problems you have to deal with. The key here is to try and develop a good professional relationship. You and the union steward may have differing viewpoints on any number of issues. That in itself doesn't mean you have to function as adversaries and deal with each other in an atmosphere of hostility. In fact, if you make a solid effort, you should be able to get along reasonably well.

This requires you to recognize that the union steward will see things from the worker's perspective, while you view them from the vantage point of a manager. Even though you don't always agree with each other, a willingness to listen to opposing viewpoints will often provide for reasonable compromises. A little bit of give-and-take also helps, so don't try to win every point on every issue. If you're willing to be conciliatory and look for a middle-ground approach to reaching agreement, the odds are the union steward will do likewise.

Of course, your ability to get along reasonably with the steward will depend on his or her attitude as well as yours. If your attempts to be reasonable are met with hostility, then you have to accept the fact you may have to spend more of your time on union-related problems. However, don't give up trying to work out a decent working relationship if your initial meetings with the union steward don't go well.

It's to be expected that the union steward will view you as an unknown quantity at the start. This may lead the union official to proceed cautiously in dealing with you, at least until your intentions are known. However, once you demonstrate an interest in being practical about resolving grievances and other issues, you may see a greater willingness to be flexible. After all, everyone wants to avoid unnecessary complications in doing their job, and the steward isn't any different in this regard.

*Chapter Nine*

# FIFTEEN SUPERVISORY MISTAKES AND HOW TO AVOID THEM

*H*ow successful you are as a supervisor will be influenced by many factors. Some of them, such as a supportive boss and good working conditions, are beyond your control. For the most part, however, the ingredients for being a good manager are within your own destiny. This chapter contains some of the most common pitfalls you want to avoid, as well as significant steps you can take to enhance your own chances of success.

Naturally, you won't always have things go smoothly. But if you concentrate on learning how to overcome some of the typical hazards, your mistakes will be minimal. Furthermore, knowing what you have to watch out for will give you greater confidence in your ability to handle any situation that comes your way.

## WHY IT DOESN'T PAY TO GET ANGRY

One of the fundamentals of successful supervision is the ability to control your emotions. The stress of your job, careless mistakes by workers, and disagreeable associates are but a few of the reasons why you might justi-fiably lose your temper. But getting angry doesn't solve anything, and it frequently makes matters worse.

Keeping your composure is crucial when it comes to dealing with your subordinates. They are also the people who are most vulnerable when a supervisor is having a bad day. After all, who else can be yelled at with little fear of adverse repercussions? Certainly not a boss, and very few peers are likely to willingly absorb verbal abuse. However, subordi-nates aren't so fortunate, which makes them an easier target for a super-visor to vent frustrations on. Even though it may not be done deliberate-ly, workers are the most likely candidates for your anger.

Workers may shrug off the anger of a boss, since retaliation isn't much of an option for anyone who values their job. However, subordi-nates are apt to react over time to a boss's angry outbursts in one of three ways. These are fear, apathy, revenge, or perhaps some combination of the three.

More than one manager has operated by using fear as the primary means of getting the job done. This type of boss yells at workers rou-tinely, publicly embarrasses them for making mistakes, and threatens dis-ciplinary action at the slightest justification. There's little two-way com-munication with workers in this kind of environment; a worker's prime goal becomes avoiding the boss, not seeking him out for guidance.

Other workers respond to management by intimidation with apathy toward their jobs. No one in their right mind is about to put in any extra effort if they are subjected to harsh treatment. And who is going to be foolhardy enough to let such a boss know about a problem? No one is, and for this reason minor mishaps may go unnoticed until they escalate into major difficulties which the supervisor then has to answer for.

Then, there are the employees who patiently wait for the opportu-nity to gain revenge on a tyrant of a boss. They go to great lengths to make a boss look bad in front of others. And if they're good at it, the boss never realizes how badly he's being sabotaged. But no matter how an individual employee responds to a boss who uses anger as a weapon against subordinates, on an overall group basis the following negative effects are probable:

&#9758;  lower unit output;

&#9758;  a greater number of errors;

✏ lack of communication between the supervisor and workers;

✏ higher absenteeism;

✏ higher than average employee turnover rates; and

✏ more complaints to the personnel office or more union grievances.

Besides the downside to anger from the perspective of your subordinates' reactions, there are personal pitfalls in getting mad. First of all, when someone is angry, they can lose control to the extent of being unable to think clearly. When that happens, the wrong decisions can be made, and things may be said to be later regretted. Furthermore, people can look pretty foolish when they get angry, so it's not the sort of behavior that generates much respect. Beyond that, it's pretty stressful, and as a consequence, won't do much to improve your health.

In substance, getting angry with workers isn't the best approach to getting the job done. Of course, no matter how hard you try there may be occasions when you lose your temper. This is to be expected, and workers understand this. However, if your personality is such that you're by nature quick-tempered, try to control it. This won't be possible at all times, but if workers know you're usually pretty reasonable, this isn't too damaging. Nevertheless, whenever it's practical, try to apologize for losing your cool.

## THE IMPORTANCE OF SETTING THE RIGHT EXAMPLE FOR WORKERS

What you expect from your workers in terms of job performance isn't always what you will get. And you may find a wide diversity in the performance levels of different individuals who work for you. There are any number of actions you can take to improve worker performance, ranging from positive measures in the form of providing training to less pleasant techniques such as disciplinary actions. One little recognized way to encourage employees to perform at a higher level of achievement is to set an example they can emulate.

This isn't as pie-in-the-sky as it might seem. After all, people are conditioned from their youth to model themselves after others. So, although the response won't be universal among your workers, at least some of them will take their cues from you. Therefore, if you set the tone in terms of being on time for work, keeping people informed, and doing your job diligently, this demonstrates first-hand what your expectations are.

On the other hand, a few of your workers may be more than willing to follow your lead if you're less than punctual, take long lunches, and so forth. It's unfortunate, but even if you work long hours, a worker who sees you arrive a few minutes late for work, will see that as an excuse to do the same. This is even more imperative, since you're a first-time boss. In fact, one of your bolder subordinates may see fit to protest if you criticize them for being late when you weren't on time yourself. Naturally, being the boss, you can always fall back on the old saw of "do as I say, not as I do." However, this sort of argument does nothing to help a first-time supervisor to earn the respect of workers.

For these reasons, although trying to set a good example for your subordinates to follow won't be a panacea for solving all of your supervisory problems, it's a sound foundation for getting started in the right direction. That in itself is a big help as you ease your way into your supervisory responsibilities.

## HOW TO KEEP YOUR DISTANCE FROM WORKERS WITHOUT BEING DISTANT

As times passes, you will get to know your subordinates better and they will get to know you. Since you're a boss who places emphasis on communicating with those you supervise, there will be a great deal of casual conversation, as well as that required for business matters. This isn't a problem in and of itself. In fact, being friendly helps establish the rapport needed to foster teamwork within your group.

However, there's a fine line you have to learn to straddle, between being a friend and a boss. As the timeworn cliché states, "Familiarity breeds contempt." If you cross the bridge from being a boss to a friend, it will be increasingly difficult to successfully supervise your department. As a supervisor, there are times when tough decisions have to be made. Some of these decisions will be unpopular with those you supervise.

To further complicate matters, if you start to socialize with subordinates, it stands to reason you will be closer to some than others. You will tend to associate with those who share your interests, whether golf or working out at the health club. Other workers may start to resent this even though nothing is said. But sooner or later, a decision will be made, which in the minds of some workers is a sign you're showing favoritism toward those you socialize with.

What happens when an undesirable task has to be assigned? If you don't give it to a friend, it signals to other workers you're playing favorites. And if you do, you may hear about it later. It's essentially a no-win situation. Once people who work for you also socialize with you, decisions you would normally make without a second thought become more difficult.

Your authority as a boss will be weakened, as workers increasingly challenge your decisions. This could ultimately place you in the unenviable position of either making decisions by committee, or relying on an "I'm the boss," edict. Whichever it is, your status as an effective supervisor will be seriously impaired.

If you develop friendships with one or two workers it can cause uneasiness for them too. They are subject to being kidded about being the boss's pet. Even worse, deep resentment can set in with co-workers at the first sign of them receiving favorable treatment. In the end, there will be a loss of cohesion in your group. Workers may divide themselves into two camps, one consisting of your friends, with the other group including everyone else who works for you. All in all, there's nothing to be gained and much to be lost when you don't separate your work from your social interests.

The difficulty you have to overcome is knowing how to remain friendly as a boss, without becoming a friend. You can establish the proper framework for this by politely refusing any invitations from workers to participate in social activities. Above all, don't socialize with them after work. Although it may seem relatively harmless, don't even join them for lunch in the company cafeteria—at least not on a regular basis. Actually, your workers will be appreciative of that too, since they won't have to watch what they say because the boss is present.

Establishing your position in terms of forming friendships won't be an ongoing problem. After you have politely turned down invitations a few times, they will cease to be made. Of course, you don't have to hide in a cave when it comes to interacting with your subordinates. In fact, once a clear pattern of not mixing business with pleasure has been established, it will be easier to mingle with subordinates on occasion.

For instance, there's certainly nothing wrong with sharing a coffee break with workers on an intermittent basis. And, of course, never fail to attend the obligatory company-sponsored social events. But even here, steer clear of discussing business with subordinates. These gatherings always have their share of ear-bending workers cornering their boss with questions about their next promotion or whatever. This is especially true when the alcohol has been flowing. In these situations, it's always wise to know when to say "good night" and head for the exit. You'll be saving yourself some aggravation and a worker or two some embarrassment the next day.

## THE NEED TO BE FAIR EVEN WHEN YOU'RE BEING FIRM

There will be occasions when you ask workers to do something and they complain about it. It may actually get to the point where you have to be insistent before the grumbling ceases. At other times, nothing will be said, even though it's obvious a subordinate wasn't happy about receiving an assignment. Some of this sort of unrest is natural, since it's impossible to satisfy everyone all of the time and still get the job done. There are unpleasant tasks that no one wants to do, and workers may not want to interrupt what they're working on to handle something else. In fact, it could be as simple as a worker expecting to leave at the regular quitting time, only to be told overtime is mandatory that night.

Whatever the reason, you sometimes have to be firm about making decisions in the face of reluctance by workers to do what you want. If everyone could set their own agenda, your group wouldn't be able to function as a productive unit. Furthermore, there's no logical reason for any worker to expect their every whim to be met. In fact, most workers take it in stride if they occasionally feel they're getting the short end of the stick. So there's nothing unusual in expecting a little grumbling from workers now and then. What you do want to guard against is preventing unfairness from creeping into the process when you're exercising your authority.

Therefore, you should make an attempt to understand why workers express dissatisfaction when you ask them to do something. Naturally, with the pressures of the job, it's not always possible to get involved in any extended dialogue with workers. Sometimes, you just have to tell someone to do something and be done with it. But the very need to do this makes it even more important to exercise care in being fair with each and every employee.

Sometimes either carelessness or a preformed judgment of a worker can lead to a supervisor being unreasonable in the equitable treatment of workers. For example, it's relatively easy to be impatient with one of your less productive workers. Therefore, if one of these individuals says something about being assigned a particular task, it's a lot harder to be tolerant than with a top-notch producer.

Then again, the reason the worker isn't too cooperative may be directly related to the employee, rather than anything you have done. Perhaps the worker is irritable because of a personal problem, or maybe the worker doesn't feel capable of being able to do the task you're giving him. Finally, the worker's apparent hostility may be nothing more than a breakdown in communication. For instance, perhaps the worker doesn't understand why he or she is being assigned the particular task.

In any event, whenever a worker alleges you're not being fair, make an effort to find out why. Usually you can persuade a worker otherwise, once you understand the basis for their complaint. On other occasions, you will find there really isn't anything of significance leading to the employee's objections, other than not liking the chore they've been asked to do. Let's look at an example of this:

## Background

Caroline has been the assistant manager in a retail clothing store for a month. Peggy, one of the sales associates she supervises, is asked one morning to open a shipment of merchandise.

*Caroline:* "Peggy, will you open the shipment that came in last night, so we can get it ready for display?"

*Peggy:* "Why me, Caroline? I'm always the one who gets stuck with that job."

*Caroline:* (Looking surprised) "I don't think that's true, Peggy. What's the big deal about opening a few boxes anyway?"

*Peggy:* "Well, in the first place, I thought I was hired as a salesperson, not as a shipping and receiving clerk. Besides that, I'm going to get all dirty doing that grubby job."

*Caroline:* (Getting aggravated, but remaining calm) "We're all here to sell, Peggy, but as you know, there are other jobs we have to do. Beth and Susan are straightening up the racks, and I'm doing an out-of-stock report. I really don't understand what the problem is. Can you help me out on this?"

*Peggy:* "Ah, I guess I'm just grumpy this morning. Let me go open the boxes and get it out of the way."

*Caroline:* "Fine, Peggy. I appreciate that."

COMMENTS: There are many times workers will protest and, as in this case, you will never get a definitive answer as to what the problem is. Sometimes, as Peggy intimates, a worker may be having a bad day, as we're all prone to have every now and then. In many instances, it's a particular task a worker doesn't like to do, rather than any unfairness on your part in making assignments. Everyone has their pet peeves in terms of little chores they don't like. Nevertheless, you can't let each employee pick and choose what they will or won't do. If that happened, then a few really grubby jobs wouldn't get done at all.

A related problem you may experience in this area is when a worker always tries to avoid certain tasks by managing to be busy doing something else at the time. You have to be on the lookout for this, since it can create resentment on the part of other workers. They probably won't say anything to you, but they won't be happy about their co-worker always ducking a particular chore.

## The Value of Establishing Credibility with Workers

Starting with your first day on the job, employees who work for you will be watching and waiting to see how you handle your supervisory responsibilities. While you're busy evaluating them, they will be checking you out. What will they be looking for? Basically, workers want to know what your management style will be. Will you get involved in every detail of the job or pretty much stay in your office? Will you be easy to talk to or difficult to get to know? These and many more questions will be answered for subordinates during your first few weeks on the job.

Until such time as your workers get to know what you expect from them, they will be tentative in their dealings with you. After all, no one wants to get off to a bad start with a new boss. No matter what your management style is, however, your subordinates will quickly adjust. What they won't be able to cope with is a lack of credibility. Will you be believable when you make commitments to them? Can they expect consistency in your actions, or will it be one way today and another way tomorrow?

Employees can pretty much adapt to any boss who is at least credible. This is exemplified by statements such as, "She's a tough boss, but at least I know where I stand." Therefore, from your first day on the job, one of your objectives should be to establish credibility with your subordinates. What you do over a period of time will gradually establish your credibility, but there are a few basic practices that will help in this regard.

### *Don't Make Careless Commitments*

First of all, don't make hasty commitments you later have to retract. This seems to be easy enough to do, but agreements can occasionally be made without thinking about them thoroughly. For example, when you're busy doing something, a worker may make a request which you quickly agree to without much thought. You may then forget about it until some time later when the employee reminds you about it. This is when you may discover the hasty commitment shouldn't have been made. As a result, you have to renege on your original agreement. Needless to say, this leaves you with an unhappy worker who thinks your word isn't worth much.

### Example

It's early on a Tuesday morning and Trudy, the supervisor, is busy working on a report which is due on her boss's desk in an hour. Tess, one of her workers, sticks her head in the door.

*Tess:*     "Trudy, can I leave an hour early on Thursday?"

*Trudy:*     (Looking up) "Sure Tess."

It's now Thursday shortly after lunch, and Trudy is going around reminding everyone overtime is mandatory that night.

*Trudy:*     "Tess, don't forget we have work tonight."

*Tess:*     "Don't you remember, I'm leaving an hour early tonight and won't be working. You said it was OK when I asked you Tuesday."

Trudy suddenly remembers she made this agreement without realizing Thursday was a regular overtime night and now finds herself in a bind. She needs everyone working that night to meet the week's production quota. On the other hand, she made a commitment which Tess relied upon.

COMMENTS: Take a moment to think about this situation that resulted from a hasty decision. If Trudy doesn't give Tess the time off, she has a very unhappy worker who doesn't think much of her credibility. On the other hand, if she sticks to her original commitment, Trudy will have an upset boss if the production quota isn't met. What would you do if you were faced with this dilemma? While you're thinking about it, let's solve Trudy's problem.

*Trudy:*     "Oh, I'm sorry, Tess. I forgot Thursday was mandatory overtime when I said you could leave early. Being new, I haven't got everything down pat yet. How important is it to you to have the night off?"

*Tess:*     "I made plans to meet a couple of friends I haven't seen for a while for dinner."

*Trudy:*     "Let's do this. Try and get someone in another department to work for you tonight. If they can, I'll clear it with their boss. If you can't, take the night off and don't worry about it. We'll do the best we can without you."

**COMMENTS:** Trudy opted to stand by her commitment and will take her chances in meeting the production goals. However, notice how a moment of forgetfulness can create a big problem out of something that seems insignificant. Of course, everyone makes mistakes, and goofs of this sort won't be fatal to a boss's credibility unless they happen on a regular basis. But when you're new on the job, you don't have a track record to reassure workers that careless mistakes are infrequent. Until you have been on the job for a while, take extra precautions to avoid making hasty commitments.

## Don't Make Promises You Can't Keep

This type of credibility hazard is closely related to making careless commitments. The difference here is you're not making a careless mistake, since you believe the promise can be fulfilled. It's relatively easy to assume many promises can be kept, when in reality, the final decision isn't within your control. Anything that requires other approvals is always subject to being vetoed. Therefore, for starters, a promise should never be made if it's dependent on factors which you have no control over. Promotions, pay raises, and job transfers are typical items that fall within this category.

Another type of promise that can cause real headaches is the contingent promise. This is the, "If you do this, I'll do this," kind of guarantee. Here, you're making a future commitment in exchange for the worker doing something for you now. This can put you in a real bind down the road if you're unable to fulfill your end of the bargain.

Many times a contingent promise is totally unnecessary in the first place. They are often made as a means of softening the blow of what would otherwise be a difficult task, such as asking employees to do something undesirable.

### Example

Anthony supervises a group in which Wanda works. He is about to ask her to skip her scheduled vacation so the group won't be short-handed.

*Anthony:* "Wanda, I know you have the first two weeks in June scheduled for vacation. If you postpone it, I'll let you pick any other two weeks after the first of July. Ordinarily, I wouldn't ask you to do this, but with two people quitting, and June being our busiest month, we won't have enough people to do the job. The hiring freeze is scheduled to be lifted the end of May, so by the end of June we'll have replacements."

*Wanda:* "Sure, boss. I haven't made my vacation plans yet anyway. How about if I take the first two weeks in July?"

*Anthony:* "You've got it."

Let's fast forward to the first week in June when a policy directive is distributed to all managers. It reads in part "The hiring freeze will remain in effect until September 30. In order to meet workload demands, and still provide for employees to take vacation time, the plant will shut down the last two weeks in August. No vacation time will be granted for the period June 15 through August 15. Any employee who has already scheduled vacation during that period can either take their vacation during the plant shutdown or, if they have additional time to use, after September 30."

COMMENTS: The supervisor is now forced to tell Wanda she can't have the first two weeks in July off after she already gave up her vacation in June. The simplest way to avoid these difficulties is to not make contingent promises in the first place. It's far easier to tell the employee outright what has to be done, without trying to soften the blow with a promise that can't be fulfilled.

## *Follow Through When You Say You're Going to Do Something*

Another credibility buster is for a supervisor to tell an employee something will be done and then fail to follow up to do what was promised. In this situation the commitment is doable, but it doesn't get done because it was forgotten. If the worker follows up and inquires about the matter, usually the boss will apologize for forgetting to act and then go ahead and do what was promised.

A problem with a boss's credibility can occur here when the boss fails to act, and the worker doesn't inquire about the matter. Some workers are more cautious than others about approaching a boss and making inquiries about actions the boss promised to take. Therefore, if the boss forgets, the worker assumes the boss was only paying lip service to the request, and never had any intention to do anything about it. If this happens frequently, then the supervisor's promises won't be believable.

To prevent this, it's a good idea to make notes of any commitments made to workers to take some form of action. If a reply was promised by a certain date and it can't be met, let workers know action has been delayed and the revised date when a response can be expected. Once you have been on the job for a few months, occasional forgetfulness will be taken in stride by workers, since you will have built a track record for following through on your commitments. At the start of your tenure, there's a greater chance workers will draw negative conclusions from any failure on your part to do what was promised.

## *Don't Be Inconsistent*

Your credibility can also suffer if you're inconsistent in your dealings with subordinates. Making a decision one way today and another way tomorrow will leave workers not knowing what to expect. Therefore, to the maximum extent possible, always try to handle similar decisions in the same fashion. There will be occasions when, for one reason or another, the same request will be treated differently than it usually is. For example, you may be very flexible about letting workers take an hour or two of leave time. However, if it becomes necessary to be more restrictive because of work pressures, let everyone know about it. Otherwise, if you suddenly say "No," to someone without an explanation, workers will think you're being arbitrary in making these decisions.

## *Don't Speculate*

Another avoidable cause of credibility problems is when you speculate on what might happen in your department. Even though you have qualified what you're saying so it shouldn't be misunderstood, speculation is subject to being interpreted as fact. If you say, "Business is picking up, so pay raises should be higher this year," your subordinates may interpret this to mean raises *will* be higher. If they're not, workers may think you have been less than honest with them. Of course, what you said was misinterpreted; but since this is a common occurrence, you're better off avoiding speculation. This particularly applies to pocketbook issues such as pay raises, which are especially meaningful to workers.

## How to Avoid the Appearance of Favoritism

The need to avoid favoritism has been mentioned previously, but there's one aspect of it that hasn't been discussed. These are legitimate actions you take which can erroneously create the appearance of favoritism in the eyes of some workers. The most common area where this can occur is when you give recognition to workers for outstanding performance. If it's not handled properly, other subordinates may perceive that the compliments or awards were based on favoritism on your part, rather than on the accomplishments of the recipients.

You may feel little need for sensitivity in this area, since there can be little doubt the workers being rewarded are truly deserving. Furthermore, nothing more significant than petty jealousy may spawn some of the resentment of a few co-workers. On the other hand, sometimes there isn't much of a performance margin to differentiate those who get awards from those who don't. In addition, it's easy to subconsciously act more favorably toward those who do the most work. And there's always the aspect of pride where workers think their own efforts were equal to those who received the awards.

Although you shouldn't dwell on this aspect of showing favoritism, it can contribute to a morale problem if you're not careful. Let's look at a typical case of such resentment.

## Example

Jeff has recently been appointed the supervisor of twelve workers in a production area for a large consumer goods manufacturer. Chuck, one of the workers, is in his office asking about how workers are selected for awards. Two other workers in the group recently received performance awards. They had been nominated for the awards by the prior supervisor.

*Chuck:* "Say, boss, what do you have to do to win one of those awards that were given out last week?"

*Jeff:* "They're given for outstanding performance over the past year. This has been done for several years now, Chuck. You ought to know about that."

*Chuck:* "Well, I know this has nothing to do with you, Jeff, but it seems the same people are always winning the awards. It's not only our department, but the same thing is true everywhere else in the company."

*Jeff:* "The awards are based on performance, Chuck, and they are voted on by a committee of people who come from outside the department. There are also several reviews that take place before the names even go before the committee. I don't know if it's true, but if some of the same people have won awards more than once, it's because they have earned them."

*Chuck:* "If you ask me, there's a little favoritism involved also. When Shawn was the boss, he always was nicer to Camille and Henry than anyone else. If you ask me, they were his favorites, and that's why they got awards."

*Jeff:* "You certainly may think that, Chuck, but it isn't true."

*Chuck:* "I'm not the only one who thinks that, boss. You can ask some of the other people."

*Jeff:*      "All I can tell you is this, Chuck. I don't play favorites, and I intend to be fair. If someone deserves an award, then they will get it. If they don't, they won't."

*Chuck:*    "I sure hope so, because it's about time someone besides those two got some recognition around here. We all work hard."

*Jeff:*      "They are eligible for future awards, just like any-body else, Chuck. Whether or not they win again remains to be seen. For now, let's get back to doing some of that hard work you mentioned."

COMMENTS: Chuck's feelings could just be petty jealousy. Conversely, they could indicate the prior boss acted in such a manner toward his star performers that other workers perceived it to be favoritism. As a first-time boss, you might encounter this sort of problem. Therefore, it's important right from the outset to show you intend to be fair in every aspect of your dealings with employees.

It's sometimes difficult to single people out for achievement awards, since there may be very little to choose from in distinguishing between the performance levels of several people. However, if you're consistently fair in your treatment of everyone, there will be little quibbling about your decisions in these matters. Nevertheless, if several people are potentially qualified, try to share the wealth, rather than selecting the same people time and again.

It also helps to take the sting out of workers showing resentment toward those winning merit awards if you give recognition to the efforts of others. For example, let hard workers who don't quite measure up to the top performers know you appreciate their efforts throughout the year. When one of these people does a good job on something, take a few minutes to let them know it's appreciated.

Avoiding the appearance of favoritism where it doesn't actually exist isn't difficult. About all you have to do is remain aware of the possibilities, and avoid unintentionally showing bias toward certain workers. If you do that, then you can't and shouldn't worry about one or two workers who would mumble about favoritism under any circumstances.

## HOW TO GET OFF THE HOT SEAT WITHOUT MAKING EXCUSES

Either at work, or in your personal experience, you probably know people who have an excuse for everything. According to their theory of life, they don't make mistakes. Someone, or something else, is always the cause of any error they make. If you have dealt with one of these people first-hand for a long enough period of time, you inevitably become immune to whatever excuse they may be offering. As a result, you're not likely to believe them even when there's justification for other factors causing or contributing to their mistake. The end result is a habitual excuse-maker never succeeds in shifting or sharing the blame with anyone else. After all, you can only use excuses so often before anything you say has little or no credibility.

Being new to your position, it's inevitable you will make mistakes as part of the learning process. In fact, long after you have become a veteran boss, an occasional error will occur. This is only natural, since the only way to avoid making errors is not to do anything at all. Whatever you do, right from the start you want to avoid using excuses as much as possible.

Aside from gaining credibility if you don't make excuses, there's an added bonus. If you refrain from using excuses when you're starting out on the job, your boss will view you as a straight-shooter who doesn't offer alibis. These initial impressions tend to stick. Therefore, later on down the line, if you find yourself in a tight predicament where an excuse would come in handy, you're in a good position to use one successfully. It will probably be accepted without skepticism, because you're not in the habit of making excuses.

Furthermore, at the beginning of your supervisory career, your inexperience in itself serves as the basis for mistakes you will make. So for the most part, when something goes wrong acknowledge the error and forget about it. It's admittedly not easy to do this, since there's a tendency to think you're not doing your job right. However, remember you're entitled to a goof here and there while you learn the job. If you keep this in mind, it helps resist the impulse to look for an alibi.

In the initial stages of your job, a good boss will go out of his or her way to shield you from any potential criticism as a result of errors you make. When this happens, be sure to express your thanks and reassure your boss the same mistake won't be repeated again.

Although accepting your own errors is one thing, taking the blame for someone else's is a different cup of tea. A few people always look for scapegoats when they do something wrong. As a new boss, you're particularly vulnerable to this sort of finger-pointing. For this reason, it's wise to be alert to people trying to blame you for their mistakes. This is most likely to happen with departments you work closely with.

If you are unfairly blamed for something by someone outside your department, the best approach is to assemble any facts to disprove the allegation. Then talk it over with your boss. There's always a temptation to deal directly with the culprit, and this is a viable course of action after you gain experience. However, at the beginning of your tenure there are too many unknowns, such as office politics, that make a direct confrontation unwise. Furthermore, you aren't likely to get the accuser to retract his or her allegation, and as an offshoot they may start a backstabbing campaign against you. So despite the unfairness, and your desire for direct retribution, keep it low-key. Besides, your boss is the only one who really counts anyway. As long as your boss knows it wasn't your goof, not much else matters.

## WHEN AND HOW TO TAKE THE BLAME FOR WORKER ERRORS

Along with facing criticism for your own mistakes, you also have to listen to people point the finger at your workers. When this happens, always keep in the back of your mind that any criticism of your workers is equally directed at you. Therefore, by defending your workers, you are also protecting your own interests. This, in itself, is added motivation to stand your ground when another department head decides to berate one or more of your people.

In fact, in a subtle attempt to question your competence in managing your department, other supervisors you do business with may criticize something your workers have done. This can happen when another boss views you as potential career competition. It may seem a little premature since you're a newly appointed boss, but there are people out there who may decide the best time to do a bit of career damage is before you have a chance to prove yourself.

Even when one of your people makes a careless mistake, it's in your best interests to accept the blame as your responsibility rather than casually admit the employee goofed. One of the messages you want to send to your workers is that you're a stand-up boss who will back them up, and fending off outside criticism is a good way to demonstrate this leadership quality.

When your employees see you are willing to defend them, they won't feel they have no one to protect their interests. This is particularly true if your workers don't have union representation. If their immediate boss isn't looking out for them, workers envision the worst. This includes fears of not getting the necessary resources to do their jobs and worries about not getting fair treatment in job assignments. Most of all, they want to be reassured they have someone to fight for them when reassignments or layoffs are planned.

Accepting responsibility when your workers make errors is one of the quickest ways to win their loyalty. It also encourages them to put forth a little bit of extra effort for you when the department is stretched thin trying to cope with an overwhelming workload. Therefore, although it may be easier to nod and agree when someone accuses one of your workers of doing a lousy job, it's a far better investment for the future to defend their performance. Let's look at how to handle such a situation.

## Background

Tom D., who is in charge of shipping and receiving, comes to see a new supervisor named Art about a labeling problem, which he alleges was caused by someone who works for Art. The following conversation takes place.

**Tom D.:** "Hey Art, how's the new job? Boy do you have your work cut out for you."

**Art:** "Why's that Tom?"

**Tom D.:** "I don't want to give you the wrong idea, since you're just getting started on the job, but you have some real duds working for you."

*Art:* "From what I've seen personally, and what I've been told, there's a bunch of hard-working people in my department."

*Tom D.:* "Who's feeding you that garbage? Yeah, well I suppose they're not going to level with you about sticking you with the misfits."

*Art:* "You certainly seem to hold a grudge against my people, Tom. Did something happen in the past that I don't know about?"

*Tom D.:* "They cause me one problem after another with their careless mistakes. If you think I'm making it up, look at this label. There are twenty-five boxes in shipping now, all being sent to the wrong address. Ingrid, one of your foul-ups, put the wrong label on the box. I had to have one of my people change every one of them."

*Art:* (Looks at the label and says,) "What's wrong with the label, Tom?"

*Tom D.:* (Frowning) "I know you're new, so it's understandable, but Ingrid has worked here for years. We've been doing business with this company at least two years and here she goes and puts the wrong address on the label. If Phil who works for me wasn't sharp enough to pick it up, the whole order would have been shipped to who knows where."

*Art:* "Let me check with Ingrid and see what happened."

*Tom D.:* "I'm not waiting for you to check with anyone. The order's going out as soon as my people finish changing the labels. You better get a handle on your people pretty quick. I'm sick of this garbage."

*Art:* "Now wait a minute, Tom. Perhaps a mistake was made. Everyone makes a mistake now and then. That's no reason for you to go around belittling people."

**Tom D.:** (Appearing obviously flustered) "Look, I don't have all day to argue with you. If you can't control your goof-ups, you won't be here long anyway." (He then storms out before Art can say anything further.)

**Art:** (Calls Ingrid into the office) "Ingrid, Tom D. was in here and he claims this label is wrong. Something about the address being different than it usually is. Do you know what he's talking about?"

**Ingrid:** (Looking at the label) "This is right."

**Art:** "Tom said the address was different from the one we've been using for the past couple of years. Is this the same address?"

**Ingrid:** "Oh, doesn't he know these are being shipped to the Kentucky facility instead of California? It's right on the paperwork with the order. We've never shipped there before, but apparently the California plant is at capacity, so the customer is shifting some work to their new plant."

**Art:** "Do you have a copy of the paperwork?"

**Ingrid:** "Sure, it's on my desk. Let's go look at it, and I'll show you what I'm talking about."

**Art:** (Looking at the paperwork) "You're right, Ingrid. I better get Tom right away. He was about to ship everything out to the old address."

**Ingrid:** "That guy thinks he knows everything. He's always blaming someone for something. It serves him right if the truck has already left."

**Art:** "Doesn't sound like you like Tom very much, Ingrid."

**Ingrid:** "You won't either, Art, after you've been here a little longer."

**Art:** (Entering Tom's office) "Hey Tom, did you ship that order yet?"

*Tom:* "It's going out now. What do you want anyway? I already did your work for you changing the labels."

*Art:* "I really appreciate that, Tom. Maybe you could do me one more favor, and change them back to what they were."

*Tom:* "What the heck are you talking about?"

*Art:* (Holding out the paperwork) "If you look at the paperwork, Tom, these are supposed to be shipped to the customer's new plant in Kentucky."

*Tom:* (Looking at the papers) "#$#$% Phil, he screws everything up. Wait here a minute." (Tom leaves and returns in a few minutes) "Hey Art, you didn't tell anyone about this did you? I'd appreciate it if you kept it between us. I'll have the labels changed back and get the shipment out today."

*Art:* "I haven't said anything and I have no problem with forgetting about it. Like I said Tom, everyone makes mistakes. I'm sure we'll have our share in the future. I'll see you later."

COMMENTS: There are several points demonstrated here. First of all, notice how Art defended his employees in the beginning by telling Tom not to belittle people. Errors will be made all of the time, and the goal should be to find out what caused the error and take corrective action. There's nothing to be gained by criticizing the worker. Of course, it's a different story if an employee continually makes careless errors without caring about how the work is done. Then, direct criticism might be appropriate. But run-of-the-mill mistakes shouldn't be an excuse for jumping all over a worker.

Art properly talked to Ingrid afterwards. If it had been an actual error he would have determined with Ingrid why it happened. They jointly could have decided what needed to be done to prevent a repetition of the error, if the nature of the mistake warranted that sort of action.

Art wisely refrained from making a major issue out of Tom's goof. There was nothing to be gained by it, and Art recognized that Tom was the type of person who is always looking for someone to blame. By keeping it quiet, Art may benefit in the future if Tom decides to be more diplomatic in dealing with Art's department. Furthermore, rest assured that everyone in Art's department knew about Tom's goof because Ingrid will probably tell other workers.

So, Art ends up with Tom owing him a favor, and Art's workers know he stands up for them and has confidence in their ability to do their jobs right. All in all, not a bad day for Art as a new supervisor, since it started out looking pretty bleak. Of course, most supervisors won't shoot from the hip with their criticism as Tom did, but whatever the situation may be, it's best to defend your people in a dignified way, and then go about correcting any errors that were made.

*Caution:* Unless it's unavoidable, when an error is made, always try to talk with the employee responsible for the mistake in private. This prevents unnecessary embarrassment for the worker in front of someone from outside your own group. The worker will appreciate this, and it's one more way to demonstrate respect for your subordinates. If you respect them, they in turn will respect you. Furthermore, by doing it this way, you have greater control over the situation, since if someone from outside your group is present they may unfairly criticize your worker. Unfortunately, the worker is likely to be angry at you for being the one who placed him in a position to be embarrassed.

## WHY YOU SHOULDN'T CUT EMPLOYEES SHORT WHEN THEY ASK FOR ASSISTANCE

As busy as you are in your new job, always resist the urge to brush off your workers when they come to you with a problem. This can be done inadvertently, especially if you feel someone else is better qualified to answer the worker's questions. Even if that is true, take the time to listen to what the employee has to say before you refer them elsewhere.

Your workers are looking to you for leadership, and if they feel you have no interest in what they're doing, the quality of their work may suffer. It doesn't take long for employees to develop an attitude of "if the boss doesn't care, why should we?" When that happens, it becomes extremely difficult to turn things around.

Employees will seek assistance from a new boss for various reasons, some valid, some not. These include:

- legitimate requests for assistance;
- testing your knowledge of the job;
- seeking an opportunity to let you know who they are;
- a need for reassurance;
- a test of your openness for discussion; and
- an excuse to talk to you about something else.

Let's look at each of these reasons separately and in greater detail.

## Legitimate Requests for Assistance

Most of the requests for assistance you receive from workers will be justified. The requests will fall into one of two broad categories. First, workers may ask for guidance in how to do a particular aspect of their jobs. It may be a new assignment which they haven't handled before, or a change in how something is done which they don't fully comprehend.

Even though you may not be on the job long enough to be fully grounded in the operational details of how the work in your department is performed, don't quickly refer these requests to someone else. Listen to what the problem is, and give the employee the appropriate guidance if you know the answer yourself. Otherwise, refer them to someone you know who would have the answer. It could be another one of your workers, or perhaps an individual outside of the department.

Whatever you do, don't send workers off on a fishing expedition to seek out a knowledgeable source for themselves. If your response to a legitimate request for assistance is "I don't know. You will have to ask around," this sends a negative message to your subordinates. Doing this repeatedly can destroy your reputation before you have even been around long enough to establish one. Employees will start to think:

- You don't know your job.
- You aren't interested in learning what you don't know.
- You won't help workers when they have a problem.
- You don't care how problems are resolved.

All of these implications are false and are caused by nothing more than what you see as a reasonable way to deal with questions you don't have the answer for. But sending workers off to find the answers on their own can lead to these assumptions in the minds of employees.

When dealing with workers, you always have to remember you're new in the job. Consequently, workers don't know what you're like, so conclusions—right or wrong—will be drawn from your interaction with them in your first few weeks on the job. So even though you're justifiably trying to save time by having the worker seek out the answer, this isn't the best approach to take when you get legitimate requests for help.

The preferred approach is to say, "I'm not sure who would have the answer to that one, but let's find out." This makes you and the employee partners in solving the problem. Of course, where this search ultimately ends depends upon the specifics of the problem. It may be a veteran employee, someone in another department, or your boss. The main thing is, you and the worker jointly sought the answer. Sure, it absorbed a chunk of your time, but look at the advantages compared to the negatives of telling the worker to try and find the answer somewhere else.

- Workers view you as being helpful.

- It demonstrates teamwork in solving problems.

- You learn the answer to something you may need to know in the future.

- Workers quickly realize that even though you're new and may not have the answers, you will do what has to be done to get them.

Most important of all, by working with the employee to seek out the right answer, you avoid the danger of workers going off on their own and not bothering to find out the proper way to do something. Instead, they just finesse their way around the problem without worrying about the end result. This, of course, can lead to subpar work and big problems for you down the road.

Up until now the discussion has focused on handling requests for assistance related to aspects of the employee's job. The second broad category of requests you will get involves administrative matters which it is your responsibility to deal with. These can include all sorts of questions workers might have on policies and procedures, but the bulk of the requests will deal with personnel matters of one kind or another.

With these questions, if you don't have the answer at your finger-tips, tell employees you will find out and let them know. Unlike questions on how to do some aspect of the worker's job, these are subjects which you're expected to have the answer for. Although you don't necessarily have to know every detail of every employee's job, administrative matters are your responsibility. So find the answers out yourself and let the employee know the results.

The only pitfall to watch for here is avoiding the habit of referring the worker to the personnel office or elsewhere for the answer to a question. Workers expect you to be the source of this information. In addition, it's wise to learn the answers to questions in this area, since other workers may have the same or similar questions. Of course, there may be specific instances where it's legitimate to refer the worker to a staff function for answers to questions. But don't do it as a substitute for avoiding leg-work on your own.

## *Testing Your Knowledge of the Job*

As opposed to workers legitimately seeking assistance, you may have one or two people come to you with questions to see how much you know about the specifics of the operation you supervise. Their motives can range from jealousy, if they fancy themselves as being qualified to supervise the group, to nothing more than perverse curiosity. If you're lucky this won't happen at all, but even if it does it's only a one-shot deal if you handle it right.

The specifics of dealing with the worker's request for help will vary. It primarily depends upon the cleverness of workers who ask questions to which they already know the answer. If it's a question you don't know the answer to, proceed exactly as you would if the employee didn't know the answer, since you have no reason to think otherwise. If the employee never admits to knowing the answer, then you have to go the full ten yards to find it.

However, if it's a question the worker should know, say "I'm surprised you don't know how to do that, Helen. You've been around here a long time." This may trigger a response such as "Well, I'm pretty sure I do, but I just wanted to check with you." If that happens, send them back to work with a comment such as "If it's worked this long, there's no reason to do it differently now." You can also refer them to a co-worker: "If you're in doubt, ask Connie. She's very capable." This is a neat way of needling someone when you're convinced they are just trying to test your knowledge of the job.

There's no reason for you to be apologetic about not knowing job-specific answers. First, you're new; second, you're not getting paid to run machines, do clerical work, or whatever the specifics of the operation are. Your job is to run the unit efficiently. Part of that responsibility is to make sure workers know how to do their jobs. When they don't, you have to provide the answers or the training, but you don't have to know every detail.

Don't feel embarrassed about not having the answer to every question that comes your way. As time passes, you'll garner a great deal of knowledge about some of the details, but even when you're a veteran you won't always have an answer to every question. In fact, the higher up the management ladder people go, the less they know about the details and the more they know about where to get the answers if they need them.

*Caution:* Don't automatically assume you're being tested by workers if they ask questions for which they should already know the answer. Sometimes workers want confirmation that what they have been doing meets the approval of a new boss. Usually they will tell you how they handled it in the past, but a few workers who are fearful of being criticized won't say anything. Of course, a good way to avoid this problem is by letting your group know everything should be done as it was previously unless you tell them otherwise.

## Seeking an Opportunity to Let You Know Who They Are

You may find workers ask you for assistance on something that seems obvious. But as the conversation proceeds, the worker will in effect give you his or her employment history, and tell you how much they know about their job. This is nothing more than asking for help as an excuse to sit down and get to know you. Although you may recognize the real reason for seeing you wasn't to get advice, don't arbitrarily rush the worker out of your office.

The sooner employees get to know you, the quicker they will be at ease in discussing legitimate matters relating to work. Besides, this won't happen repetitively, so seize the chance to establish good rapport with the worker. You can also use this as an opportunity to learn about the specifics of the worker's job.

### A Need for Reassurance

You may have workers come to you not so much for assistance as for reassurance. Some people are naturally insecure, and this insecurity is heightened by the arrival of a new boss. Therefore, these workers will ask question after question about whether they are doing their work the way you want it done.

This isn't a major problem the first time or two this takes place. However, this kind of worker will continually pester you if you don't find a way to persuade them otherwise. Nevertheless, you don't want to admonish them, since it's more of a personality quirk than anything else. Beyond that, despite the nuisance it can become, it's reassuring for you to know someone cares enough about their job to ask questions.

Your best bet is to try and build their confidence gradually so they don't feel the need to consult with you on every little detail of their work. However, even if you're ultimately successful, this process will take place over a long time. Therefore, in the meantime try to pair the worker with a knowledgeable subordinate. Be diplomatic about this, and explain that you have complete confidence in the person who you delegate to answer their inquiries. Incidentally, be sure you pick an employee who has the personality and willingness to take on such a task. Otherwise, the person delegated by you may serve to heighten rather than lessen the insecurity of the person they're supposed to be helping.

### A Test of Your Openness for Discussion

One or two workers may approach you with questions as part of a feeling-out process to see what type of boss you are. What they're trying to find out is if you will be the sort of boss they can discuss things with. Workers know from experience that even though managers will say in a meeting they have an open-door policy, this isn't always true. So at the start of your job, you may have people test your sincerity on this issue.

Although after you have established a reputation for openness you might move these people along rather quickly, it pays to be patient at first. Even though the time might apparently be better spent doing other things, look at it as making a contribution toward demonstrating your willingness to listen to what your employees have to say.

## *An Excuse to Talk to You about Something Else*

Sometimes you may find a worker asking for help as a pretext to talking with you about something else. This is frequently the case when the employee is hesitant about raising the subject with you. In fact, in some of these situations you may find yourself in a discussion that's rambling around so much you have to ask if there's anything else bothering the worker. It's at this point that the troublesome issue will be raised.

Some people are more forceful than others, so after you have been on the job a while, you will pretty much know who will be open about what they want to discuss and who will beat around the bush. At least then you will be much more adept at saving time when a less forceful employee isn't getting to the point. Until then, you have to feel your way along in handling these conversations.

## THE CORRECT WAY TO GET A NEW EMPLOYEE OFF AND RUNNING

Before you have even had a chance to get your feet on the ground as a new supervisor, you may find yourself having to assimilate a new employee into your group. This isn't difficult to do, but it can be time consuming. Even though it is an added, perhaps unexpected burden, it's important to do the job right. In fact, how well the new worker does on the job will be influenced by the effort you put into getting the person off to a good start.

The successful introduction of a new worker into your group will start the minute she arrives for the first day on the job. The first thing you want to do is put the person at ease. So spend some time in casual conversation getting to know the person. Incidentally, don't start the first day of a new worker's job by saying how busy it is. The worker will find that out soon enough, so there's no point in adding stress to the typical queasiness a new employee experiences.

In your initial meeting with a new worker there are several points you want to cover; but, since everything is new, it won't all be remembered. So don't overload the worker with information at your first encounter. Incidentally, if you were hired into the company for your job rather than promoted from within, your own indoctrination will be fresh in your mind. Use this as a reference point for covering anything you feel was lacking in your own start.

Probably the best place to begin is with administrative basics that are of major interest to the person. The most fundamental is how and when the person gets paid. Ironically, this is a detail that isn't always covered properly. Sure, the worker is told payday is Thursday or whenever. But what's sometimes left out is the precise mechanism for getting their check: Do you hand them out, or does someone else? In the morning or the afternoon? If there are arrangements for employees to cash their checks, what are they?

Besides pay, give the worker the details on time and attendance, vacations, and so forth. Once those are out of the way, go over the specifics of what the worker will be doing on the job. Reassure the employee that it will take a while to learn the job and not to worry about making mistakes. Most of all, in a convincing fashion, let the employee know you're available at any time to answer questions.

Before the worker has even arrived on the scene, some preparatory groundwork should have been laid. First, the employee's work station should have been set up, so the individual can get off to a clean start without looking for supplies or other resources.

Even more important, you should have made arrangements for the worker to be under the wing of an experienced worker. This person should be given the responsibility for the day-to-day indoctrination and training of the new employee. Selecting someone for this assignment is a critical decision. First of all, be certain the person has the personality to handle this sort of an assignment. You want someone with both the necessary job skills and a positive outlook toward the job. The last thing you need is a disgruntled worker helping to train a new hire. Above all, satisfy yourself the person selected is willing to take on the assignment. If not, the person won't be willing to put more than the minimum effort into the task.

For the first week or two, follow up closely on a daily basis to see how the new hire is doing. In fact, on the worker's first day on the job, take the time to show the person around and introduce her to co-workers. Don't overlook making certain the person is taken care of for lunch. This seems minor, but people have well-established lunch routines at work, and there's a real possibility everyone might take off for lunch without anyone thinking to invite the new arrival. So if lunch arrangements aren't settled, take the employee to lunch yourself.

After a few weeks when you have been able to assess the capabilities of the new worker, you may want to arrange for training in any deficient areas. By that time, you should also have a fair idea of the worker's overall capabilities. Above all, make sure the worker is sufficiently challenged. Sometimes new hires are given lesser assignments until they learn the ropes. There's nothing wrong with that, but once the employee settles into the routine, the workload should be adjusted to a level consistent with the person's abilities. Otherwise, boredom will set in, and this can contribute to the worker being unhappy on the job.

You may find yourself putting a good deal of effort into making a new employee a solid, contributing member of your team. This isn't wasted energy, since good workers are at a premium. Therefore, the more you can do to ensure the satisfactory development of a new hire, the more productive the person will be in the long term. In essence, the initial investment of your time will pay dividends for a long time to come.

On a more personal note, any new employees you acquire after becoming a supervisor won't be comparing you to the previous boss. Since new workers won't have any preconceived notions about how the department should be run, you will be their sole supervisory role model. For this reason, just as a new football coach is judged on his own recruits, your supervisory success will to a large extent be based on how well you develop your new employees.

## WAYS TO SCHEDULE WORK SO SUBORDINATES DON'T GRUMBLE

You may recall the discussion back in Chapter 3 on being fair in making work assignments. It primarily dealt with situations where workers try to avoid unpleasant assignments, as well as the importance of not overburdening your best workers. There's another situation you may have to deal with if your department has a cyclical workload with sharp peaks and valleys in the amount of work. This might be on a year-round basis where the company's business fluctuates widely, or it might be during a specific time-frame, such as the retail peak during the holiday shopping season.

Here, unlike in Chapter 3, the concern isn't how much or how little work or what kind of assignments employees are given. Instead, it's the problem of scheduling employees, which if it isn't done right can create real morale problems. Scheduling difficulties are particularly acute in any business that uses large numbers of part-time or temporary workers. To a lesser degree, work scheduling can cause problems where set hours are worked by everyone. For example, scheduling can be a headache for any supervisor during the summer when vacations can create short-handed situations at work, or even on long holiday weekends. Although a regular work schedule minimizes these problems, it doesn't always eliminate them.

Whatever the specifics of scheduling you personally face, if you have a large number of part-time employees your hassles will be multiplied. To illustrate this, let's look at what happened during a fairly typical period for one supervisor.

## Background

Claire supervises a department in a large discount store. She has four full-time workers, one of whom is the assistant manager, and twelve part-timers who work varied hours.

August 1 — One employee calls in sick, and another calls to say he will be two hours late because of car trouble. Claire asks one part-timer to work two hours to cover one slot, and goes one shift short one worker.

August 2 — One worker doesn't show up, and two others ask to leave early. Claire calls three workers and finally gets one to come in early to cover for the no-show. Claire herself covers for the two workers who have to leave early.

August 3 — One worker says she can no longer work nights because of her family situation. Claire makes a note to just schedule her days.

August 4 — Claire is told one of her full-timers is being transferred to another store. A part-time employee says he is quitting to go back to school.

August 5 — Claire arrives for the late shift to be told two part-timers won't be in, so her crew works two people short.

COMMENTS: Rather than being unusual, this is fairly typical of the scheduling hassles for a business that uses a lot of part-time help. It's unavoidable to be a supervisor in these situations without having to do a lot of juggling to keep your department adequately staffed. Although scheduling can be a nightmare, there are several things you can do to alleviate the problems. First of all, try to put individual workers on set schedules rather than juggle them around from days to nights and the other way around.

This gives employees some certainty as to when they will be working. At the same time, you should reasonably expect the people to work the scheduled hours. When people are on varied schedules, it's more likely they will have conflicts in their personal life which makes it difficult to be at work. It's easy to say fire them and get someone else. But when you're dealing with part-timers, the job doesn't generally have the same significance as a full-time job. Therefore, workers are prone to quitting at the proverbial blink of an eye.

To give yourself some flexibility in coverage for scheduled absences and other short-handed situations, try to find a core of willing part-timers who are willing to work anytime on short notice. You can then use these people to fill-in during the inevitable emergencies. Of course, if you have a core group of full-time workers, schedule them so you have at least one full-timer on any given shift.

Beyond these specifics, there is a related factor that influences the dedication of part-timers, namely how much they like their boss. If you are easy-going and considerate of the special problems associated with part-time workers, the people who work for you are less likely to let you down when you need them on the job. So, if you have part-time workers, don't overlook your personal ability to keep them on the job and productive.

Even if you don't have any part-time worker problems, you may still hit a scheduling fiasco or two at vacation time or around holidays. The basic problem occurs when everyone wants time off at once. All that is required here is consistency on your part. Whatever practice you use to determine who works and who gets the time off, as long as it's fair and consistent, you shouldn't have too many problems. Naturally, one or two people may do a bit of grumbling, but it's usually those who always find something to complain about.

## HOW TO PLAN ON-THE-JOB TRAINING SO IT DOESN'T DISRUPT OPERATIONS

As you become more familiar with the skills of your subordinates, you will notice differences in the abilities of individuals as reflected in their job performance. Part of this variation in worker performance can be attributed to individual initiative, because some people work harder than others. Another factor which may contribute to subpar performance is a lack of adequate training.

Of course, the training needs of your department will be dictated by several considerations. First and foremost is the nature of the work performed by your group. If it involves the continuous introduction of new machinery and technology, a great deal of formal training may be necessary on a fairly regular basis. On the other hand, if the work is relatively routine and little or no complex machinery is involved, not much in the way of formal training will be required.

No matter how extensive the overall training needs of your group may be, however, some amount of on-the-job training will be needed on an individual or group basis. Some of this training can be anticipated. For example, new employees will have to be trained from scratch in their job, unless they have had prior experience elsewhere. Even then, specific procedures and tasks will be new to them.

The introduction of new equipment or changes in existing procedures for doing the work will also involve varying levels of on-the-job training. Finally, as you observe your workers performing their duties over a period of time, you are likely to find workers who need additional on-the-job training to improve their performance. In some cases, workers may never have been trained properly from the outset, while in other instances some bad work habits have been picked up along the way.

Whatever the circumstances in your department, on-the-job training is something you will have to plan for. Most of it will be relatively informal, such as showing a worker an easier way to do a particular task. At other times, as with new employees, more extensive training will be required. The two major problems you face in this area are first, identifying on-the-job training needs, and second, providing the training without disrupting the daily operations of your group.

When you have extensive on-the-job training requirements that consume a good deal of time, try to delegate this duty to one of your experienced workers. This particularly applies to the training needs of new employees. You can't devote the time needed to train a new worker and still adequately perform your supervisory duties. Unless a new employee has extensive experience in the same job with a previous employer, a lot of instructional time will be needed to get the worker up to speed. So your best bet is to delegate the training duties to a subordinate.

In picking an employee to train a new hire, a great deal of care is needed. Otherwise, the training won't be done right and you'll find yourself continually correcting the way the new employee is doing the job. As a result, your time will be nickled and dimed away to the extent that you might as well have done the initial training yourself. To avoid this pitfall pick a trainer who:

- knows the job;
- can communicate easily with others;
- is patient;
- shows a willingness to accept the assignment; and
- will be able to train the worker without falling behind in his or her own job.

Obviously, you may have to make some compromises if someone isn't available who meets all of the qualifications. But to the maximum extent possible, look for a worker who substantially conforms to these requirements.

In terms of routine on-the-job training, as you become familiar with the operation, you will notice certain workers making more mistakes than others. When you see this happening, be careful to accurately pin-point the cause. Be careful not to be overly critical with workers when mistakes occur. It's easy to assume the worker was careless or goofing off, when something else may be responsible for deficient workman-ship. Working conditions or inadequate equipment may be responsible. Then again, maybe the errors were caused by someone else. For instance, poor quality material might be causing an excessive number of defects.

Then again, perhaps the employee is doing something wrong that can be easily corrected. Talk it over with the employee and explain what is being done wrong. Show the employee the right way to do it, but don't automatically assume this will correct the problem. Usually it will, but old habits are hard to break, and it may take several attempts on your part before you succeed in getting the task done the right way. Don't lose your patience when this happens. Nothing discourages employees more when they're trying to learn something than to be yelled at. Always keep in mind that everyone isn't a quick learner, and some workers will require more time than others to get it right.

Aside from individual on-the-job training, you may have instances where everyone has to be trained, such as when a new piece of equip-ment is introduced. In these situations, you're better off having everyone undergo instruction at the same time. This way, there's less chance of some workers receiving less adequate instruction than others. If your work situation makes this impractical, however, don't postpone anyone's training indefinitely. The longer training is delayed, the less likely it will take place at all.

There are some types of on-the-job training which you can hold off on until your group has a less hectic work schedule. By doing this, you can use downtime periods to bring everyone up to speed in their on-the-job training. Instruction in minor procedural changes are the sort of rou-tine training that can be done during slack periods. Incidentally, if the nature of the work in your group has significant peaks and valleys, use the slower periods to train workers to do other jobs in the group if this is feasible. This form of cross-training will ensure you always have someone qualified to fill-in in the absence of a co-worker.

## WHAT YOU CAN AND SHOULD DO WHEN MORALE IS LOW

Shortly after assuming your supervisory position, you may notice the morale isn't good in your department. There can be any number of reasons for this. If it's a company-wide problem, there's little you can do on an individual basis to improve morale. Overall morale problems can be caused by anything from layoffs to employees overworked because of hiring freezes and stringent cost controls.

If it's obvious this is the case, then mention it to your boss and see what sort of feedback you get about whether any top-management initiatives are being taken to improve the situation. Even when you can't identify the cause of low morale, your boss may be able to fill you in as to the possible cause. This may not always happen though, since the higher up on the management ladder people are, the less likely they are to be aware of morale problems.

Another reason you find morale low upon your arrival may be the result of the actions of the prior supervisor. If things didn't go smoothly with the previous boss, you may find workers not particularly motivated when you arrive on the scene. Although inheriting a morale headache because of poor supervision by your predecessor isn't the best of situations, there is a positive aspect to it. Once workers see they have a new boss who is concerned about them, morale should slowly improve.

Although you might think about mentioning overall morale at a meeting with your group, this probably isn't the best approach. After all, no employee wants to tell the boss what's wrong in front of everyone. The best way to approach the problem is on an individual basis. Feel your employees out in casual conversation. As they get to know you, the chances of them leveling with you about what's wrong will increase.

You may find workers giving you different reasons as to what's bothering them, since they are looking at their problems from an individual basis. For example, where a long-time worker may be concerned about job security, a younger person might be more upset about a lack of advancement opportunities. In fact, the diversity of views may surprise you. Let's look at a typical example of this.

## Background

There has been widespread publicity in the media about forthcoming employee cutbacks at a large manufacturer with facilities in several different locations. Nothing has been announced formally within your company, although rumors are widespread and morale is understandably low. Elaine supervises a department in one of the plants, and in discussions with workers receives the following feedback from individuals on their personal concerns.

### Job security

Frank, a twenty-year veteran of the company says, "I'm concerned if the cuts are deep enough, I'll be hit. Where else could I get a job paying these wages? And I'm too old to start all over."

### Loss of benefits

Alice is worried about losing an extensive package of company-paid benefits, since her husband is self-employed and they could not afford the cost of replacing medical, dental, and life insurance and other benefits.

### Optimism

José isn't worried at all, since he thinks the cuts will be made at other plants.

### Restrained glee

Joe is twenty-one years of age and has been on the job two years. He would love to be laid off so he could spend the summer hanging out with his friends.

### Future opportunity

Carol has been with the company four years and is in line for a promotion. She is afraid that even if she survives a layoff, her future with the company won't be bright.

As you can see here, though the cause of the morale problem is the same, the forthcoming layoffs affect people differently. Whenever your group has a morale problem that is caused by factors beyond your control, do your best to project a positive attitude, since your confidence may help in picking up the spirits of some of your workers. Conversely, if you appear glum, it's almost guaranteed to make a bad situation even worse.

Nevertheless, don't attempt to downplay an obvious problem, since workers will resent it. It also helps employees if you're willing to listen while they vent their frustrations. Even when times are tough, if you are respected by those who work for you, they will give you a greater level of effort than a boss who simply shrugs and says, "There's no point in talking to me, since I can't do anything about it."

Of course, if the morale problem is localized to your group, you should make every effort to eliminate the cause if it's feasible to do so. Sometimes you may find a worker's performance slipping, and after talking with the individual discover the worker is upset about something you're not aware of. It may be a pre-existing condition which you inherited because the previous boss wasn't accessible or didn't place any emphasis on worker concerns. This isn't unheard of, as some managers have an attitude which implies "You're getting paid for doing the job, so don't gripe."

You may discover that your inexperience inadvertently caused a morale problem. For example, perhaps you were assigning work randomly, when previously workers handled certain jobs. Sometimes someone will bring something of this nature to your attention, but that isn't always so. Don't be afraid to reverse a decision if you find out it wasn't the best move to make. A boss who is willing to admit he was wrong will always have better channels of communication with subordinates, since people know what they say isn't going to be ignored. Therefore, by holding open and frank discussions with your subordinates you can bring hidden problems to the fore and resolve them. Even when a problem can't be resolved to the satisfaction of workers, your willingness to listen to their opinions can turn things around and improve morale.

## THE RIGHT WAY TO DEAL WITH CHRONIC COMPLAINERS

One thing that can get under your skin faster than anything else is a chronic complainer. To make matters worse, as a new boss you're a prime target for a constant griper. Yet until you get to know the people who work for you, it's hard to give one of these types the brush-off. In the first place, you may not be able to tell immediately if the gripes are legitimate. Furthermore, you don't want to be seen as a boss who isn't willing to listen to what workers have to say. At least initially you may have to suffer through a few sessions of griping and groaning. But once you peg someone as a constant complainer, there are some measures you can take to solve the problem.

The starting point for any complaint is to determine whether it has any validity. On occasion, even a chronic griper may have a legitimate beef. If the complaint is genuine, see what can be done to resolve the problem. There will be occasions when a workable solution can't be found. When this happens, explain to the worker why the complaint can't be resolved.

When you are faced with a chronic complainer, always try to figure out the basis for the constant griping. It may have little or nothing to do with the job. Some people are never able to command any attention, and complaining may be a way for them to get someone to listen to them. This is fine and you may even be sympathetic, but there are limits to the amount of time you can spend as an amateur counselor. So even here, you will eventually have to learn to cut the person short. There are a variety of techniques you can use to do this. Some of them will work better than others in certain situations. A few tried and true methods are the following:

- Give them a job to do whenever they bother you. This makes you a poor choice for future complaints.

- Try teaming them up with another worker who is a good listener. While one talks, the other can listen.

- Refer them to someone else to handle their complaint. This is a great way to get even with people.

- Have them put complaints in writing, but make sure the person doesn't like to write as much as he likes to talk.

- Try out-complaining them. Even gripers don't like to listen to complaints.

- Go about your business and let them keep talking. They may not take the hint, but at least you'll get your work done.

- Tell it like it is. Simply say, "I'm too busy to talk now."

- Give them a time limit. For example, say, "I'm busy. You have five minutes, Sue."

✎ Leave whenever they show up. Go anywhere, but walk fast since they'll probably tag along.

Even the most hardened complainers will eventually find an easier target once they get the message that you don't want to hear their constant carping. You may feel reluctant to give them the cold shoulder, but it's certainly preferable to falling far behind in your work. Besides, while you're listening to foolish complaints, other workers may be left waiting to see you for legitimate reasons. Therefore, at times you will have to draw the line with constant complainers, or you will find yourself griping about not getting your job done.

## HOW TO BE A BOSS WITHOUT BEING BOSSY

One of your personal concerns as a first-time supervisor may be how you can act with the authority of a boss without being dictatorial and demanding. Some bosses manage primarily by using the concept of fear. In other words, "do what I say, or else." However, this sort of leadership isn't going to spur workers to do anything more than the minimum necessary to avoid the wrath of the boss. By the same token, you will at times have to make tough decisions and make them stick. So you can't run your department as a free-wheeling democracy with everyone getting to vote on what gets done next.

Nevertheless, with a little practice and foresight, you can develop a management style which allows you to exercise leadership without wielding a big stick. The most basic consideration for being a thoughtful boss starts with your attitude. When dealing with workers, ask yourself these two questions:

✎ If I were the worker, would I want to be treated this way?

✎ Would I act this way toward my boss or other senior managers who control my destiny at work?

If you can answer these questions with a yes, you're on the right track to showing the sort of self-restraint that's sometimes needed when dealing with subordinates. In fact, nothing more difficult than being polite is a step in the right direction. Look at the difference in the following requests by a supervisor and think of the worker's reaction.

*Poor:*     "I need this done right away."

*Good:*     "Can you help me out, Charlie? I need this information by noon for the boss."

COMMENTS: The most important difference here is that the first comment is phrased like a direct order, while the second is in the form of a request. You sound bossy in the first request and solicitous in the second. The second request is personalized by addressing the worker by name, and it also explains the urgency of the request. It helps when you make a request to explain the purpose. In the second example, if Charlie is busy, he can understand why it's necessary to do what you want promptly because it's for your boss. Not knowing this, he might think "If she needs it right away, why doesn't she do it herself? Doesn't she see I'm busy?"

Some people might think if you ask for something by phrasing it as a request rather than an order the worker will be more inclined to refuse. This isn't apt to happen, since the worker recognizes you're the boss and will respond accordingly. But even assuming it wasn't true, or you have someone who decides to challenge you, you haven't lost anything. If necessary, you can always fall back on being direct about wanting a worker to do something for you. What you're striving for is to make this the exception rather than the rule when dealing with your subordinates.

Naturally, there will be times when you are abrupt in talking with an employee. It's not always easy to keep your composure when it's busy and you're overburdened with work. Don't worry about this, since workers will see this as an exception to your normal behavior and not think anything about it. As a general rule, strive to be polite and thoughtful in dealing with others, and for the most part they will reciprocate. Of course, there will be occasions when you have to be fairly blunt. When a worker isn't following the rules and requires some form of supervisory discipline, don't hesitate to assert your authority. Workers who are doing their jobs will respect your need to be firm. It will send the necessary message to the one or two people who respond only when forced to by a boss who knows when it's time to be tough.

# Chapter Ten

# PERSONAL ASPECTS FOR SUPERVISORY SUCCESS

*O*ne of the keys to supervisory success is learning how to operate within your own limitations. You will find that it's impossible to please everyone all of the time. For this reason, it's important to know how to handle the priorities of your job. You also will have to justify many of your decisions to your boss, as well as avoid overreacting when workers make mistakes.

Then, there are some basic measures that will make your job less difficult, such as establishing a daily routine and not taking disappointments personally. You also have to be persuasive in making your case for additional help when you need it. Otherwise, you'll always be operating under the added stress of too few people doing too much work. This chapter discusses how to deal with these varied issues.

## HOW TO AVOID AND COPE WITH PANIC SITUATIONS

Back in Chapter 7 there was a discussion of the steps to take when a crisis erupts and your boss comes running with a top-priority job. Here the focus is on avoiding the run-of-the- mill panics that occur periodically. Some of these panics are perpetual, such as a push to meet end-of-the-month production quotas or the hassle of quarterly inventories. In other instances, the panic is a one-time event in response to some sort of extraordinary request. No matter what sort of operation you supervise, an occasional panic to get something done in a hurry is a virtual certainty.

What's also a certainty is after you have experienced your first such panic, you will probably vow to do something so you won't be caught in the same bind twice. As you go on to other tasks, the project that had everyone running around like chickens with their heads cut off will be forgotten. Then, when pandemonium hits again, you will remember your forgotten vow.

Any of these pressure-cooker projects which are repetitive in nature can be made more manageable with a little bit of planning. Therefore, when you encounter your first one, as you're coping to meet commitments keep an open mind about what you can do to make the task easier the next time around. Ask yourself questions such as:

- What can I do to be better prepared for this situation when it happens again?

- What actions can I take on my own to get ready?

- Will I need assistance from people outside of my group?

- Is anything being done this time that can be eliminated in the future?

- Is there an easier way to handle this project?

- Is someone or something in particular causing this panic?

- Is this a self-induced panic?

Let's look at how you can respond to these questions to minimize future crunch-time problems. When you have the same work demands causing periodic panics to meet a deadline, such as meeting production or sales quotas, much of this is beyond your control. However, even here you can anticipate possible demands being placed upon your department at specific times, such as the end of every month. Knowing this, you can take steps to be ready when you're called upon to swing into action to meet an extraordinary workload within a short period of time.

For example, don't approve time off for employees during the period of anticipated heavy activity. Mark these times in your calendar so you don't inadvertently grant leave ahead of time. Otherwise, you may put yourself in the embarrassing position of having to cancel an employee's leave at the last minute. If it's feasible, see if you can schedule your work so the department won't be busy with other chores when the panic is due to hit.

In some situations, you may be able to do work ahead of time to prepare for a periodic deadline that always finds you scrambling to finish something in a hurry, for example, recurring reports that always seem to come just when you're busy doing something else. Although you may not be able to complete the report until the last minute, much of the preparatory work can be done ahead of time. This is one of those easy pressure relievers people tend to overlook in any facet of their lives. If you don't think this is true, visit any post office on April 15 as people rush to file their income tax returns.

Some recurring panic situations may require assistance from outside your department. If so, try to coordinate with these people beforehand so they will be ready to furnish the necessary assistance. This is particularly true if you can't finish the task without the necessary support. The need for planning here is even greater if the people furnishing assistance aren't under any pressure to complete the task you need help with. In fact, they may have higher-priority work from their perspective, so if you're going to get their help, you'd better schedule it before the last minute.

The first time you face a pressure situation which you know will happen again, look for nonessential work involved in the project to see if it can be eliminated the next time around. Being new on the job, you're well situated to look at things from a fresh vantage point. Often, many tasks are performed in a certain way only because this develops as a habit over a period of time. So you may be able to determine ways to cut corners to save some work the next time around.

Besides eliminating unnecessary effort to help cope with panic situations, try finding easier ways to do the work. Can aspects of the job be combined, done by other departments, or somehow made simpler? The specifics will vary, but it's something that should always be kept in mind when you're dealing with a dreaded project.

There are some panic situations that exist only in the eyes of the beholder. A few people treat everything they do in life as a last-minute, panic-provoking crisis. You may have the unfortunate experience of having to do work for people who operate in this fashion. Of course, just because they are in a panic doesn't mean you have to react the same way. However, watch the political angle here, since if higher-ups are convinced that what someone is doing is top priority, your department has to respond as if it is—even though you know otherwise.

The easiest form of panic situation for you to resolve is one that is self-induced. Being new, you naturally want to do your best to impress others. In doing this, you may unwittingly place unneeded pressure on yourself to do more than is necessary. As a result, you may treat routine requests as priorities that require immediate action. To avoid this, you have to learn to establish priorities in terms of your work, the subject of the next section.

## SOME SIMPLE TACTICS FOR HANDLING THE PRIORITIES OF YOUR JOB

Once you have mastered the details of your work, you will readily know the priorities to assign to individual tasks. How to sort these priorities out was covered back in Chapter 2 in the topics on deciding what is and isn't important, and what to do first. Beyond the specifics of determining the priority of individual assignments, there are a number of general considerations in establishing where you will focus your energies to do your job most efficiently.

As you may have already discovered, there's no end to the amount of work available to fill your work day. You will find as time passes and you become more experienced that all the routine tasks become easier. You may also discover additional duties you have to perform that you weren't even aware of when you first started work. In addition, as you become more competent, your boss is going to give you added responsibilities. As a result, you'll never catch a breather unless you adopt some strategies for coping with an endless flow of work.

Let's look at some tactics to help put the overall burden of your job in perspective.

## 1. Recognize There Will Always Be Work to Do

You will become extremely frustrated if your goal is to master your job to the point where you actually have time to put your feet up on the desk and grin at an empty in-basket. This is a fantasy similar to winning millions of dollars in a lottery and retiring. In fact, your chances of winning the lottery are probably better. This isn't to imply that there won't be times when you can take a break. There will be—and there should be—since you have to allow yourself periods of relative calm to recharge your batteries. However, there will always be work waiting for you, whether you're returning from a ten-minute coffee break or a two-week vacation.

This isn't a problem unless you make it one. If you're willing to recognize there will always be a backlog of work, you won't stress yourself out trying to do everything at once. Concern yourself with what you're working on without worrying about anything else. This is the most important priority you have in terms of dealing with the realities of your job. Once you're able to accept the fact you'll always have something else needing to be done, then you'll be better able to concentrate on the priority of the moment without worrying about what you have to do tomorrow.

## 2. Do what Counts and Ignore Everything Else

Don't lock yourself into jumping back and forth from one thing to another. The end result is that nothing gets finished. At any given time, there's only one important priority task for you to finish. Not so, you may say, as you sit with three jobs to do, all with tight deadlines. Remember, tasks aren't always as important as they seem, and they're seldom as crucial as someone else says they are.

The longer you're on the job, the better you will be able to recognize those tasks which aren't anywhere near the priority status someone claims. Always keep in mind that what's top priority with someone else, may be very low on your scale of what gets done next. You will run into people who allege everything they bring to you is urgent. This is the way some people operate, and once you learn who they are, it will be easier to ignore their demands.

Of everything you have to do at any given time, one task will take precedence over others. Work that one through and then move on to the next, or you may find yourself doing a little on both and finishing neither on time. Naturally, there is sometimes work that can be done concurrently, but don't lose sight of the number-one priority of the moment.

### 3. Don't Waste Time on Hopeless Tasks

You will occasionally find yourself with an assignment that wouldn't matter much if it were never done. However, it's a requirement given to you by your boss, or some staff function, so it has to be completed. That it does, but you shouldn't spend more time on it than is necessary to minimally comply with the request. In fact, many tasks of this nature are great candidates to be delegated to a subordinate. They are low-risk in terms of receiving criticism if not completed properly, so there's little to be lost in farming it out to one of your workers.

### 4. Always Look for Shortcuts

Whenever you're tackling any task always look for quicker and better ways to complete the chore. This is particularly true when your workload is at a peak. Often things are done as a matter of habit, with little thought given to simplifying the job. You have a distinct advantage here, since being new on the scene you won't be conditioned to do tasks a certain way. Therefore, it will be easier for you to be objective about looking for and using time-saving shortcuts.

### 5. Let Your Boss Know You're Overburdened

There's always the tendency to follow the path of least resistance when it comes to handing out work. Therefore, once you have conquered the fundamentals of your job, you may find your boss giving you more and more work. At first, the boss may be considerate enough to inquire if you're up to handling the chore. Something may be said such as, "Are you ready to try something new?" You, of course, will say, "Sure."

Once you successfully complete that assignment, more will follow. This is likely to continue up to the point where you eventually have to tell the boss you're overburdened. Don't be hesitant about doing this, since the alternative may be assignments not finished on time. At that point, it sounds like a shallow excuse if you blame it on too much work. The obvious response to this by your boss would be, "Why didn't you tell me you were busy? I could have given that job to someone else." So tell the boss beforehand and save yourself the embarrassment of looking foolish.

You can use a little finesse when you decide to let the boss know you can't handle anything else. Say something such as, "I'll do this project if you want boss, but I don't know if I'll be able to finish it on time with all of the other work I have." Even if you get the assignment, you have covered yourself if it isn't completed on schedule. However, generally a boss will recognize your plight and find someone else for the task. Incidentally, when you let the boss know you have too much work, be prepared to prove it with facts.

## SEVERAL EASY WAYS TO JUSTIFY DECISIONS TO YOUR BOSS

Being a supervisor will give you the opportunity to make decisions on your own. That's the good news. From a negative aspect, it gives your boss an opportunity to second-guess every decision you make. That isn't likely to happen, but there will be times when your boss asks the question, "Why did you do that?" This means you have to be ready to justify what you have done. Even when your boss doesn't agree with you, if you offer good reasons for what you did, it probably won't be criticized.

There are several general ways to justify decisions aside from those which apply to any specific action you take. These include the following:

### 1. It Was the Best Available Choice

Tell the boss you considered several alternatives and after doing so decided the course of action you took was the most practical. As the basis for choosing the option you did, try to show how it saved time and money, required fewer resources, or whatever. If you can't do that, perhaps you can claim it was the choice that offered the least potential for future problems such as customer complaints or whatever else could occur from the action you took.

## 2. Precedent

The action you took may have been how the particular situation was handled in the past by your predecessor. This doesn't necessarily preclude your boss from asking you about it. For one thing, your boss isn't going to be aware of why every decision was made the way it was by everyone working for him. Then again, he might know the reason, but be asking the question to test your understanding of the situation. Don't take offense at this, since your boss may be making sure his new supervisor doesn't make a careless mistake. After you've been on the job for a few months, you'll notice considerably less interest in your reasons for doing something.

## 3. Necessity

Sometimes you may have to do something a little out of the ordinary to get the job done. For example, perhaps you skipped a required approval, or cut corners somewhere along the way. If you're questioned about this, be ready to prove it was necessary to meet an urgent deadline. Even when your boss doesn't agree with what you did, you won't be criticized if your actions were preferable to being late in completing the work.

## 4. "No One Told Me Differently"

In the beginning, you're bound to make a few bad decisions owing to your inexperience. Rather than fumbling around for a feeble excuse if the boss criticizes you for doing something wrong, just admit you weren't aware of the proper way to proceed. Your boss will probably tell you what should have been done and say "Do it this way the next time." Needless to say, make sure you do, or your boss won't be as considerate in the future.

*Caution:* If you had prior experience with another company in the type of work you're now supervising, never use this as the basis for justifying something you did. There's nothing that can get under a boss's skin faster than having someone say, "I did it that way because that's how they do it at Acme." If a boss questions a decision, you will never justify it on that basis. It's the old "if it wasn't done here, it wasn't done right" attitude, and right or wrong, it doesn't pay to argue the merits.

## How to Think Like a Worker And Act Like a Boss

Somewhere along the line before you became a supervisor, you may have had a chance to experience first-hand how unpleasant some bosses can be to work for. You may have vowed then to never be like that when you became a boss. If so, you now have the opportunity to fulfill that pledge. If you haven't already done so, you will soon discover that it isn't easy to supervise other people. And when a boss does get upset, it's not always the boss who is to blame. A troublesome worker or two can drive a boss to distraction just as easily as an ornery boss can aggravate workers. Nevertheless, despite the work pressures, personality differences, and other work-related obstacles, it's both possible and practical to strive to be a supervisor who both gets the job done and is respected by his or her subordinates.

One key to straddling the line between being a demanding boss who is disliked and a pushover who isn't respected is to look at decisions you make from a worker's perspective. This isn't hard to do, especially since you're starting out new to the supervisory ranks and haven't had time to become cynical. However, it does require you to think before you act. That in itself isn't as simple as it sounds when you're under pressure trying to do ten things at once. But even though you may not always have time to think about worker reactions, if you keep this idea in mind, you will avoid most of the blunders that disrupt a good working relationship with your subordinates.

To be successful at thinking like a worker and acting like a boss, you have to be able to anticipate how workers will react when you ask them to do something. By doing this you avoid careless actions that upset workers, such as asking an already overburdened worker to do something when co-workers are sitting on their duffs. It can be summed up by the old cliché, "Think before you act." This sounds good, but it's not always easy to do when you're busy, so if you're not conscious of the need to view your actions from the eyes of your workers, it isn't likely to happen.

It's worth looking at a few examples of routine requests that can cause trouble if they're made without anticipating the worker's reaction.

| | |
|---|---|
| *Supervisory Action:* | A worker walks by the boss's office and the boss says, "Hey, Alex, since you're going that way, would you drop this off in Joe's office." |
| *Worker's Thoughts:* | "What's he think I am, a courier? I can't even go to the bathroom without being asked to do something. You'd think I had nothing better to do." |
| *Rationale:* | The worker is unhappy because he is (1) busy, (2) doesn't like being treated like a messenger, and (3) thinks the boss should do his own chores. Circumstances vary, and although you can't spend your working day analyzing possibilities, little spur-of-the-moment requests can antagonize people. Under slightly different conditions the worker wouldn't have objected. For example, if Alex had stopped in to chat with the boss, and when he was leaving the boss had said, "Say Alex, if you're going by Joe's office, could you drop this off for me? No problem if you can't," the request would be taken in stride. |
| *Solution:* | Try to avoid making casual requests without thinking about the implications. Workers resent it when they perceive a boss to be asking them to do something because it's beneath the dignity of the boss to do it. |
| *Supervisory Action:* | The supervisor says to Marlene, who is the best worker in the group, "Will you hold off on what you're doing, and help Barbara out? She's way behind in her work." |
| *Worker's Thoughts:* | "Am I getting Barbara's salary too? I'm asked to help everyone out around here. Why doesn't the boss get people to do their jobs?" |
| *Rationale:* | The worker isn't pleased about having to drop her own work to help someone who |

works at a slower pace. The worker also feels that she is penalized rather than rewarded for excelling.

*Solution:* It's frequently simpler to take the easy way out to get work done rather than dealing with a problem. For this reason, hard workers are sometimes asked to pick up the slack for their slower peers. This situation should have been handled by finding out why Barbara is behind in her work rather than by having Marlene help her out. Workers won't resent pitching in to help others if it's a one-time deal. But if they sense they're being taken advantage of, it will create resentment. Always think about the fairness issue when you ask workers to do something extra.

*Supervisory Action:* Peggy asks for Friday off and the boss says, "I'm sorry, Peggy, but I can't spare you."

*Worker's Thoughts:* "He could spare Joe last Friday, though. This guy plays favorites like you wouldn't believe."

*Rationale:* People make comparisons, so if one worker's request is granted and then a similar request is denied, it's virtually automatic that the person rejected will think favoritism is the reason.

*Solution:* If the supervisor had thought about this from the worker's perspective, he would have explained to Peggy why she couldn't have that Friday off. Knowing there was a valid reason for the denial, she wouldn't have been perturbed. The boss could have said, "I'm sorry Peggy, but it's the end of the month and production goals have to be met. Therefore, I can't give anyone time off this week." When you normally agree to something, and then circumstances require denial of a request, an explanation will prevent dissatisfaction.

| | |
|---|---|
| *Supervisory Action:* | Marsha is working at her desk when Shelby, her supervisor comes by, throws some papers on her desk, and says, "You made three errors yesterday. What's wrong with you?" Shelby then stalks off without waiting for a reply. |
| *Worker's Thoughts:* | "Why didn't she give me some training? All she does is criticize people." |
| *Rationale:* | No one likes to be scolded, particularly if they think they don't deserve it. Workers won't respond well to negative criticism, so it serves no useful purpose. |
| *Solution:* | The supervisor should have refrained from being critical and instead asked if Marsha was having a problem with her work. A discussion should have followed to find out why mistakes were being made and what could be done to correct the problem. |

In these examples, as in many other circumstances, it's not difficult to anticipate the reaction of a worker in given situations. However, it does require an awareness of the possibilities. Carelessness can also creep into the process, since in most instances workers aren't going to express their feelings to the supervisor. So if you're not thinking about how a worker may feel about something you say or do, the damage can be done without you realizing it.

**Note:** Although it's important to be sensitive to employee reactions, this shouldn't be the overriding factor in your decision making. Some people will be negative about anything, while at other times tough but fair decisions won't sit well with workers. As long as you're reasonably sensitive in your day-to-day dealings with subordinates, you won't have problems in this area.

## WHY IT'S IMPORTANT NOT TO OVERREACT WHEN SUBORDINATES MAKE MISTAKES

Obviously you want to get off to a good start as a boss, so anything that goes wrong may bother you. Furthermore, being new, you have to rely on your workers to a larger degree than a more experienced boss. After all, until you fully understand the operation you're now supervising, it will sometimes be hard to figure out if everything is going as smoothly as it should be. This feeling of not having full control of the situation can put you on edge. As a result, without meaning to, you may find yourself snapping at workers when mistakes are made. Even if you don't lose your temper, you may be overly cautious in checking to be sure employees are doing their jobs right.

All of this is well intentioned on your part, but your subordinates won't see it that way. From their vantage point you'll be seen as an insecure boss who has no confidence in their ability. As they see it, since you have no confidence in them, there's no reason for them to have any confidence in you. This leads to an atmosphere where workers decide you won't tolerate mistakes, so they will take various measures to avoid your oversight and criticism.

Your workers may work more slowly so as to better avoid the possibility of even an occasional error. This may indeed reduce the number of mistakes your workers make, but it will also blow a huge hole in the productivity of your group. If production goals, or any other quantitative measures, are used to determine the productivity of your group, the yardsticks by which output is measured will plummet. Even if the operation you supervise isn't subject to these kind of measurements, the drop in performance will be obvious. All of this means, you can expect to hear your boss say, "What's the matter with your group? Their performance is going down the tubes."

What do you do then? You may decide that since you were reprimanded, you better lay the law down to your people. You tell them they better pick up the pace pretty darn quick, or else. What happens next?

They either speed it up and errors resume, or they ignore you and give every appearance of working harder without actually doing so. To make a long story short, you're caught in a no-win situation. As a result, productivity will remain low until you find and cure the cause of the mistakes.

Workers slowing down to avoid your wrath is just one of the possible outcomes if you overreact when mistakes are made. It's also likely workers won't let you know about potential problems for fear of having you blame them. As a result, it isn't always easy to track and correct serious problems. Let's look at an example.

## Background

Jack, a supervisor who is vocal in criticizing anyone who makes mistakes, is called to the working area by a subordinate. Let's pick it up there.

*Jack:*   "What's the problem, Hank?"

*Hank:*   (Pointing at a machine) "It's gone on the fritz again. We're out of action until it's repaired."

*Jack:*   "This is the fourth time in two months that machine has failed. I'm going to get it replaced. In the meantime, work on a job that doesn't require you to use that thing."

A week later a new machine is in place, and within a month the new machine breaks down twice, causing work delays. Shortly after that, Jack gets a transfer to another department. Bob, a newly promoted supervisor, takes Jack's place. Within a matter of weeks the workers discover Bob is the type of supervisor who looks for answers instead of criticizing people when something goes wrong. About then, the infamous machine breaks down again, and Bob talks to Hank about it.

*Bob:*   "Hank, you know this job better than anyone. Got any ideas as to why the machine keeps going down?"

*Hank:*   "Well, I'm not positive, Bob, but I think I know what the problem is. I've been keeping track, and whenever we run over a hundred units at one time it starts to overheat and then it fails. It has never broken down when we run jobs of less than a hundred or so. I think it's just not built to run large-quantity orders."

**Bob:** "I wonder why the manufacturer didn't tell us that?"

**Hank:** "Well for one thing, they don't make larger machines, so maybe they're happy as it is. Then again, maybe they don't realize it either."

**Bob:** "I'm going to see about getting a heavy-duty replacement from another supplier. I'm sure glad we have you around here, Hank."

The machine is replaced and the problem is eliminated.

COMMENTS: Hank never bothered to tell Jack about his suspicions because he didn't want to be criticized. He knew if the machine was replaced and it didn't solve the problem, he would be the one to take the blame. Furthermore, since Jack was always yelling at workers, none of them were in the least bit interested in helping to solve problems.

In summary, there's little to be gained and much to be lost by jumping all over people when something goes wrong. Instead, take occasional errors in stride and work with the employee to determine the cause. Then take whatever corrective action is necessary to prevent it from happening again.

*Note:* You may run into a situation that does require you to be firm with a worker about errors. For instance, if you have an out-and-out screw-up who continually makes careless mistakes, you have little choice but to tell him to get with the program. However, this should be the exception rather than the rule.

## How to Ask for—and Get—Additional Help

As was mentioned in the section on getting the resources you need back in Chapter 8, your boss may try to accommodate you when you ask for necessary equipment and supplies. However, when it comes to asking your boss for additional people, you have a much longer road to travel. Hiring more help is a last resort for any cost-conscious company, and every manager involved in approving such requests is ready to say no before, during, and after your pitch for another person.

In any event, you have to supervise the unit for a few months before you can accumulate enough evidence to justify why you need another person. In the unlikely event it's obvious by the end of your first week on the job, the boss won't listen to you until you've been around long enough to have some credibility.

Adding to your woes is your status as a new supervisor, since veteran supervisors may also be pleading for help. Their comments to your mutual boss will be similar to these:

- ✆ "I've been asking for help for a year, so I should get it before anyone else."

- ✆ "She hasn't been here long enough to know whether she really needs help."

- ✆ "He hasn't learned how to manage that group yet, or he wouldn't be asking for help."

After all, when bosses aren't rushing to approve new job slots, there's going to be plenty of competition fighting for any opening that may be approved. All of this means if you need help, you will not only have to go to great lengths to prove it, but you'll also need better justification than anyone else. So where do you start?

Once you decide you need another worker, plan to spend some time campaigning with your boss. Mention the fact casually whenever you can, without actually making a specific request. All you're doing here is planting the seed which you hope to harvest later. If you work up justification and present it to your boss without any prior mention, you're guaranteed a negative answer. Since you have been turned down after presenting a full-blown case for approval, you won't have any ammunition left for future requests. It's far preferable to hear your boss tell you there's no hope for help several times. Then, when you do present your hard justification to prove your need it will have a greater impact.

This raises the question as to the best way to justify a request for an additional worker. Simply put, facts work best, but not just any old facts. What you have to prove to the boss is how hiring someone will benefit the company from a profit-and-loss standpoint. This is crucial, since if the boss does go along with your request, he has to get approval up the line, and the higher you go in management, the broader the outlook.

The "big-picture" people at the top are interested in the bottom line: profits. You get profits by making more money than you spend. When you add a worker, you're spending money for salary, fringe benefits, training, and so forth. This means you have to show where spending the money for another worker will make even more money for the company. Equally effective is to be able to show that adding a worker will save the company money over and above the cost of the new employee.

By this time you may be thinking this is too complicated. It isn't, but it will take some time and thought. However, the advantages for you will be worth the effort. First of all, it gives you the edge over veteran supervisors who don't even think of this angle. Beyond that, it creates a real impression on your boss and everyone up the line who reviews your analysis. This is the sort of stuff that gets you moving toward your next promotion even before you have settled into your current position. Most important of all, it stands the best chance of getting you the help you need. This in the long run means you will have fewer job pressures and probably won't have to work as long or hard to get the job done.

As the basis for your justification, work up some figures to show how adding a worker will increase output. Alternatively, if your group has been continually working overtime, you can show it's cheaper to hire someone full-time than pay the overtime costs. You may also be able to show how working extensive overtime results in lower output per worker due to fatigue or causes costly mistakes. The possibilities will vary with the specifics of the work your group does. The important point is to quantify what you do in dollar terms, since that's what will sell your pitch.

The figures you use shouldn't be hard to come by, and you probably have many of them in the numerous reports you have to do as part of your job. Crank the raw data into a spreadsheet on a computer and see what you can come up with. If juggling numbers isn't your strong suit, get a friend to help you out. The better your presentation is, the stronger the chances of it meeting with success.

You may be wondering what happens down the road if you can't prove your assumptions panned out in terms of making money or saving money. Don't worry about it, since no one will ever ask. People do this day in and day out to justify all sorts of financial transactions, and the likelihood of the future facts jibing with the current assumptions aren't much better than none to nil. There's a certain mindset when it comes to numbers that influences people to accept them as fact when they're only projections, and you can use this to your advantage.

**Note:** Although the discussion in this topic has focused on strategies for hiring additional people when you need them, there are other times you may have to use similar tactics. For instance, if an employee quits, you may be told the worker isn't going to be replaced. An equally bad scenario is if your boss tells you someone is being transferred out of your unit to a group that needs the worker more. Here too, you have to swing into action and prove your need for the employee. The better you are at proving these types of decisions are bad for the company, the greater your chances of saving the job slot.

## USING THE GRAPEVINE TO GET ADVANCE WARNING

Your prime source of information on matters that will directly affect you and your group will be your boss. However, it's always nice to be tuned into what's happening in other areas of the company. Further, it's really helpful to get advance notice on all sorts of administrative and operational matters before you are told about them officially. For example, if you hear there is going to be a meeting on a certain subject, this gives you a chance to prepare for any questions you may be asked. Actually, the possibilities for putting advance information on a wide range of topics to good use are endless.

Of course, being new, you will have to start from scratch to build a network of contacts who can feed you the latest scuttlebutt. For this reason, it's good to get to know as many people as you can throughout the company. You will meet most of these people while going about doing your job. Others you may get to know through any athletic or social groups the company sponsors. And serving as a volunteer on various company committees can provide still other opportunities for making contacts who may serve as a future source of information.

Naturally, building a network of contacts takes time, but right from your first day on the job, your subordinates will be a good source of information. However, you will have to learn to distinguish between those employees who are fairly reliable and those who are less so. Furthermore, workers won't generally have access to the sort of management information which would be of the most interest to you. Nevertheless, you may be surprised at some of the tidbits of gossip that come your way from subordinates.

Beyond these sources, if you are really desperate to know what's going on within the company, there are always the tried and true office gossips. These people will feed you a continuous stream of what they swear is the latest information. Don't bet your last dollar on anything gossips tell you, however, since they have little interest in whether their stories are fact or fiction. Finally, if your workers are union members, the union steward can frequently clue you in to forthcoming developments long before you hear them from official channels. This is particularly true when the lines of communication in your company aren't too efficient.

## How to Establish a Daily Routine that Works for You

In your first days and weeks on the job, you may find yourself being pulled in nine different directions as you try to learn everything you need to know. There will be questions from your subordinates and assignments from your boss. A seemingly endless stream of people will introduce themselves to you, and you wonder if you'll ever learn to remember all their names. If that's not bad enough, your in-basket will fill with paperwork as you fervently wish so many people didn't know who you were. You may also find you're working on several tasks simultaneously but having trouble getting any of them completed.

The apparent chaos you may encounter at first is nowhere near as bad as you might be envisioning it. As you gradually figure out the details of your job, things will fall into place. However, you can help the process along by adopting a daily routine for dealing with many of your duties. So once you're beyond the first week or so of playing it by ear, it's time to start planning how to gain control over your workload.

Everyone has their own working rhythm in terms of energy levels. Some people are all fired up and ready to go early in the morning, while others don't shift into high gear until later in the day. It's helpful to recognize the peak periods when you're most alert and ready to tackle anything. Once you do this, use these times to work on the tough tasks, and save the more mundane activities, such as routine paperwork, for low points in your day.

By using this approach, you will be able to do more during the day than if you operate on a first-in, first-out basis with your work. The reason behind this is simple: If you're trying to work on a difficult assignment that requires a good deal of concentration, it will be very slow going if you're doing this when your energy levels are running low. On the other hand, during these low points in your day you can move along fairly well on routine tasks that don't require much thought.

Another common problem everyone faces with certain tasks is an inability to start work on them. It may be a difficult report you have to write or some other loathsome chore you wish would simply vanish. Unfortunately, these burdens don't disappear, so you have to do them sooner or later. However, when you put them off, they're still in the back of your mind and no closer to completion. When you get one of these projects, the best way to conquer it is to dig right in and go to work. You may find your progress to be distressingly slow at first, but if you plug away a little at a time, you will be moving ahead toward completion. In fact, once you get over the initial hurdle of getting started, you may be surprised to find the task is nowhere near as difficult as you had originally envisioned.

As you start to develop your work routine there are a number of issues you will have to consider, such as how to get the quiet time you need for tasks that require a good deal of thought. The simplest solution would be closing your office door so no one will bother you. If the layout of your working area doesn't give you this luxury, then you may want to find an empty conference room you can use on occasion.

Since you're just starting out, however, it's important to emphasize your availability to subordinates, and a closed door may send the wrong message. So at the beginning, you may want to do your heavy-duty thinking early in the morning before other people arrive or after everyone leaves for the day. No doubt, you're not thrilled with this suggestion, but it would only be necessary for a month or two until workers get to know you better.

Naturally, as you settle into a regular work routine you will develop habits in the way you handle different tasks, as well as specific times when you generally do them. However, a supervisory position doesn't lend itself to the same structured method of working that some other jobs might. With a number of people working for you, there will always be a degree of unpredictability to each working day. Therefore, always be flexible about adapting your working routine to the varied interruptions of the job.

## LEARNING TO AVOID TAKING THINGS PERSONALLY

There may be a time or two in your early days as a supervisor when you wonder if you made the right move in taking the job. You may feel you're sandwiched between upper management and your workers, receiving respect from neither group and abuse from both directions. At times this may not be too far from the truth. The objectives of management and workers may clash on occasion, and when they do, you're in the middle of the conflict. Although you're a member of the management team, your proximity to those you supervise puts you in a different position than someone who is not in the first tier on the management ladder.

It's one thing to be able to analyze reports from the relative seclusion of an enclosed office and say "We've got to increase worker productivity." When senior managers do this, the word comes down the line to pick up the pace. Unfortunately, you're the one who has to figure out how to get your workers to do more than they already are. From your vantage point, you may know what's really needed are more workers, not greater productivity from people who are already overworked. You also know the futility of trying to convince senior management of this.

From the other end of the spectrum, you have workers who seem to be always looking for pay raises. They don't want to hear about business being slow, competition being tough, or the company struggling to stay in business. From their perspective, the answer to management's desire for increased productivity is, "Get real, we're not even being paid enough for the work we already do." As you know, but don't want to say, some of these workers are paid more than they're worth.

If you feel like the person in the middle, it's because you are. However, it's essential to avoid taking the comments from both sides personally. Actually, there's no reason to, since you're only the conduit—not the target—for the complaints that flow back and forth. Once you accept this fact, it's much easier to deal with the realities of being a supervisor.

It's a people-oriented job, which means you will encounter the whole range of human emotions at one time or another. Even though at times it may seem difficult, you will have to admit that at least your job isn't dull. There are a couple of things to do to help lessen the amount of aggravation which comes your way.

First and foremost, don't give either workers or other managers ammunition to fuel their complaints. Therefore, if workers gripe about management decisions, even if you agree with them, do so silently. If you openly express your own dissatisfaction, this only reinforces worker convictions and leads to further moaning and groaning. It follows also, that when supervisors sit around the lunch table and gripe about their subordinates, don't chime in with your own complaints.

Another way to avoid being the innocent victim of someone's ranting and raving is to be conscious of those times when people aren't in their best moods. Of course, there's no foolproof way to do this with complete certainty, but much useless flak can be dodged by not approaching people at the wrong time. As you observe the people you work with, you will notice there are certain times of the day when they're not at their best.

For instance, your boss may be a bear early in the morning. If so, you're asking for trouble by approaching him at the start of the business day. In fact, many people get off to a slow beginning in the morning, and even those who aren't rude may not be particularly helpful. So unless you're dealing with a morning person, barring absolute necessity, let people unwind before you approach them on business. Along the same lines, your subordinates won't appreciate you showing up to discuss work right at quitting time.

Although you may feel you get more than your share of complaints from all directions, it's probably not as bad as you think. Everyone grumbles now and then, and some people have perfected it as an art form. Accept it for what it usually is: nothing more than people releasing their frustrations. Much of the time these attitudes may not even be related to something at work. If it's any consolation, at least as a supervisor you're in a position to be the messenger for those with complaints rather than the recipient.

---

## How to Recognize and Deal with Limitations on what You Can Do

---

Your desire to succeed in your new job can lead to a great deal of frustration if you're not careful. No matter how fast you learn the fundamentals of supervision, and even though you work long hours on the job, influences beyond your control will place limits on what you can accomplish. Unless you both recognize and learn to deal with these obstacles, you will find yourself wondering what you're doing wrong when in reality there's nothing more that can be done. The various factors that can influence your degree of success as a supervisor include the following:

### Your Boss

Just as a good boss can make your job easier, a bad boss can make it a nightmare. If your boss is indecisive, you won't be able to secure necessary approvals or perhaps even get action on routine requests. Maybe your boss won't back you up when it's necessary, which can lead you to be cautious for fear of making mistakes. Then again, your boss may simply be nasty to deal with to the extent you avoid all but essential contact. Whatever the tendencies may be, if your boss isn't the best, it makes it that much harder to do your job successfully.

### Top Management

Company policy can have an influence on your ability to do your job. For example, company decisions on such matters as hiring, layoffs, reorganizations, and pay and benefits can determine whether you have enough people to operate your department efficiently.

### Your Employees

The experience, skill levels, and training of those who work for you are a prime determinant as to how effective you can be in running your department. Since you're probably inheriting these people from the previous boss, they might not fit the mold of the type of worker you would like to have. Nevertheless, even though you didn't choose them, your effectiveness will depend in large part on how well you can get them to do their jobs.

## Resources

Using old equipment and difficulty in getting supplies will hinder the ability of your department to operate at maximum efficiency. Equipment that's always breaking down can not only cause work delays but also affect the morale of your workers. Even the layout of the working area can influence the productivity of your group.

## Unions

If your company is unionized, then the provisions of the labor agreement will have to be adhered to. The constraints of work rules and the like can hinder your ability to operate effectively.

As you can see, there are all sorts of factors beyond your control that can make your job harder to do. Don't worry if everything doesn't always go as smoothly as you would like. When you encounter obstacles, whatever they might be, look for alternatives to get the job done. Strive to do the best you can and don't get discouraged even if your efforts fail. Over the long haul, your ability to handle adversity will be a significant factor in your success as a supervisor. So take everything in stride—both good and bad—and you will find your job a lot easier to do.

# Index